# CAKE DECORATING MOTIFS

# CAKE DECORATING MOTIFS

150 Designs for Making Your Cake Unique

*Sheila Lampkin*

**APPLE**

A QUARTO BOOK

First published by Apple Press
in the UK in 2007
7 Greenland Street
London NW1 0ND
www.apple-press.com

ISBN 978-1-84543-173-0

This book was designed and produced by
Quarto Publishing plc
The Old Brewery
6 Blundell Street
London N7 9BH

**Senior Editor** Liz Dalby
**Art Editor and Designer** Julie Francis
**Managing Art Editor** Anna Plucinska
**Assistant Art Directors** Penny Cobb,
Caroline Guest
**Photographer** Karl Adamson
**Illustrator** Kuo Kang Chen
**Proofreader** Laura Howell
**Indexer** Diana LeCore
**Art Director** Moira Clinch
**Publisher** Paul Carslake


Manufactured in Hong Kong by Modern Age
Repro House Ltd
Printed in China by Midas Printing
International Ltd

Acknowledgements

Quarto would like to thank the following
suppliers for tools and materials used to
make the motifs in this book:

Tools and equipment:
Knightsbridge PME Ltd
Chadwell Heath Lane, Romford,
Essex, RM6 4NP, UK
tel: +44 (0)20 8590 5959;
fax: +44 (0)20 8590 7373
email: sales@cakedecoration.co.uk;
website: www.cakedecoration.co.uk

Icing supplies:
The fondant used for all designs
was Regalice by Renshaw. Available
in 16 colours, Regalice is a favourite of
professional bakers, cake decorators
and sugarcrafters across the UK. It's a
ready-to-use paste that can be pinned
or sheeted straight from the box, and
sets firmly and cuts cleanly. For details of
stockists please call +44 (0)870 870 6954.

Torbay Cake Craft
5 Seaway Road, Preston, Paignton,
Devon, TQ3 2NX, UK
tel: +44 (0)1803 550178
www.crafty-creations.co.uk

Quarto would also like to thank:

Earlene Moore for the use of selected text
extracts from her website, Earlene's Cakes
(featured in the article on pages 30–33,
Using colour).
www.earlenescakes.com

Elaine MacGregor for three cakes (pictured
on pages 36–37).

# Contents

How to use this book     6

## Materials and Techniques

Making cakes     10
Pound cake     12
Carrot cake     14
Rich fruit cake     16
Chocolate cake     18
Royal icing     20
Buttercream icing     21
Fondant     22
Pastillage     23
Tools and equipment     24
Using colour     30
Covering cakes     34
Making a template     38
Using a template     40
How to pipe     42
Working with fondant     44
Design ideas     48

## Design Directory

Pattern selector     52
Animals     62
Plants     90
Seasonal     118
Celebrations     146
Novelty ideas     174
Surfaces and textures     202
Cupcakes     230
Alphabets     232

Conversions     248
Glossary     250
Index     252
Contacts and suppliers     256

# About this book

These sample pages with explanations will help you get the most from this book. Turn to page 50 to find all the patterns collected together, so you can view them quickly and make a selection.

*B*ake a delicious cake and decorate it with a selection of handmade motifs of your choice – simply add a name or message to make the design that bit more personal. This book gives you the know-how to create a stunning centrepiece for any occasion.

## Materials and techniques

A 40-page technical section equips you with the skills you need to start decorating cakes, and includes four delicious and versatile basic cake recipes.

1 **Photographic sequences**
Step-by-step photographs clearly demonstrate the stages.

2 **Clear step-by-step text**
Core techniques are explained for perfect results.

3 **What you need**
Ingredients and baking times for a range of tin sizes.

4 **Tips**
Handy hints to ensure the best possible results.

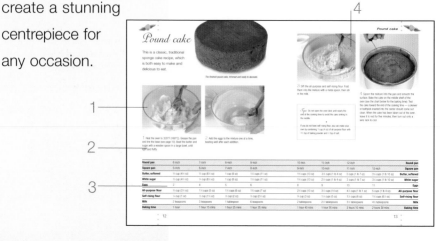

5 **Template**
Template for copying
and scaling the motif up
or down (full instructions
given on page 38).

6 **Order of work**
Detailed instructions for
assembling the motif.

7 **Full-colour photograph**
The finished motif is shown.

8 **Spiral binding**
The binding prevents the
book from snapping shut!

5  7  8  6

---

## Key to symbols used in the Design Directory

There are more than 200 motifs organized into categories and arranged by degree of difficulty.

### Degree of difficulty
Skill level required on a scale of 1–3:

◌ Easy

◍ Moderate

◍◍ Complex

### Use for
Ideas for designing with decorative elements:

▢ Cake edging (for borders)

▤ Side designs (for deep cakes)

◯ Cake tops (for all shapes of cake:
circular, square or rectangular)

♡ Cupcake (individual cake designs)

▥ Whole cake (integral motifs
that act as coverings)

### Mix & match
Ideas for mixing the featured motifs
with others in the directory.

### Motif uses
The motifs divide into four categories, providing
very different finished effects, from flat to
three-dimensional. Different types of icing
(see pages 20–23) are suitable for each.

⌒ Flat (rolled-out fondant or pastillage)

⌒ Low relief (moulded fondant or pastillage)

◯ 3-D (moulded fondant)

⬩ Linework (piped buttercream or royal icing)

### Tools
Lists the tools you will need.

# Materials and techniques

The motifs shown here are mainly made from fondant, although the designs also lend themselves to other materials such as royal icing or chocolate modelling paste. Every cake will be a unique creation composed by you.

Each page describes how to make the motif and gives hints on where to mix and match the designs to complete a unique cake top. The cakes can be coated with the covering of your choice – be it royal icing, buttercream, chocolate ganache or fondant. Go to the pattern selector on pages 50–61 to make your choice.

With few exceptions, the designs can be prepared off the cake and then placed in position once the cake has been covered. Motif sizes can easily be adjusted to fit a variety of cake sizes and shapes, according to your choice.

# Making cakes

It is important that the cake tastes as good as it looks. Chocolate, carrot, fruit or sponge – everyone has their favourite cake recipe. All share some basic techniques for success.

It is important to know how many people are going to share a cake so there will be enough for everyone. Use the recommended amounts of ingredients for the size of cake tin you wish to use (see pages 12–19).

A celebration cake may be used during a meal as the dessert – in this case, allow for a portion size of about 2.5 x 5 cm (1 x 2 inches) per person. If the cake is to be cut at the end of a meal, a portion of about 2.5 cm (1 inch) square should be enough.

## Lining the tin

Before baking a cake, you will need to line the tin.

1 Use a pastry brush or a piece of kitchen towel to grease the inside of the tin with vegetable shortening. Sprinkle it with flour and shake gently to cover the whole area. Remove any surplus flour by turning the tin upside down and tapping it gently but firmly.

2 Cut a sheet of greaseproof paper a little larger than the base of the tin. Make a fringe of short inward cuts around the outside.

3 Press the greaseproof paper into position. Make sure the paper is pressed firmly against the base of the tin, or it may distort the shape of the cake.

*Choose a tin that will suit your cake design.*

4 Cut a strip that will fit around the side and fit this into the tin so that it sits snugly against the base. Add a little more grease to make the paper stick.

10

## Storing

**Undecorated cakes** can be preserved in a variety of ways. Rich fruit cakes will keep for many months and do not need to be frozen; wrap them tightly to keep air out and store in a box in a cool, dry place. Sponge cakes and carrot cakes are better frozen until required. Cover them tightly in clingfilm before freezing. Defrost them thoroughly before decorating.

*Store a cake in a covered container.*

## Cooling the cake

Once the cake is baked, remove it from the tin and leave it to cool on a wire rack. Bake a sponge cake the day before decorating to allow the mixture to cool and the cake structure to hold together firmly. Rich fruit cakes should be made three weeks before they are decorated to allow the cake time to mature. During this time you can brush the top and bottom with alcohol.

**Decorated cakes** should be kept in a covered carton or cake saver box. Once they are cut, the cut edge will begin to dry out. To keep the cake moist, press a strip of greaseproof paper or clingfilm against the cut side.

> *Tip* If you do not bake regularly and your larder is not stocked with baking supplies, then consider using a cake mix. These are available in most food stores in a variety of flavours, and will contain most of the ingredients that you need (you will usually have to add eggs and liquid). Simply prepare the mix and bake as instructed on the packet.

## Levelling the cake

Almost all cake mixtures will bake with a domed surface. Once the cake has cooled, trim the top of the cake to give a level surface before you decorate it.

1 Move a long, serrated knife backwards and forwards horizontally across the top surface of the cake.

2 The levelled cake is now ready to be covered (see pages 34–37) or stored (see above).

# Pound cake

This is a classic, traditional sponge cake recipe, which is both easy to make and delicious to eat.

*The finished pound cake, trimmed and ready to decorate.*

1 Heat the oven to 160°C (320°F). Grease the tin and line the base (see page 10). Beat the butter and sugar with a wooden spoon in a large bowl, until light and fluffy.

2 Add the eggs to the mixture one at a time, beating well after each addition.

| Round tin | 15 cm (6 in) | 18 cm (7 in) | 20 cm (8 in) | 22 cm (9 in) |
|---|---|---|---|---|
| Square tin | 12 cm (5 in) | 15 cm (6 in) | 18 cm (7 in) | 20 cm (8 in) |
| Butter, softened | 135 g (4½ oz) | 200 g (6½ oz) | 250 g (8 oz) | 310 g (11 oz) |
| Caster sugar | 135 g (4½ oz) | 200 g (6½ oz) | 250 g (8 oz) | 310 g (11 oz) |
| Eggs | 2 | 4 | 5 | 6 |
| Plain flour | 110 g (3½ oz) | 150 g (5 oz) | 185 g (6 oz) | 230 g (7 oz) |
| Self-raising flour | 35 g (1 oz) | 50 g (1½ oz) | 60 g (2 oz) | 75 g (2½ oz) |
| Milk | 2 teaspoons | 3 teaspoons | 1 tablespoon | 6 teaspoons |
| Baking time | 1 hour | 1 hour 15 mins | 1 hour 25 mins | 1 hour 35 mins |

3 Sift the plain and self-raising flour. Fold them into the mixture with a metal spoon, then stir in the milk.

4 Spoon the mixture into the tin and smooth the surface. Bake the cake on the middle shelf of the oven (see the chart below for the baking time). Test the cake towards the end of the cooking time – a skewer or cocktail stick inserted into the centre should come out clean. When the cake has been taken out of the oven, leave it to rest for five minutes, then turn out onto a wire rack to cool.

*Tips* Do not open the oven door until nearly the end of the cooking time to avoid the cake sinking in the middle.

If you do not have self-raising flour, you can make your own by combining 100 g (4 oz) of plain flour with 1½ tsp of baking powder and ½ tsp of salt.

| | | | | |
|---|---|---|---|---|
| 25 cm (10 in) | 28 cm (11 in) | 30 cm (12 in) | | **Round tin** |
| 22 cm (9 in) | 20 cm (10 in) | 28 cm (11 in) | 30 cm (12 in) | **Square tin** |
| 400 g (13 oz) | 610 g (1 lb 4 oz) | 715 g (1 lb 7 oz) | 810 g (1 lb 10 oz) | **Butter, softened** |
| 400 g (13 oz) | 610 g (1 lb 4 oz) | 715 g (1 lb 7 oz) | 810 g (1 lb 10 oz) | **Caster sugar** |
| 8 | 9 | 10 | 11 | **Eggs** |
| 300 g (10 oz) | 460 g (14 oz) | 535 g (1 lb 1 oz) | 610 g (1 lb 4 oz) | **Plain flour** |
| 95 g (3 oz) | 150 g (5 oz) | 175 g (6 oz) | 200 g (6½ oz) | **Self-raising flour** |
| 2 tablespoons | 2½ tablespoons | 3½ tablespoons | 4½ tablespoons | **Milk** |
| 1 hour 40 mins | 1 hour 55 mins | 2 hours 10 mins | 2 hours 30 mins | **Baking time** |

# Carrot cake

Traditional carrot cakes are extremely popular and have the great advantage of feeling healthy rather than sinful.

*Carrot cake can be layered with buttercream or cream cheese icing.*

1 Heat the oven to 170°C (340°F). Sift the flours, spices and bicarbonate of soda into a large bowl.

2 Whisk the oil, sugar, eggs and golden syrup together in a bowl.

| Round tin | 15 cm (6 in) | 18 cm (7 in) | 20 cm (8 in) | 22 cm (9 in) |
|---|---|---|---|---|
| Square tin | 12 cm (5 in) | 15 cm (6 in) | 18 cm (7 in) | 20 cm (8 in) |
| Self-raising flour | 90 g (3 oz) | 125 g (4 oz) | 150 g (5 oz) | 170 g (5½ oz) |
| Plain flour | 90 g (3 oz) | 125 g (4 oz) | 150 g (5 oz) | 170 g (5½ oz) |
| Ground cinnamon | 1 teaspoon | 1 teaspoon | 1¾ teaspoons | 2 teaspoons |
| Ground ginger | ½ teaspoon | ¾ teaspoon | ¾ teaspoon | 1 teaspoon |
| Ground nutmeg | ¼ teaspoon | ¼ teaspoon | ½ teaspoon | ½ teaspoon |
| Bicarbonate of soda | ½ teaspoon | ½ teaspoon | ¾ teaspoon | 1 teaspoon |
| Vegetable oil | 100 ml (3½ fl. oz) | 120 ml (4 fl. oz) | 175 ml (6 fl. oz) | 200 ml (6 ½ fl. oz) |
| Brown sugar | 115 g (4 oz) | 140 g (4½ oz) | 200 g (6½ oz) | 225 g (7 oz) |
| Eggs | 2 | 3 | 4 | 4 |
| Golden syrup | 60 ml (2 fl. oz) | 70 ml (2½ fl. oz) | 100 ml (3½ fl. oz) | 125 ml (4 fl. oz) |
| Grated carrot | 250 g (8 oz) | 315 g (10 oz) | 450 g (14 oz) | 500 g (1 lb) |
| Pecans or walnuts | 30 g (1 oz) | 50 g (1½ oz) | 50 g (1½ oz) | 60 g (2 oz) |
| Baking time | 1 hour 20 mins | 1 hour 30 mins | 1 hour 35 mins | 1 hour 45 mins |

3 Make a well in the centre of the flour, and gradually pour the mixture into it. Use a wooden spoon to combine with the flour.

4 Stir in the grated carrot and chopped nuts. Spoon the mixture into a greased and lined tin (see page 10). Bake the cake (see the chart below for the baking time). Test towards the end of the time – a skewer or cocktail stick inserted into the centre should come out clean. Remove the cake from the oven, leave it to rest for 15 minutes, then turn it out onto a wire rack to cool.

| | | | | |
|---|---|---|---|---|
| 25 cm (10 in) | 28 cm (11 in) | 30 cm (12 in) | | **Round tin** |
| 22 cm (9 in) | 20 cm (10 in) | 28 cm (11 in) | 30 cm (12 in) | **Square tin** |
| 250 g (8 oz) | 350 g (11 oz) | 400 g (13 oz) | 450 g (14 oz) | **Self-raising flour** |
| 250 g (8 oz) | 350 g (11 oz) | 400 g (13 oz) | 450 g (14 oz) | **Plain flour** |
| 2¼ teaspoons | 3 teaspoons | 4 teaspoons | 4¼ teaspoons | **Ground cinnamon** |
| 1¼ teaspoons | 2 teaspoons | 2¼ teaspoons | 2¾ teaspoons | **Ground ginger** |
| ¾ teaspoon | 1 teaspoon | 1¼ teaspoons | 1½ teaspoons | **Ground nutmeg** |
| 1 teaspoon | 1½ teaspoons | 2 teaspoons | 2 teaspoons | **Bicarbonate of soda** |
| 250 ml (8 fl. oz) | 400 ml (13 fl. oz) | 485 ml (15 fl. oz) | 520 ml (17 fl. oz) | **Vegetable oil** |
| 280 g (9 oz) | 460 g (15 oz) | 500 g (1 lb) | 600 g (1 lb 4oz) | **Brown sugar** |
| 5 | 6 | 8 | 8 | **Eggs** |
| 140 ml (5 fl. oz) | 250 ml (8 fl. oz) | 265 ml (8½ fl. oz) | 320 ml (10 fl. oz) | **Golden syrup** |
| 620 g (1 lb 4 oz) | 1 kg (2 lb) | 1.1 kg (2 lb 3 oz) | 1.3 kg (2 lb 10oz) | **Grated carrot** |
| 70 g (2½ oz) | 90 g (3 oz) | 110 g (3½ oz) | 125 g (4 oz) | **Pecans or walnuts** |
| 1 hour 55 mins | 2 hours 10 mins | 2 hours 20 mins | 2 hours 30 mins | **Baking time** |

# Rich fruit cake

Fruit cake tastes delicious and
is full of plump dried fruits and
candied cherries. It provides
a firm base for decorations.

*Fruit cake will keep for many months.*

1 Mix together the dried fruit, chopped candied cherries and brandy in a bowl. Cover and leave for several hours until the liquid is absorbed.

2 Heat the oven to 140°C (280°F). Grease and line the tin (see page 10). Beat the butter and sugar with a wooden spoon until light and fluffy.

| Round tin | 15 cm (6 in) | 18 cm (7 in) | 20 cm (8 in) | 22 cm (9 in) |
|---|---|---|---|---|
| Square tin | 12 cm (5 in) | 15 cm (6 in) | 18 cm (7 in) | 20 cm (8 in) |
| Mixed dried fruit | 440 g (14 oz) | 625 g (1 lb 4 oz) | 875 g (1 lb 12 oz) | 1.1 kg (2 lb 4 oz) |
| Glacé cherries | 45 g (1½ oz) | 60 g (2 oz) | 90 g (3 oz) | 100 g (3½ oz) |
| Brandy (or boiled water) | 40 ml (1½ fl. oz) | 40 ml (1½ oz) | 40 ml (1½ fl. oz) | 60 ml (2 fl. oz) |
| Butter, softened | 100 g (3½ oz) | 150 g (5 oz) | 200 g (6½ oz) | 280 g (9 oz) |
| Muscovado sugar | 100 g (3½ oz) | 150 g (5 oz) | 200 g (6½ oz) | 280 g (9 oz) |
| Eggs | 2 | 3 | 3 | 4 |
| Plain bread flour, sieved | 125 g (4 oz) | 185 g (6 oz) | 250 g (8 oz) | 375 g (12 oz) |
| Mixed spice | ¾ teaspoon | 1 teaspoon | 1½ teaspoons | 2 teaspoons |
| Ground almonds | 25 g (¾ oz) | 30 g (1 oz) | 45 g (1½ oz) | 60 g (2 oz) |
| Baking time | 2 hours | 2 hours 15 mins | 3 hours 15 mins | 3 hours 30–45 mins |

3 Gradually add the eggs one at a time, beating well after each addition. Add 1 tbsp of flour.

5 Spoon the mixture into the tin and smooth the surface. Tap the tin on the work surface to remove air bubbles. Bake the cake (see the chart below for the baking time). Place a heatproof bowl of water in the base of the oven to keep the cake moist. Test towards the end of the baking time – a skewer or cocktail stick inserted into the centre should come out clean.

6 After baking, drizzle the cake with a little brandy if required, then cover it with a sheet of greaseproof paper and a sheet of aluminium foil, and leave it to cool in the tin. When the cake is cold, remove it from the tin and wrap tightly in clingfilm (leave the greaseproof paper on). Store until ready to decorate. Make the cake at least three weeks in advance; this allows time for the cake to mature and the flavours to develop.

4 Stir in spoonfuls of soaked fruit alternately with the rest of the flour, spices and ground almonds.

| | | | | |
|---|---|---|---|---|
| 25 cm (10 in) | 28 cm (11 in) | 30 cm (12 in) | | **Round tin** |
| 22 cm (9 in) | 20 cm (10 in) | 28 cm (11 in) | 30 cm (12 in) | **Square tin** |
| 1.5 kg (3 lb) | 1.8 kg (3 lb 12 oz) | 2.2 kg (4 lb 8 oz) | 2.6 kg (5 lb 4 oz) | **Mixed dried fruit** |
| 150 g (5 oz) | 200 g (6½ oz) | 250 g (8 oz) | 280 g (9 oz) | **Glacé cherries** |
| 60 ml (2 fl. oz) | 80 ml (2¾ fl. oz) | 120 ml (4 fl. oz) | 160 ml (5 fl. oz) | **Brandy (or boiled water)** |
| 410 g (13 oz) | 470 g (15 oz) | 560 g (1 lb 2 oz) | 690 g (1 lb 6 oz) | **Butter, softened** |
| 410 g (13 oz) | 470 g (15 oz) | 560 g (1 lb 2 oz) | 690 g (1 lb 6 oz) | **Muscovado sugar** |
| 6 | 8 | 8 | 10 | **Eggs** |
| 500 g (1 lb) | 625 g (1 lb 4 oz) | 750 g (1 lb 8 oz) | 875 oz (1 lb 13 oz) | **Plain bread flour, sieved** |
| 3 teaspoons | 4 teaspoons | 4 teaspoons | 5 teaspoons | **Mixed spice** |
| 90 g (3 oz) | 125 g (4 oz) | 160 g (5 oz) | 200 g (6½ oz) | **Ground almonds** |
| 4 hours | 4hours 30–45 mins | 5 hrs 15 mins | 5hrs 15–30 mins | **Baking time** |

# Chocolate cake

Chocolate cakes are always popular and are many people's favourite.

1 Heat the oven to 180°C (360°F). Grease and line the tin (see page 10). Put the sugar, butter and vanilla extract in a bowl. Beat them with a wooden spoon until light and fluffy.

2 Add the eggs one at a time, beating well after each addition.

| Round tin | 15 cm (6 in) | 18 cm (7 in) | 20 cm (8 in) | 22 cm (9 in) |
|---|---|---|---|---|
| Square tin | 12 cm (5 in) | 15 cm (6 in) | 18 cm (7 in) | 20 cm (8 in) |
| Butter, softened | 90 g (3 oz) | 140 g (5 oz) | 165 g (5½ oz) | 185 g (6 oz) |
| Caster sugar | 165 g (5½ oz) | 250 g (8 oz) | 300 g (10 oz) | 330 g (11 oz) |
| Vanilla essence | 1 teaspoon | 1½ teaspoons | 2 teaspoons | 2½ teaspoons |
| Eggs | 2 | 2 | 3 | 3 |
| Self-raising flour | 40 g (1½ oz) | 55 g (2 oz) | 65 g (2 oz) | 75 g (2½ oz) |
| Plain flour | 115 g (4 oz) | 165 g (5½ oz) | 200 g (6½ oz) | 225 g (7 oz) |
| Bicarbonate of soda | ½ teapoon | ¾ teaspoon | 1 teaspoon | 1½ teaspoons |
| Cocoa powder | 40 g (1½ oz) | 60 g (2 oz) | 70 g (2½ oz) | 80 g (2¾ oz) |
| Milk | 140 ml (5 fl. oz) | 210 ml (7 fl. oz) | 250 ml (8 fl. oz) | 280 ml (9 fl. oz) |
| Baking time | 50 mins | 1 hour | 1 hour 10 mins | 1 hour 15 mins |

Build up layers of chocolate cake
with tasty buttercream fillings.

3 Sift the flours, baking soda and unsweetened cocoa.
Gradually fold into the mixture in small quantities,
alternating with small quantities of milk.

4 Spoon the mixture into the tin and smooth the top
surface. Bake the cake (see the chart below for the
baking time). Test towards the end of the baking time –
a skewer or cocktail stick inserted into the centre
should come out clean. Leave the cake to cool in the tin
for 15 minutes before turning it out onto a wire rack
to cool completely.

| 25 cm (10 in) | 28 cm (11 in) | 30 cm (12 in) | | **Round tin** |
| --- | --- | --- | --- | --- |
| 22 cm (9 in) | 20 cm (10 in) | 28 cm (11 in) | 30 cm (12 in) | **Square tin** |
| 225 g (7 oz) | 325 g (11 oz) | 465 g (15 oz) | 560 g (1 lb 2 oz) | **Butter, softened** |
| 410 g (13 oz) | 570 g (1 lb 2 oz) | 660 g (1 lb 5 oz) | 825 g (1 lb 1 oz) | **Caster sugar** |
| 3 teaspoons | 4 teaspoons | 5 teaspoons | 6 teaspoons | **Vanilla essence** |
| 4 | 5 | 6 | 7 | **Eggs** |
| 95 g (3 oz) | 125 g (4 oz) | 150 g (5 oz) | 190 g (6 oz) | **Self-raising flour** |
| 280 g (9 oz) | 350 g (11 oz) | 445 g (14 oz) | 560 g (1 lb 2 oz) | **Plain flour** |
| 1¾ teaspoons | 2¼ teaspoons | 2½ teaspoons | 2¾ teaspoons | **Bicarbonate of soda** |
| 90 g (3 oz) | 110 g (3½ oz) | 120 g (4 oz) | 160 g (5 oz) | **Cocoa powder** |
| 350 ml (11 fl. oz) | 500 ml (16 fl. oz) | 560 ml (18 fl. oz) | 700 ml (22 fl. oz) | **Milk** |
| 1 hour 20 mins | 1 hour 30 mins | 1 hour 40 mins | 1 hour 50mins | **Baking time** |

# Royal icing

Royal icing is a heavy meringue mixture that can be used at various stages of firmness for line and border piping. Use it softened to flood into outlines to make a 'run out'.

*Whisk the meringue powder and water together to a foam.*

**Large mix – for coating and piping detail**
250 ml (½ pint) cold water
40 g (1½ oz) meringue powder
1.75 kg (3½ lb) icing sugar, sifted

**Small mix – for adding detail**
75 ml (3 oz) cold water
15 g (½ oz) meringue powder
500 g (1 lb) icing sugar, sifted
1 teaspoon glycerin (optional) – use to give a softer coating icing, but do not use in icing for piping

1 Place the water in a bowl and whisk in the meringue powder until dissolved (see above). Pure albumen powder may take several hours to dissolve.

2 Place half the icing sugar on top of the liquid and beat in with a wooden spoon until smooth. Add half the remainder and beat in, then add the remainder.

3 Beat the icing at a slow speed in a food processor until it forms peaks that will stand when drawn upward with a palette knife. This is known as full peak consistency.

4 Store the icing in an airtight container with clingfilm pressed onto the surface. When you use the icing, cover the bowl with a damp cloth to avoid a crust forming on the icing while you work.

5 Always re-beat the icing to the correct consistency before use (see left).

*Tip* One of the main factors influencing successful piping is the icing consistency. Two terms are used to describe this:

**Full peak (top):** when the icing is pulled upward with a palette knife, it retains a peak without bending over.

**Soft peak (bottom):** the icing keeps a peak when pulled upward but bends over at the top.

*Tips* Achieve a sparkling icing by adding the sugar in stages. Adding too much sugar too quickly will result in dull, grainy icing that is difficult to pipe.

Royal icing can be purchased ready to use in tubes, for writing on cake tops.

# Buttercream icing

Buttercream icing is versatile and quick to make, and can be flavoured and coloured. It can be spread or piped onto the cake.

110 g (4 oz) butter, softened
225 g (8 oz) icing sugar, sifted
2 tsp milk
1 tsp vanilla extract

*Tips* Multiply the quantities in this recipe to cover large cakes.

•

Chill the cake before covering with buttercream icing for a firm surface that will be easier to coat.

*Add delicious flavourings to the basic buttercream icing mix (see below).*

1 Beat the butter with a wooden spoon until it is light and fluffy.

2 Stir in the sugar, milk and vanilla extract. Beat well until light and smooth. Add a little more liquid or sugar, as needed, to adjust the consistency.

## Alternative flavourings

A few simple alterations will change the flavour of the buttercream icing:

**For a citrus cake**, replace the milk and vanilla with orange or lemon juice, and 2 tsp of finely grated lemon or orange rind.

**For a chocolate cake**, mix 1 tbsp unsweetened cocoa blended with 1 tbsp boiling water. Leave to cool before adding to the butter icing.

**For a coffee cake**, add 2 tsp of instant coffee granules blended with 1 tsp boiling water, or a strong espresso coffee, to the icing.

# Fondant

You can buy pre-made fondant or use this recipe to make your own. Fondant can be rolled out and shaped, and is used to make most of the motifs in this book.

### Fondant
2 dessertspoons gelatin
50 ml (2 fl. oz) cold water
125 ml (4 fl. oz) glucose
2 tbsp white vegetable shortening
1 tbsp glycerin
Colouring and flavouring, as desired
900 g (2 lb) icing sugar

3 Knead in the remaining sugar until the fondant is smooth and pliable. Adjust the consistency of the mixture, adding a little more liquid or icing sugar as necessary. Place the fondant in a plastic bag in an airtight container, and allow to rest overnight. Knead it again before use.

1 Sprinkle the gelatin onto the water. Soak the gelatin in the cold water until softened, then dissolve it over a bowl of hot water or in the microwave using short bursts of power (don't let the mixture boil).

2 Add the glucose, shortening, glycerin, colour and flavouring (if required). Cool until lukewarm. Sift half the icing sugar into a bowl, make a well in the centre, and pour in the gelatin mixture. Mix together with a wooden spoon, gradually incorporating the sugar.

*Tips* The basic mix is white. Colour fondant with paste or gel, not liquid food colouring (see page 32); neither of these will alter the consistency too much.

•

Made a fondant adhesive by working together a golf-ball size of fondant with a little water until it becomes soft and sticky. Brush a small amount onto the parts to be joined together.

•

Add a small amount of gum tragacanth to the fondant to give a firmer texture. This is particularly useful for making drapes (see page 221) or for basketweave (see page 223).

# Pastillage

Pastillage (also called gumpaste) sets like a hard tablet, or pastille. Use a shop-bought mix or make up your own using this recipe. It should not be used for decorations that people will bite into, as it is too hard – use it for motifs that can be removed before the cake is eaten.

450 g (1 lb) icing sugar, sifted
1 tbsp gum tragacanth
4 tbsp warm water
1½ tbsp glucose

3 Pour the glucose mixture into the centre of the icing sugar and mix with a palette knife. Cover with a damp cloth and leave to rest until cold. Blend in the remaining icing sugar to give a firm, pliable paste.

1 Place three-quarters of the sifted sugar into a bowl. Sprinkle the gum tragacanth over the top and make a well in the centre.

2 Mix the water and glucose in a microwave-safe bowl. Microwave for 30 seconds (until it is clear).

*Tips* Roll out pastillage on a light dusting of icing sugar, and keep any spare paste well wrapped to keep it from drying out.

•

Smear a little vegetable shortening on your hands when you are kneading the pastillage, which will help prevent it from sticking.

•

When the pieces of pastillage are drying, place them on a foam pad and turn them over every few hours to enable all sides to dry evenly.

# Tools and equipment

All the motif designs in this book can be produced with the minimum of basic equipment. Once you have experienced the thrill of creating your own cakes, you may want to buy some of the many tools available that will help you take the craft further.

### Cake making

To make the cakes you will need a few basic pieces of equipment that you may already have in your kitchen.

### Plastic mixing bowls

Plastic mixing bowls are useful as they have a firm rubber base that grips the table while the mixing takes place, as well as a lip to pour out the mix and a grip to hold at the top.

### Electric mixer

If you make cakes often it is very handy to have an electric mixer that does the beating and whisking required in cake-making procedures.

### Glass bowls

Weigh or measure out all the ingredients into various glass bowls. It helps to have a selection of sizes.

### Moulds and cake cases
These moulded curves are useful to dry icing shapes in either a concave or convex shape. Use gold, silver or pastel-coloured cake cases for the cupcakes (see page 230) to show them off.

### Sieves
Icing sugar, flour and other dry ingredients can be passed through a sieve to ensure that there are no lumps in the fine powder.

### Whisk
Use a whisk to introduce air into a mixture, for example when mixing egg whites to make royal icing.

### Cutting wire
Use a cutting wire to cut level sections of cake.

### Measuring spoons
Sometimes small amounts are required in a recipe; these are listed as a spoonful or part of a spoon. Measuring spoons can be filled and levelled off to provide the correct amount. Some recipes also require cups or parts of cups – these are measured out with the larger set of measures.

### Spoons
Metal and wooden spoons and plastic spatulas are used for mixing cakes and icing and putting icing into a piping bag (see page 42).

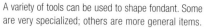

# Cutting and modelling

A variety of tools can be used to shape fondant. Some are very specialized; others are more general items.

### Flower and leaf cutters

Making the shapes for flowers and leaves can be quite complicated; cutters cut out the same shape from rolled-out fondant quickly and easily time after time.

### Plastic and metal cutters

Plastic and metal cutters are a great help in making shapes – here is a selection including round, square, teardrop, star, calyx and plunger cutters for small blossoms.

### Stamens

Stamens are non-edible cotton-based inserts for the centres of certain varieties of flower.

### Brushes and rolling pins

Small, soft brushes can be used to apply lustre and vegetable shortening to motifs.

Pastry brushes are used to spread jam onto a cake surface when covering it with marzipan or fondant, or to moisten a cake surface with boiled water or alcohol when coating with marzipan.

Rolling pins press out the fondant to an even surface. Textured pins make a pattern in the fondant. Also shown are two straight edges that are used to flatten buttercream or royal icing over the top surface of a cake.

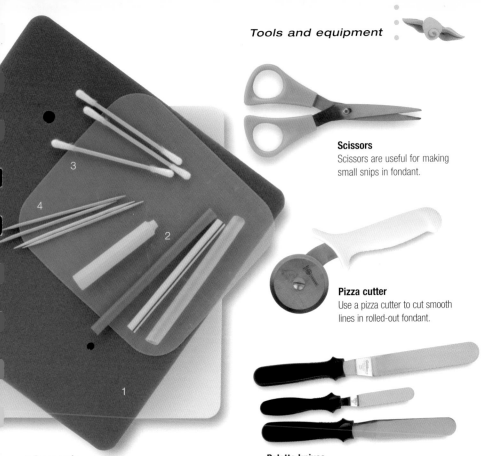

**Scissors**
Scissors are useful for making small snips in fondant.

**Pizza cutter**
Use a pizza cutter to cut smooth lines in rolled-out fondant.

1 **Foam pads**
Foam pads are used for holding the cutout fondant while you are manipulating it with other tools.

2 **Straws**
Various sizes of straws provide markers for curves such as mouths, beaks and claws.

3 **Cotton buds**
Cosmetic cotton buds can be used to blush colour onto models.

4 **Cocktail sticks**
Cocktail sticks are used to indent holes and add small dots of colour to fondant.

**Palette knives**
Large palette knives are generally used for coating a cake with buttercream or royal icing and spreading fillings. The smaller ones are very useful for modelling. Some have a cranked handle or bend so that fingers are kept away from the cake surface.

**Garlic press**
Push fondant softened with vegetable shortening through a garlic press to form a mass of strands to use for hair, for example.

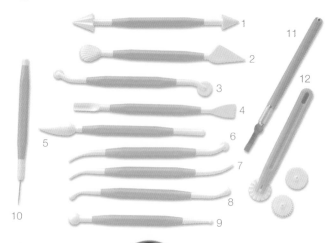

## Modelling tools

1  Serrated and taper cone tool
2  Blade and shell tool
3  Cutting wheels
4  Scallop and comb tool
5  Bulbous cone tool
6  Quilting tool
7  Veiner
8  Bone tool
9  Ball tool
10  Scriber needle
11  Sugarcraft knife
12  Designer wheel

## Sugar shaker

A sugar shaker distributes small amounts of icing sugar onto the work surface.

## Smoothers and side scrapers

A pair of icing smoothers helps to create a good surface on the top and sides of a fondant cake. Side scrapers can be either straight or serrated to spread buttercream or comb a pattern onto the cake side.

## Piping tools

Store piping bags in an upright container, so they are ready on hand when needed. Once the bag is filled with icing keep the tip moist and ready to work by placing it in a stand with a moist foam base. Piping nozzles are available in many sizes to accommodate the medium being used – for delicate detail and fine piping use small nozzles. Larger nozzles are particularly useful for buttercream and bold piping. Disposable bags can be ready-made plastic cones or made from greaseproof paper triangles curled into shape (see page 42). The brush cleaner removes any residue from the inside of the nozzle. A coupler can be used to join the icing bag and the nozzle.

## Finishing touches

Emboss patterns and textures, add colour, and display and store your finished creations.

### Tilting turntable

For detailed work and to allow you to work on the cake side or top, a tilting turntable will angle the cake to make the work area more visible.

### Turntable

A large, flat turntable is useful to move the cake around to work on from all angles.

### Embossing tools

Embossing tools imprint words or patterns into fondant or buttercream and can provide a guide for piping.

### Colouring

Colouring to add to icing is available in various types (see page 32); there are spray and paste colours, powders, liquids and lustre, as well as pens that contain edible food colouring.

### Cupcake stand

Use a cupcake stand to present a display of decorated cupcakes (see pages 230–235) to accompany a large cake.

### Storage drawers

Fondant motifs can be made in advance and stored in drawers, ready to be used on the appropriate occasion.

### Crimpers

Crimpers are shaped tweezers that press fondant into interesting shapes. They are particularly useful for imprinting a design around the top edge of a cake.

# Using colour

Mix and match vibrant colours to make your cake designs stand out, or learn how to add subtle tones for a more delicate finish. Your skill with modelling and piping is important; but a stunning end result hinges upon your ability to combine and use colours.

## The colour wheel

The colour wheel helps you to see how one colour relates to another. If colours are close together on the colour wheel and have colours in common, they are said to be related. Related colours go well together. The colour wheel is made up of primary, secondary and tertiary colours.

1 **Primary colours**
*Red, yellow and blue are the primary colours – they are pure colours and all other colours come from a mix of these three. Red and yellow are warm colours, and blue is cool.*

### Complementary colours
*Complementary colours are directly opposite one another on the colour wheel and have no colour in common – for example, red is opposite green and a combination of these colours works well in a design.*

2 **Secondary colours** *Secondary colours are an equal mix of two primary colours. Blue and yellow produce green, red and blue produce violet, and yellow and red produce orange.*

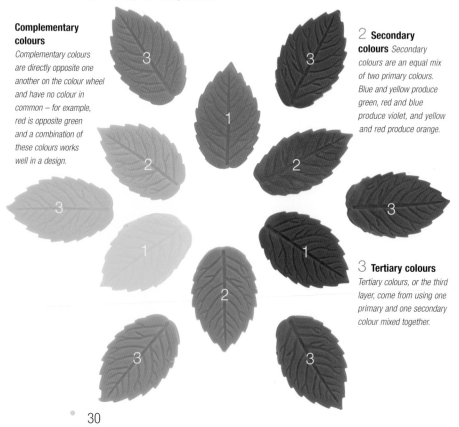

3 **Tertiary colours**
*Tertiary colours, or the third layer, come from using one primary and one secondary colour mixed together.*

## Non-colours

Neutral colours, black and white are not considered part of the colour wheel. White is an absence of colour, and black is a collection of the three primary colours in intense form. Neither are considered true colours. Because it takes such a strong concentration of colour to produce black, it is easiest to buy black colour.

Brown is a combination of opposites on the colour wheel such as red and green or yellow and violet. (Essentially brown is a combination of the three primary colours in a less intense form than black.)

*White, black and a neutral shade*

## Manipulating colours

If you want a pastel colour, start with a pastel coloured icing. For example, hot pink and bright yellow will not produce a soft apricot without adding a lot of white icing. In mixing soft colours, add soft colours. When trying to get exact colours, add very small amounts of colour (or icing) until you get the colour you require.

Some colours that you might want to mix will require a 'dulling' effect, such as moss green and dusty rose. This requires that you go to the opposite side of the colour wheel. For example: leaf green plus orange equals moss green: pink plus pale green equals dusty rose.

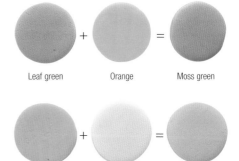

Leaf green + Orange = Moss green

Pink + Pale green = Dusty rose

---

## *Colouring variables*

There are no absolutes in mixing icing colours because of the many things that can affect the colour, such as ingredients, temperature and humidity, time and light.

### Ingredients

Shortening, margarine and butter make colours turn darker, whereas lemon juice softens colours. If you use salt in your buttercream icing, mix your colours the night before; if the salt is not thoroughly dissolved, it will leave little light spots in your icing.

### Temperature and humidity

In icings that contain shortening, margarine or butter, the temperature of the room, heat of your hands and warmth of the liquid you add can affect the icing colour. Warmth seems to make the colour darken or become deeper.

### Time

When using buttercream icing, soft or light colours can be made and used immediately and will only darken slightly. But when you are striving for dark colours, mix in the colours and then let the icing sit overnight before decorating: you won't have to use quite as much colour. Charcoal grey will turn black, and an 'almost' red will turn bright red.

### Light

When your creation is finished, be careful to protect your work from sunlight or other bright lights. Pinks are especially susceptible to fading. Purples fade to blues; blues to grey; black to purple or green.

## Types of colouring

**Paste colours** are a very concentrated form of colour designed to be used in very small quantities. Some are very thick and almost dry.

**Gel colours** come in small to medium size bottles with a small hole at the top to allow for a drop of colour at a time to be squeezed from the bottle. They provide very strong colour, are easy to use and are refillable.

**Powder colours** are the driest form of colour available. They must be dissolved in a small amount of liquid before use otherwise there may be specks of undissolved colour in the icing.

**Liquid colours** come in two varieties: specialized airbrush colours and liquid colours. The latter are not always strong enough to colour icing without altering the consistency. For best results choose dedicated cake decorating colours.

**Tubes of icing** are available, in white and various colours, pre-mixed so that a quick written message may be added to the cake.

**Lustres** add a soft, subtle sheen when applied to icing with a soft brush. Lustre sprays add sparkle to special cakes.

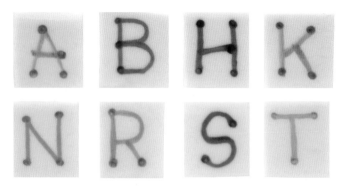

> *Tip* Prepare and store tiles of finely rolled-out pastillage. These can be used for adding lettering quickly and cleanly to a finished cake design. The letters can be written on neatly with a food colouring pen (as shown here) or piped (see page 43).

## Using food colouring pens

Edible colouring pens contain an edible ink and so are useful for writing messages either onto parts of motifs or directly onto cakes, as well as adding small details and accents to the motifs. They have the advantages of being easy to control and drying very quickly.

32

## Adding colour to fondant

Use the following technique to distribute food colouring evenly through white fondant. When a ball of the coloured fondant is cut in half, it should not contain any streaks or swirls of darker colour.

1 Dip a cocktail stick in the food colouring and draw it across the surface of the fondant. Take care not to dig into the fondant, which might introduce pockets of air.

2 Start to roll the fondant on the work surface to distribute the colour evenly. For a marbled effect, simply stop before the colour is evenly mixed.

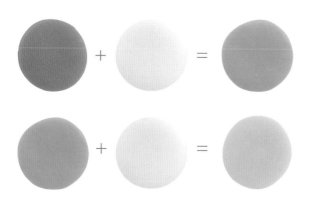

*Tips* Many colours mixed together create a dull, muddy colour. Try to keep colours bright and crisp by mixing them selectively.

•

Colours should be wrapped up individually as the colour migrates from one to another if pieces of paste are pressed together in one container.

3 Adjust the colour of the mixed fondant if necessary by adding white, as shown here. Remember, though, that the fondant may fade over time.

# Covering cakes

Fondant provides a smooth, firm surface to decorate, and buttercream icing may be piped and textured successfully.

## Covering a cake with fondant

A smooth surface on the cake makes all the difference to the appearance of the fondant covering. Use the following technique to get a smooth and even finish with neat edges and straight sides.

2 Cover the cake with rolled-out marzipan. This provides a smooth base for the fondant and a better finished result. Use a smoother to make the surface of the marzipan completely flat.

1 The cake should have a flat top and bottom so that it sits snugly on the board and has a smooth surface for the decoration (see Levelling the cake, page 11). If there are any large indentations, fill the space with a plug of fondant. If the base has loose crumbs, chill it for a few minutes to firm up the surface. Use a pastry brush to coat the cake with a warm apricot masking.

3 Knead the fondant into a neat ball with any cracks on the underside. Sprinkle the work surface lightly with icing sugar, and use the rolling pin to roll backwards and forwards over the surface of the fondant. Rotate the fondant through 90° every few rolls – there is no need to turn it over. Keep rolling until the fondant is about the right size to cover the cake, and about 0.5 cm (¼ inch) thick.

*Tip* A turntable is a useful piece of equipment that allows the cake to rotate while it is being coated and decorated.

6 To neaten the edges, hold a palette knife with the flat blade vertically against the cake side, and press the point down to the cake board. Trim off any surplus fondant all the way around the cake, turning the cake so that the cutting is always done at the front. Polish the sides once again to tuck the edges in and make the base neat. Any crimping or embossing must be done at this stage before the surface of the fondant starts to firm up.

4 Move the cake adjacent to the rolled fondant. Holding the rolling pin over the centre of the rolled fondant, flip half of the fondant over the pin so that it is well supported. Lift up the rolling pin with the fondant draped across it, and move it over the cake, allowing the fondant to drape over the cake.

7 Finally, decorate the cake with your chosen motifs. Crimping around the top of the cake makes a neat border.

5 Use a smoother to polish the surface of the cake and remove any air from under the fondant coating. Check around all the sides and smooth them down until the fondant meets the board. Try to avoid any pleats by gently smoothing and stretching the fondant until it sits easily around the sides of the cake. Polish the sides of the cake with a smoother.

## Covering a cake with buttercream

Buttercream is a versatile medium that will take flavour and colour to suit the cake's design and the purpose for which it is made. It can be spread and piped onto the cake surface to make interesting textures and patterns. Use the embossing tools to mark out designs and then pipe over them for consistent results. Buttercream cakes are best stored in cool conditions as the mixture will soften with heat.

2 The first coating is called a 'crumb coat' as it adheres any loose crumbs to the cake surface. Use a palette knife to spread a very fine coat of the buttercream all over the sides and the top of the cake. Put the cake back in the freezer or fridge to chill again.

1 Prepare the cake by trimming it to the correct size. If required, split the cake into several layers and add a filling of buttercream. If the cake was baked in several layers, build up the layers and fill in any gaps with extra buttercream. Turn the top layer upside down to provide a level surface for decorating. Trim any surplus cake so that the sides all line up correctly – this makes it much easier to apply the buttercream in the next stage. Place the cake into the freezer for half an hour or chill in the refrigerator for several hours. This provides a firm surface to apply the first thin coating of buttercream.

3 Spread a layer of buttercream over the top surface of the cake with a long palette knife. Use the edge of the knife to form a smooth, level surface. Don't add too much at once – it is better to add a thin coat, chill again and add a second coat if you need a thicker layer. When you are satisfied with the surface remove the palette knife as it comes to the edge. Chill once again.

*These cakes show a few of the decorative possibilities of buttercream.*

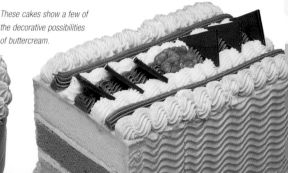

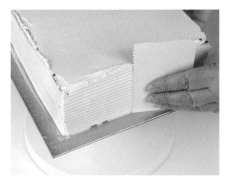 

4 Use a palette knife in an upright position to add a layer of buttercream icing to the cake sides. If you want a smooth surface, scrape the side edges with a plain side-scraper that has a flat surface. Use a serrated side-scraper to give the sides a texture, in this case horizontal lines. With a sharp knife, trim the top edges level with the surface of the cake top. A piped border will cover the joins.

5 Prepare a piping bag (see page 42) for decorating the edges. Press out even shells or swirls all around the top edge, and the bottom edge if required, to complete the coating of the cake.

6 Add the motif carefully to the top of the cake, moving the pieces in stages on the tip of a palette knife until they are all assembled. To complete the cake, pipe words and add design elements to suit the occasion.

*Tips* To coat a square cake, work on two opposite sides, chill it, and then work on the other two opposite sides.

•

Work with the cake placed on a turntable, except for coating the cake top, when the cake must be still.

•

A crumb coat is especially important if a dark cake is being covered by a light buttercream.

*Buttercream icing is a tasty, versatile coating. Texture the surface with straight or wavy lines, and add piped edgings.*

# Making a template

If you like a motif design but need to change the dimensions to suit your cake, there are easy ways of doing this. Each design in the book is presented as a template on a grid to enable you to resize it easily.

Make every cake unique by changing the design to fit the size, shape and intention of the cake. A template can be made for an individual motif, or for the whole cake top. There are several simple ways of changing the size of a motif template to suit your needs.

## Using a grid

1 On a sheet of white paper, draw a square or rectangle the size you want the finished motif to be. Use a ruler to divide this box into squares – the number of squares should match those in the original grid.

2 Recreate the original image by replicating the lines that appear in each grid box on the template on your grid. Work square by square until the design has been completely transferred.

*The completed motif is shown alongside the template used to create it.*

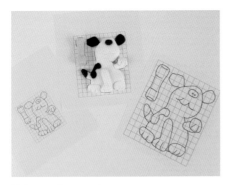

## Using a photocopier

If you have access to a photocopier, use it to enlarge or reduce the motif. Work out the enlargement in terms of a percentage. For example, if the size of the original picture is 100 per cent and you want it twice as big, set the photocopier at 200 per cent.

### *Paired motifs*

Many of the motifs in this book would look good as a pair, facing in opposite directions. They could be used to frame a message, for example. To do this, you can either scan the template and use imaging software to flip it, or trace the motif over a lightbox (see below) and turn the paper over.

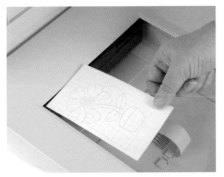

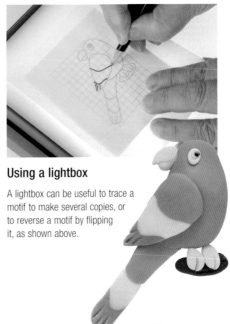

## Using a scanner

If you have access to a computer with a scanner, scan the template and use image software to adjust the size of the template to your requirements.

## Using a lightbox

A lightbox can be useful to trace a motif to make several copies, or to reverse a motif by flipping it, as shown above.

# Using a template

Use the instructions on pages 38 and 39 to make a template at the required size. Here you can see the usual order of work to follow to make your motif.

Once you have made the template, put it in a plastic sleeve to protect it. The pattern of the motif can be built up on top of the plastic sleeve and then moved to the top of the cake using a palette knife.

Build up the motif, starting with the bigger, main pieces, and then moving on to the detail. Where coloured sections are the same, it is a good idea to work on all these pieces together, which will both save time and prevent colours cross-mixing on the work surface.

*The finished motif, ready for transfer to the cake.*

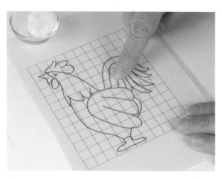

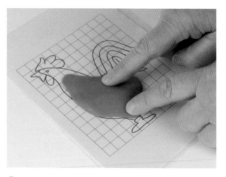

1 Use your finger to smear a little vegetable shortening over the template in the plastic sleeve. This will help to keep the components in place as you work on them, but also enable you to remove them easily to transfer the finished motif to the cake.

2 Working from the back of the design, shape the main body elements. Roll a ball and then flatten it into the shape of the template, leaving a bulge in the centre of the fondant and smoothing out the edges to fit within the lines.

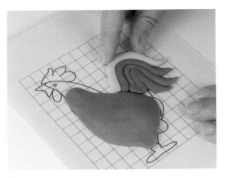

3 Still working with the back components, roll and shape the next section of detail.

6 Carefully brush on lustre where appropriate. If a denser coating of lustre is required, brush over the areas with a very small amount of vegetable shortening. This provides a surface that will hold the lustre better.

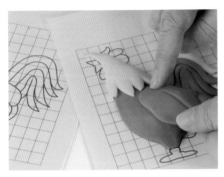

4 Moving toward the front of the design, continue adding the components.

*Tips* Build up a file of templates so that the designs you use regularly are quickly available when needed. Make a note of the colours and quantities used for your design, so that a quick reference guide is instantly on hand. It is sometimes useful to have two copies of the template – one to work on and the other as a guide to making the components.

Motifs can be made and stored in advance of the event. Keep them in a storage container and lift them on the tip of a palette knife to transfer them to the cake. Don't worry about moving the whole motif all it once; it may be easier to transfer the components in several parts. As they have all been moulded together originally they will fit closely against one another when reassembled. A very small amount of water brushed onto the back surface will be sufficient to attach them into position.

5 Finally, work on the small details, including any marks or textures mentioned in the detailed instructions.

41

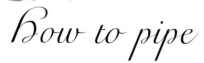 

# How to pipe

Decorate the edges and base of your cake with neat designs piped from buttercream or royal icing. Or make abstract patterns and even piped motifs on the cake top.

## Making a piping bag

You can buy conical icing bags or make them yourself. The size depends on the work to be completed; generally, buttercream piping uses a larger bag and a coupler – this joins the bag to the icing nozzle.

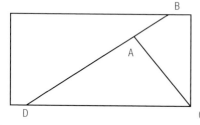

3 Make a little cut through the combined layers of paper and turn one edge of the cut downward to secure the bag. Cut the tip off the bag and sit the piping nozzle in the neck of the bag before the icing is inserted.

1 Cut the shape of the piping bag from silicone paper. From the oblong of silicone fold a diagonal line (shown as DB in the diagram). Slit the paper with a sharp knife along this line. Fold the paper to create a crease from A to C. A becomes the point of your piping bag and C is at the wide end.

2 Take point B and turn it over in a circle until the line AB fits along the line C. Take point D and curve it around in a circle the opposite way to create a cone shape. Fold all the pointed paper ends inwards. It is not essential that they all sit exactly on top of one another.

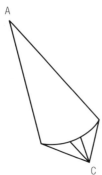

4 Ensure the icing is at the correct, full-peak consistency (see tip, page 20). Use a palette knife to fill the bag half to two-thirds full of icing. Push the icing down into the bag but take care not to overfill it or it may burst. Fold the edges of the bag in toward the centre. You are now ready to pipe. Hold the bag between your middle and index fingers and push down with your thumb.

**Bulb** A bulb is a rounded ball of icing. To make one, hold the bag upright, directly above the surface, and squeeze with an even pressure to form a ball of icing. Release the pressure and take the piping bag off gently. Tap any small peaks down with a damp paintbrush.

**Pressure piping** In pressure piping, softer icing is used to fill in shapes to form the motif. Finer details can then be piped over the top of the larger, filled-in shape.

**Line** Lines can be piped will both plain and serrated icing nozzles. Hold the bag at a slight angle and press out the icing with an even pressure while moving slowly in the direction required. To finish, release the pressure and lift away the piping bag.

**Zigzag** The zigzag technique can be used to fill in spaces or to create shapes with either plain or serrated nozzles. Move the nozzle over the surface of the cake in a Z shape.

**Scroll** A scroll makes a useful edging for the cake. It is usually piped with a serrated nozzle. Press out a bulb with the icing and, maintaining the pressure, move in a C or S shape, gradually releasing the pressure to form a tail.

**Cornelli** Cornelli piping fills in shapes and consists of a continuous line piped in curved Cs and Ws in no particular pattern.

*Tip* When piping letters to add to a cake (see pages 236–247), prepare some finely rolled pastillage tiles large enough for a single letter to sit on. Allow the tiles to dry before adding any letters. Place a tile over the pattern of the letter you require. The shadow of the letter should show through (a lightbox may help you to see the pattern more clearly). Pipe over the letter outline with royal icing. Allow the icing to dry thoroughly before attaching each tile to the cake with a little of the remaining royal icing. Using this method avoids the need to pipe lettering directly onto the finished cake top and risk mistakes.

**Twisted rope** The secret to piping twisted rope is constant pressure and even piping. Hold the bag and gradually rotate it to create a coiled effect.

# Working with fondant

All the motifs can be made using a small range of basic techniques and shapes. All the shapes are created from the basic ball.

## Basic modelling shapes

Whatever size of fondant you are working, first roll a ball in the palms of your hands to remove any crease marks, then manipulate it into the shape required.

A ball is always the starting point.

*Roll the ball in the palms of your hands with a circular motion until it is nicely rounded and has no creases.*

*To achieve two equal pieces, cut the ball in half.*

*To divide again, place the flat side down onto the work surface and cut in half again.*

Once you have the right size piece of fondant, re-roll it into a ball and then form other shapes from there.

*To make a cone, roll the base of the ball into a V shape by pressing your palms closer together and rolling backwards and forwards.*

*To make an elongated cone, continue to roll one end backwards and forwards until the cone becomes longer and thinner.*

*To make a sausage shape, place the ball onto the work surface and roll backwards and forwards so the sides are parallel.*

*To make smaller shapes, continue to roll balls and divide them in half, down to very small sizes.*

Some motifs require a development of these shapes to form new shapes.

*To make a carrot shape, continue rolling the elongated cone until it is long and much thinner.*

*To make a thin tube, continue rolling the sausage on the work surface until it reaches the length required.*

*To make a double-ended cone, turn an elongated cone around and taper the other end to make it pointed.*

## Order of work for a simple motif

Work on the motif starts with preparing the template to the correct size, then creating the various components and assembling them on the template.

*A heart-shaped petal is formed by marking a central line into the base of a cone and flattening it with a palette knife.*

*The centre of the flower is textured with piping nozzles pressed into the fondant.*

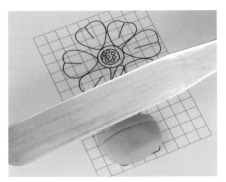

1 Spread the fondant out to the edges of the template. A round shape can be suggested by leaving the centre of the fondant thicker at the edges.

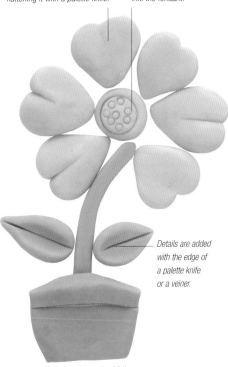

*Details are added with the edge of a palette knife or a veiner.*

*With love (see page 101)*

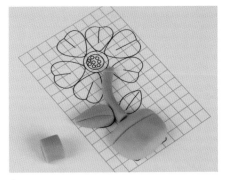

2 Work on all the pieces of one colour, then move onto the next colour.

3 Use a small palette knife to help shape the components and then place them in position. Add textures as necessary.

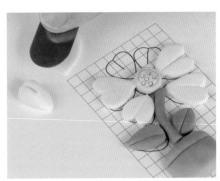

## Adding detail to a complex motif

More complex motifs are built up using the same basic principles. Work methodically for the cleanest and most professional end result.

1 Roll balls of fondant to smooth onto the template for large background shapes. All other shapes are formed from the basic ball.

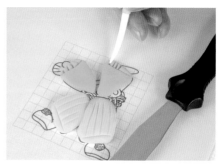

3 Add texture with the veiner or other embossing or texturing tools. Wipe the tools clean between colours.

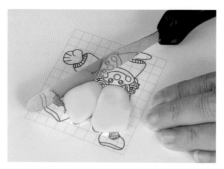

2 Use a palette knife to tap the edges of shapes straight where needed.

4 Work colour by colour to avoid cross-mixing of colours. Move finished sections aside if necessary.

*Tip* The basic motif templates could also be used for different applications, such as motifs formed of piped outlines, as shown here.

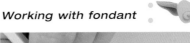

5 Use tools to add details. As well as specialized tools, you can use the ends of piping nozzles, pens or drinking straws. Experiment with different effects.

6 Place small details with the pointed tool to avoid touching the finished parts of the motif.

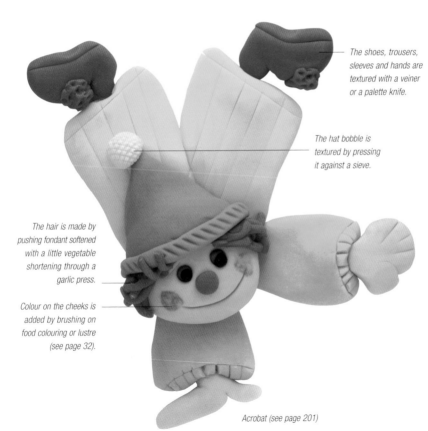

The shoes, trousers, sleeves and hands are textured with a veiner or a palette knife.

The hat bobble is textured by pressing it against a sieve.

The hair is made by pushing fondant softened with a little vegetable shortening through a garlic press.

Colour on the cheeks is added by brushing on food colouring or lustre (see page 32).

*Acrobat (see page 201)*

# Design ideas

The motif designs in this book can be positioned and combined in an almost infinite variety of ways to make your cake a unique creation.

## Motif positions

### Large, central

Make a feature of one motif. Enlarge it to a suitable size for the finished cake.

### Small, repeated

Make many small, identical motifs for a completely different effect.

### Repeated around the sides

Small motifs repeated around the sides of a cake provide a neat finish.

### Side plaque

A side plaque provides a focal point, to which a message could be added.

### Off-centre

Your cake design does not have to be symmetrical – play with ideas.

### Different sizes (same motif)

The same motif in an array of sizes gives the effect of perspective.

### Different motifs on a theme

Try grouping motifs together, linked by shape or theme.

### Design incorporating text

Some motifs lend themselves to displaying a message. Or incorporate piped letters into your design.

## Adding embellishments

Use texture and piped embellishments to add the finishing touches to a celebration cake.

1 **Imprinting a design**
Use a scallop tool to imprint a delicate edging.

2 **Piping lace**
Use royal icing to pipe a lace edging (see page 225).

3 **Adding ribbon**
Choose a decorative ribbon to tie around the cake.

# Mix and match

Take a selection of ideas from the design directory and combine them to form your own unique cake creation. For example, add bamboo to the panda motif, a message envelope to the dog, or a frog on a pond to a lilypad and leaf.

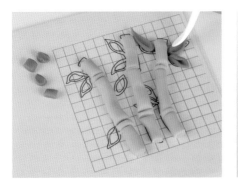

### 1 Make bamboo
Make the bamboo motif following the instructions on page 90.

### 2 Position panda
Make the panda motif following the instructions on page 74. Position the motifs on the cake when dry.

*The finished cake, featuring the combined design elements.*

*Tips* Motifs can be prepared in advance and stored until needed. This is particularly useful when you make a cake base that has a short storage time. Decide on all the design elements that you want to include on the cake and collect these together on the cake board, along with any decorative ribbon.

Once they have been baked, the cakes need time to rest before being decorated. It is a good idea, too, to chill the cakes before decorating them (with the exception of the rich fruit cake), as this provides a firm base on which to work. Place in the freezer for 30 minutes, or refrigerate for two hours.

49

# Design Directory

All the design motifs are shown over the next few pages, so that you can select those appropriate for your cake and then move on to the instructions given for the motif of your choice. Make the motif templates larger or smaller, depending on the size of your cake (see Making a template, page 38–39).

# Motif selector

The design directory contains more than 150 stunning motif designs. The motifs are organized into themes and are arranged in order of increasing complexity within each section.

## Animals

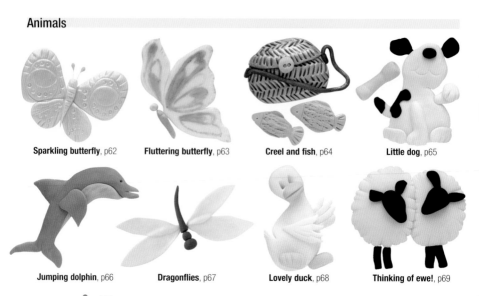

**Sparkling butterfly**, p62          **Fluttering butterfly**, p63          **Creel and fish**, p64          **Little dog**, p65

**Jumping dolphin**, p66          **Dragonflies**, p67          **Lovely duck**, p68          **Thinking of ewe!**, p69

**Happy tortoise**, p70

**Wacky whale**, p71

**Ice-bucket bunny**, p72

**Cool kitten**, p73

**Playful panda**, p74

**Friendly elephant**, p75

**Party penguin**, p76

**Horse's head**, p77

**Leo the lion**, p78

**Wise owl**, p79

**Dapper dog**, p80

**Frisky frog**, p81

**Pair of geese**, p82

**Pretty parrot**, p83

**Lovebirds**, p84

**Puppy love**, p85

**Cock-a-doodle-doo**, p86

**Birdhouse**, p87

**Fishy friends**, p88

**Prickly hedgehog**, p89

# Flowers, fruits and leaves

**Bamboo canes**, p90

**Blossom frame**, p91

**Colorful cosmos**, p92

**Spring daffodils**, p93

**Ivy ring**, p94

**Lilypads**, p95

**Holly sprig**, p96

**Rose leaves**, p97

**Rudbeckia**, p98

**Snazzy sunflowers**, p99

**Springtime tulips**, p100

**With love**, p101

**Bouquet**, p102

**Pretty parasol**, p103

**Blossom basket**, p104

**Poppy**, p105

**Arum lily**, p106

**Fancy fuchsias**, p107

**Oak leaves and acorns**, p108

**Pine cones**, p109

**Wild rose**, p110

**Rose**, p111

**Dogwood branch**, p112

**Bunch of grapes**, p113

**Daisy spray**, p114

**Exotic orchid**, p115

**Pretty pansy**, p116

**Fan with roses**, p117

## Seasonal

**Seasonal sleigh**, p118

**Sugar cane**, p119

**Red-nosed reindeer**, p120

**Christmas tree**, p121

**Christmas bells**, p122

**Mistletoe**, p123

**Peace dove**, p124

**Party crackers**, p125

**Plum pudding**, p126

**Christmas stocking**, p127

**Santa Claus**, p128

**Jolly snowman**, p129

**Robin redbreast**, p130

**Prayer book**, p131

**Easter egg**, p132

**Easter chick**, p133

**Menorah**, p134

**Star of David**, p135

**Top hat and shamrock**, p136

**Pumpkin witch**, p137

**Halloween ghosts**, p138

**Pumpkin family**, p139

**Christmas candle**, p140

**Christmas angel**, p141

**Christmas rose**, p142

**Easter bunny**, p143

**Fourth of July**, p144

**Thanksgiving turkey**, p145

## Celebrations

**Flower basket**, p146

**Baby's bib**, p147

**Baby bootees**, p148

**Champagne bottle**, p149

**Champagne glasses**, p150

**Baby in a cradle**, p151

**Mortarboard and diploma**, p152

**Sending a message**, p153

**Golf bag**, p154

**Mailbox**, p155

**Cup of love**, p156

**Pram**, p157

**Rattle**, p158

**Shirt and tie**, p159

**Signpost**, p160

**Do-it-yourself**, p161

**Wedding bells**, p162

**Rubber boots**, p163

**Torah scroll**, p164

**Book**, p165

**Watering can**, p166

**Golf ball and club**, p167

**Little girl**, p168

**Ocean liner**, p169

**Lucky horsehoes**, p170

**Pink rabbit**, p171

**Holding the key**, p172

**Candle power**, p173

## Novelty ideas

**American heart**, p174

**Anchor**, p175

**Ballet slippers**, p176

**Baseball mitt**, p177

**Beer mug**, p178

**Bucket and spade**, p179

**Convertible car**, p180

**Footsteps in the sand**, p181

**Acoustic guitar**, p182

**Flying high**, p183

**Top hat and gloves**, p184

**Toy steam train**, p185

**Racing car**, p186

**Umbrella**, p187

**Tennis racquet**, p188

**Helicopter**, p189

**Sailing boat**, p190

**Mobile phone**, p191

**Dashing Stetson**, p192

**Drum**, p193

**Over the moon**, p194

**Teddy bear in a box**, p195

**Girl in the snow**, p196

**Gone fishing**, p197

**Classic car**, p198

**Little boy**, p199

**Clown**, p200

**Acrobat**, p201

## Surfaces and textures

**Multi-looped bow**, p202

**Flat-looped bow**, p203

**Gift box**, p204

**Rope and shells**, p205

**Inscription banner**, p206

**Message labels**, p207

**Hearts**, p208

**Hearts and flowers**, p209

59

**Tassels**, p210

**Scrolls and shells**, p211

**Star on flag**, p212

**Wishing on a star**, p213

**Strips and flowers**, p214

**Formal bow**, p215

**Rounded scroll**, p216

**Rosebud circle**, p217

**Cutout lace**, p218

**Chunky lace**, p219

**Balloons**, p220

**Pleated drape**, p221

**Draped braid**, p222

**Basketweave**, p223

**Flat lace embroidery**, p224

**Piped lace**, p225

**Repeated stencil**, p226

**Individual stencil**, p227

**Rosette**, p228

**Curved lace embroidery**, p229

## Cupcakes

**Pair of hearts**, p230

**Horseshoes**, p231

**3-D bootees**, p232

**Certificate**, p233

**Wedding bells**, p234

**Golden keys**, p235

## Alphabets

**Linked lines**, p236–p239

**Flower fun**, p240–p243

**Lots of dots**, p244–p247

# Sparkling butterfly

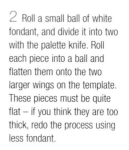

**Degree of difficulty**

Easy

**Use for**

Cake top

Use this simple and effective sparkly butterfly motif as a pretty addition to a special party cake.

**Mix and match**

Snazzy sunflowers, *page 99*

Poppy, *page 105*

Daisy spray, *page 114*

**Motif uses**

Low relief

Flat

**Fondant colours**

White

Gold lustre

**Tools**

Plastic sleeve

Palette knife

Cutters or other indenting tools

Soft brush

*See also*

Using colour, *page 30*

Making a template, *page 38*

Working with fondant, *page 44*

## Order of work

1 Adjust the design to the size required. Make a template and place in a plastic sleeve. Try making many small butterflies to cover a cake, rather than a single large one, to retain the delicate effect.

2 Roll a small ball of white fondant, and divide it into two with the palette knife. Roll each piece into a ball and flatten them onto the two larger wings on the template. These pieces must be quite flat – if you think they are too thick, redo the process using less fondant.

Two tiny flower stamens can be used for the antennae.

3 Roll another, smaller ball of white fondant, and cut it into two pieces. Roll each piece again and flatten them onto the smaller wings at the base of the template.

4 Roll a tiny piece of white fondant into a small carrot shape for the body. Attach it between the wings in the centre of the template.

5 Roll two tiny carrot shapes and add these to the head for antennae.

6 Use cutters and tools to indent the fondant with a pattern – make it the same on both sides of the butterfly. Use a soft brush to gently dust gold lustre all over the butterfly to add a delicate sheen.

7 Transfer the motif to the cake when dry.

# ℱluttering butterfly

This is a different view of a butterfly from the side – make it face in either direction and decorate it using vibrant colours.

## Order of work

1 Adjust the design to the size required. Make one template and place in a plastic sleeve, then make another to cut round.

2 Roll out some white fondant with the rolling pin. Use a sharp knife to cut round the second template. Cut two separate pieces – the full wing-top and bottom in one piece, and the partially hidden wing as another piece.

3 Place the pieces onto the template and smooth them into shape. Roll a small tube and ball of white fondant for the body and head.

4 Paint a pattern on the wings using a damp, soft brush and pink lustre, and coat the head and body of the butterfly with lustre. (One colour is used here, but a variety of different colours could be used.)

5 Transfer the motif to the cake when dry. Position the main wing first and then add the other bits.

Add more butterflies, rather than making them too big.

**Degree of difficulty**

◌ Easy

**Use for**

◯ Cake top

**Mix and match**

Rudbeckia, *page 98*

Springtime tulips, *page 100*

**Motif uses**

◠ Low relief

◠ Flat

**Fondant colours**

◯ White

Pink lustre

**Tools**

Plastic sleeve

Rolling pin

Sharp knife

Soft brush

*See also*

Using colour, *page 30*

Making a template, *page 38*

Working with fondant, *page 44*

# Creel and fish

**Degree of difficulty**

Easy

**Use for**

Cake top

**Mix and match**
Gone fishing,
*page 197*

**Motif uses**

Low relief

Flat

**Fondant colours**

Brown

Orange

Green

Copper lustre

**Tools**
Plastic sleeve
Palette knife
Veiner
Small piping nozzle
Soft brush
Small, sharp scissors

*See also*
Making a template,
*page 38*
Working with fondant,
*page 44*

This fish-themed motif would be ideal to decorate a fishing enthusiast's cake for a range of special occasions.

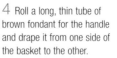

## Order of work

1 Adjust the design to the size required. Make a template and place in a plastic sleeve.

2 Take some brown fondant and flatten it onto the pattern, leaving some height in the centre and making the edges thin. Use the side of the palette knife to make an indent across the creel, one-third of the way down, to define the lid of the basket.

3 Use a veiner to make the basketweave texture, marking the basket at a slanting angle in a row from left to right. Change the direction of the angle on the next row of the basket to make the markings slant from right to left. Continue until the basket is covered with texture.

4 Roll a long, thin tube of brown fondant for the handle and drape it from one side of the basket to the other.

5 Add the basket catch, using a small piece of orange fondant pressed onto the join of the basket and lid. Mark it twice with a small piping nozzle. Use a soft brush to dust the basket all over with copper lustre.

6 Form two small, oval shapes from green fondant. Flatten them to a point at one end and press out a fishtail shape at the other. Use a veiner to texture the tail, and a small pair of sharp scissors to mark the scales. Mark an eye and a tiny indent for the mouth. Lightly brush with copper lustre to give a sheen.

7 Transfer the motif to the cake when dry.

Change the shape of the fish to suit the type of fishing!

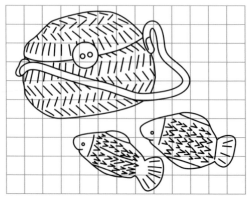

# *Little dog*

This friendly little dog is a suitable motif for dog lovers of all ages, for any occasion from a birthday to a retirement celebration.

## Order of work

1 Adjust the design to the size required. Make a template and place in a plastic sleeve.

2 Roll a carrot shape of white fondant, place it on the pattern (broad end down), and press into shape for the dog's body and head. Trim it to fit with the palette knife.

Replace the bone with a newspaper or a bouquet.

3 Roll two small sausages of white fondant, and mould a paw at one end. Add one to the centre of the body and indent the paw using the veiner. Add the other to the right of the body, bend it forwards, and indent the paw. Roll two small balls of white fondant, add to either side of the base, and indent to make back paws. Tuck a tail of white fondant behind the dog.

4 Add patches of black fondant to the coat and tail, smoothing them into position. Cut a small ball of black fondant in half, shape into teardrops, press flat, and insert behind the head as ears. Add a black nose with two indentations for nostrils. Use a veiner to mark the mouth as shown.

5 Transfer the motif to the cake when dry.

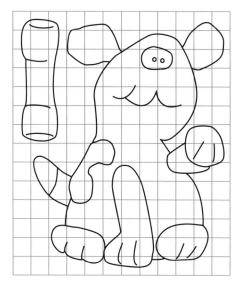

**Degree of difficulty**

 Easy

**Use for**

 Cake top

**Mix and match**
Blossom basket, *page 104*
Sending a message, *page 153*
Rubber boots, *page 163*

**Motif uses**

 Low relief

 Flat

**Fondant colours**

 White

 Black

**Tools**
Plastic sleeve
Palette knife
Veiner

*See also*
Using colour, *page 30*
Making a template, *page 38*
Working with fondant, *page 44*

# Jumping dolphin

**Degree of difficulty**

Easy

**Use for**

Cake top ○

**Mix and match**
Wacky whale,
*page 71*
Rope and shells,
*page 205*

Use a dolphin that appears to be leaping out of the water to decorate a water-themed cake. Mix and match with other marine motifs.

**Motif uses**

Low relief ⬭

Flat ⬭

**Fondant colours**

Dark blue ●

Light blue ●

**Tools**
Plastic sleeve
Palette knife
Pointed tool

## Order of work

1 Adjust the design to the size required. Make a template and place in a plastic sleeve.

2 Make two shades of blue fondant. Roll a tube the length of the template from the darker blue fondant. Add a smaller tube of lighter blue fondant alongside the centre part of the dark blue tube. Smooth the edges of the tubes to fit the outlines of the dolphin, leaving quite a depth of fondant through the body, and smooth the fondant thinner at the nose and tail. Use the palette knife to make a slit in the tail, and smooth the flippers onto the template to get the correct shape.

3 Shape the nose of the dolphin. Use the side of the palette knife to indent the mouth. Mark the eye with the pointed tool.

4 Flatten some darker blue fondant onto the template to make two flippers, one sticking out from the back and the other curved over towards the front.

5 Make more dolphins if required.

6 Transfer the motif(s) to the cake when dry.

Use several different-sized dolphins to create an interesting and effective design.

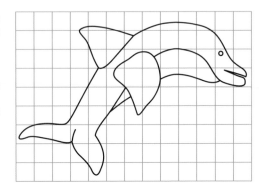

*See also*
Making a template,
*page 38*

# Dragonflies

Pairs of dragonflies hovering and darting, perhaps with some waterlilies, make a charming and versatile cake decoration for many special occasions.

## Order of work

1 Adjust the design to the size required. Make a template and place in a plastic sleeve.

2 The wings of the dragonflies must be very fine, so pastillage is more suitable than fondant. The sideways dragonfly has two wings and the one seen from above shows all four. Roll out some pastillage with the rolling pin and cut out six pointed ovals for wings. Use a round cutter to cut first one curve of a wing and then the other.

3 Roll two carrot shapes of blue fondant for the bodies, and curve them a little to fit onto the template. At the broad end of each, add a small ball of blue fondant, then a slightly larger ball, flattened into an oval shape for the head.

4 Add the wings as shown, overlapping them slightly.

5 Use a soft brush to dust the wings with ivory lustre to make them glisten.

6 Transfer the motifs to the cake when dry.

Don't make this design too big. The wings should be very fine and almost translucent.

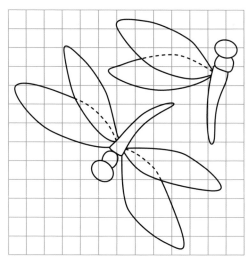

**Degree of difficulty**

⬙ Easy

**Use for**

◯ Cake top

**Mix and match**
Lilypads, *page 95*

**Motif uses**

⬬ Low relief

⬭ Flat

**Fondant colours**

◖ White pastillage

⬤ Blue

Ivory lustre

**Tools**
Plastic sleeve
Rolling pin
Round cutter
Soft brush

*See also*
Using colour, *page 30*
Making a template,
*page 38*
Working with fondant,
*page 44*

# Lovely duck

**Degree of difficulty**

Easy

**Use for**

Cake top

Side design

**Mix and match**

Frisky frog, *page 81*
Lilypads, *page 95*
Champagne glasses,
*page 150*
Gift box, *page 204*

**Motif uses**

Low relief

Flat

**Fondant colours**

White

Yellow

**Tools**

Plastic sleeve
Palette knife
Veiner
Rolling pin

*See also*
Making a template,
*page 38*

This duck motif can be used to present champagne glasses or a gift box. Alternatively, team it with water-themed motifs.

## Order of work

1 Adjust the design to the size required. Make a template and place in a plastic sleeve.

2 Roll a carrot shape of white fondant, a little longer than the shape on the template. Fold over the thin end – this makes the head – and lay the fondant down over the shape. Ease it over the template to form the duck's body and head.

3 Make a little cut in the middle of the left side, pull it away from the body to form a tail, and indent two lines on this with the veiner.

Reverse the template to create two ducks facing each other.

4 Roll out some white fondant with a rolling pin and cut two triangles for the wings, using the template as a guide. Cut zigzags on the short edges with the palette knife, and impress lines with the veiner. Place one wing beneath the body and one over the body, as shown.

5 To make the feet, cut a ball of yellow fondant in half and roll each piece into a cone. Indent the base of the body on the left, press in the point of one cone and fold the rest outwards. Press the base flat and indent with the veiner. Indent the duck's body, near the centre, and insert the pointed end of the other cone. Mark with the veiner.

6 To make the beak, form a flattened cone with a small ball of yellow fondant. Indent the head just above the neck, and add the pointed end of the flattened cone. With a knife, cut across the beak and open it out a little. Mark eyes with the veiner.

7 Transfer the motif to the cake when dry.

# Thinking of ewe!

Make a couple of cosy sheep to celebrate an engagement or maybe a move to a new home.

**Degree of difficulty**

◇ Easy

**Use for**

○ Cake top

 Side design

**Mix and match**

Inscription banner, *page 206*

**Motif uses**

◇ Low relief

◯ Flat

**Fondant colours**

⚪ White

⚫ Black

## Order of work

1 Adjust the design to the size required. Make a template and place in a plastic sleeve.

*Incline the sheep's heads towards each other.*

2 Divide a ball of white fondant in half. Roll each half into a ball, squash into ovals, and arrange side by side on the template. Use the veiner to indent all round the edges to form the sheep's woolly coats.

3 Divide a small ball of black fondant in half, squash into teardrop shapes, and position on each body. Divide a tiny ball of black fondant in half, and mould two ears by shaping the pieces into flattened teardrops. Insert a pair of ears behind one head, and then make another pair of ears for the other head. Mark two eyes on each head using a cocktail stick.

4 Make a thin tube of black fondant. Use the palette knife to cut four equal pieces, and add to the sheep for legs.

5 Transfer the motif to the cake when dry.

**Tools**

Plastic sleeve
Veiner
Cocktail stick
Palette knife

*See also*

Making a template, *page 38*

# happy tortoise

**Degree of difficulty**

Easy

**Use for**

Cake top ⬭

**Mix and match**

Inscription banner,
*page 206*

**Motif uses**

Low relief ⬭

Flat ⬭

**Fondant colours**

Light brown ◖

Mid brown ●

Dark brown ●

Black ●

**Tools**

Plastic sleeve
Veiner

*See also*
Using colour, *page 30*
Making a template,
*page 38*
Working with fondant,
*page 44*

Slow but sure, this cheerful little tortoise motif could be used on cakes for all sorts of events.

## Order of work

1 Adjust the design to the size required. Make a template and place in a plastic sleeve.

2 Use a light brown fondant for the tortoise's body. Roll a generous-sized ball of fondant to remove any cracks. Place it on the template and smooth it down to the edges, leaving some depth in the centre. Make the bottom edge curved. Draw a line just above the base using a veiner.

3 Roll some balls of mid brown fondant in different sizes and press them onto the shell, placing smaller ones towards the top of the dome.

4 Make the head using the dark brown fondant. Roll a medium-sized ball into a chunky cone, and form the nose from the broader end. Ease the pointed end of the cone underneath the edge of the shell. Use the veiner to mark the curved mouth and indent the eye sockets. Add tiny black balls of fondant for the eyes.

5 Roll two small balls of dark brown fondant and take one-third off each. Roll each separate piece into a ball and flatten them to form rectangles. Use these for the tortoise's feet – one large foot, and a smaller one behind it – at either end of the tortoise. Use the veiner to mark claws.

6 Transfer the motif to the cake when dry.

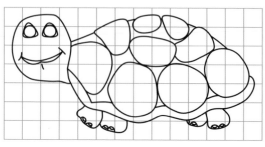

A curved indent for the mouth indicates a smile.

# 𝒲𝒶𝒸𝓀𝓎 𝓌𝒽𝒶𝓁ℯ

This fun marine motif is an ideal decoration for any cake with a nautical theme.

**Degree of difficulty**

◇ Easy

**Use for**

○ Cake top

**Mix and match**

Rope and shells, *page 205*

**Motif uses**

⬭ Low relief

⬯ Flat

**Fondant colours**

 Dark blue

 White

Gold lustre

**Tools**

Plastic sleeve
Palette knife
Pointed tool
Drinking straw
Rolling pin
Soft brush

## Order of work

1 Adjust the design to the size required. Make a template and place in a plastic sleeve.

2 To make the body of the whale really chunky, use a fairly large ball of blue fondant. Roll the ball into a cone and thin out the pointed end. Make a cut through the cone along a quarter of its length, from the pointed end. Curve the pieces outwards to form the whale's tail flukes. Flatten the fondant onto the template and use the side of the palette knife to tap the edges to the correct shape.

3 Make a cut for the mouth with the palette knife, and open it a little. Mark the crease where the mouth ends. Just above the mouth, indent a hole for the eye socket with the pointed tool. Add a tiny ball of white fondant for the eye. Mark the pupil of the eye and indent a curve just above the eye with the end of a drinking straw.

4 Add a curved V of white fondant for the whale's water spout. Roll a tube of white fondant, form it into a rippling shape, then flatten it with a rolling pin. Lay it over the base of the whale for waves. Use a soft brush to dust the waves with gold lustre.

5 Transfer the motif to the cake when dry.

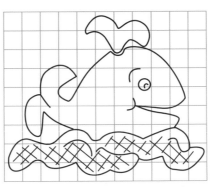

You could add more foaming waves, as shown in the photo.

*See also*
Using colour, *page 30*
Making a template, *page 38*
Working with fondant, *page 44*

# Ice-bucket bunny

**Degree of difficulty**

Easy

Celebrate good news with this cheery little bunny peeping over the top of an ice bucket.

**Use for**

Cake top ⬭

Side design

## Order of work

1 Adjust the design to the size required. Make a template and place in a plastic sleeve.

**Mix and match**

Champagne glasses, *page 150*

Sending a message, *page 153*

2 Use pink fondant to press out the bucket shape so that it is wider at the top than at the base. Trim the top and bottom edges with the side of a palette knife. Roll two fine tubes of dark brown fondant and add to the bucket as banding. Add a circle formed from a finely rolled tube of dark brown fondant to the top band, and a tiny band of fondant to complete the handle and hide the join.

**Motif uses**

Low relief ⬭

Flat ⬭

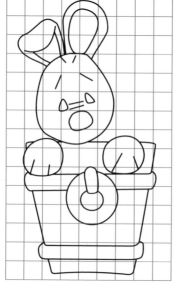

**Fondant colours**

Pink ⬤

Dark brown ⬤

**Tools**

Plastic sleeve
Palette knife
Triangular veiner

3 Use dark brown fondant to make an egg shape to fit over the template for the head. Mark the eyes with the triangular veiner, pointed end up. Indent a hole for the nose and add a small teardrop of dark brown fondant, tapping it down into the hole to form a flattened oval. Mark the eyebrows with the veiner. Take a ball of the same fondant, cut it in half, and shape each half into flat teardrops to create a pair of long ears. Tuck these in behind the head.

4 Place the head at an angle, peeping over the top of the bucket. Finish the motif with two fondant paws holding onto the edge of the ice bucket.

5 Transfer the motif to the cake when dry.

*See also*
Making a template,
*page 38*

72

Place the head at an angle to add character.

# Cool kitten

Make this cute kitten motif, and match it with a birthday gift box or a message for a cat lover's special day.

## Order of work

1 Adjust the design to the size required. Make a template and place in a plastic sleeve.

2 Take a small ball of white fondant, divide it in half, and shape each to fit the back legs on the template. Stretch them right up to the neck.

3 With a similar sized ball of white fondant, roll a carrot shape, and press it into a triangular shape on the template, to form the cat's body. With the side of a palette knife, make a cut through the fondant at the base to divide the legs. Mark the paws on all four legs with the veiner.

4 Add a small sausage of white fondant on one side for the tail.

5 Mould a white, oval face to fit the template, pinch out two ears at the top with your fingers and place on the cat's neck, placing it at a slight angle to suggest a mischievous look.

6 Mark the nose in the centre of the face with a veiner, and add a very small pale pink fondant nose. Add tiny ovals of pale pink inside the ears. Use a cocktail stick to indent eyes. Mark some whiskers and a mouth with the veiner.

7 Transfer the motif to the cake when dry.

To make a pair of kittens, reverse the template so the tails are on opposite sides.

**Degree of difficulty**
 Easy

**Use for**
 Cake top

**Mix and match**
Gift box, *page 204*

**Motif uses**
 Low relief
 Flat

**Fondant colours**
 White
 Pale pink

**Tools**
Plastic sleeve
Palette knife
Veiner
Cocktail stick

*See also*
Using colour, *page 30*
Making a template, *page 38*
Working with fondant, *page 44*

# Panda

Bamboo canes,
page 90

**Degree of difficulty**

Easy

**Use for**

Cake top

**Mix and match**

Bamboo canes,
*page 90*

**Motif uses**

Low relief

Flat

**Fondant colours**

White

Black

**Tools**

Plastic sleeve
Veiner
Palette knife
Black food
colouring pen

*See also*

Making a template,
*page 38*
Working with fondant,
*page 44*

74

Use this panda motif on its own
for a striking look, or team it with
bamboo for a more natural effect.

## Order of work

1 Adjust the design to the size
required. Make a template and place
in a plastic sleeve.

2 Roll two balls of white fondant, one
slightly smaller than the other. Flatten
them onto the template for the
panda's body and head.

3 Mark indents round the panda's
head and body with the veiner, to
give the impression of fur and define
the outline.

4 Roll a very small ball of black
fondant, divide it in half and shape it
to fit the panda's back arm and foot.
Indent these with the veiner as shown.

5 Use a slightly larger ball of black
fondant, again divided in half, to
create the front arm and leg. Shape
these onto the template and indent the
edges with the veiner.

6 Add tiny ears of black fondant,
indented in the same way. Indent two
eye sockets halfway down the head.
Add two tiny balls of black fondant,
and repeat with even smaller balls of
white fondant. Finally, mark the mouth
and the eyes with a black food
colouring pen.

7 Transfer the motif to the cake
when dry.

Curl the panda's arms and legs round some
bamboo canes (see page 90).

# *Friendly elephant*

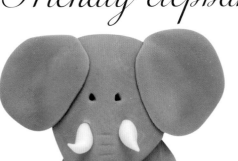

How about an elephant motif to trumpet a message of good wishes to someone on a special occasion?

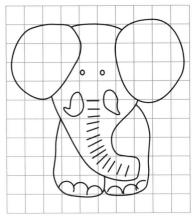

Try adding a small crown between the ears as a fun party hat.

## Order of work

1 Adjust the design to the size required. Make a template and place in a plastic sleeve.

2 Roll a ball of grey fondant into a chunky cone, and flatten this onto the base of the template with the thinner end pointing upward. Tap in the sides of the fondant with the side of a palette knife. Cut a line to mark the two legs. Use a drinking straw to mark the feet.

3 Roll a ball of grey fondant into a carrot shape. Elongate the thin end to create the elephant's trunk, flatten this onto the template. Curve the trunk as shown.

4 Use the veiner to indent two small eyes. Make two indents under the eyes where you will slot in the tusks. Use white fondant to make the tusks by rolling two small tubes, pointed at both ends. Set these into the prepared slots, and curve them upward.

5 Use the edge of the palette knife to mark lines across the trunk. Cut a small ball of grey fondant into two equal pieces, re-roll each into a ball and flatten out. Place these as ears, half on the head and half off.

6 Transfer the motif to the cake when dry.

**Degree of difficulty**

 Easy

**Use for**

◯ Cake top

**Mix and match**
Inscription banner,
*page 206*

**Motif uses**

▱ Low relief

▱ Flat

**Fondant colours**

 Grey

 White

**Tools**
Plastic sleeve
Palette knife
Drinking straw
Veiner

*See also*
Making a template,
*page 38*

75

# Party penguin

**Degree of difficulty**

Moderate

**Use for**

Cake top

Side design

**Mix and match**
Party crackers,
*page 125*

**Motif uses**

Low relief

Flat

**Fondant colours**

Black

White

Yellow

Orange

Red

**Tools**
Plastic sleeve
Veiner
Palette knife
Rolling pin

*See also*

Making a template,
*page 38*

Try making a row of these fun penguin motifs to decorate a winter party cake.

## Order of work

1 Adjust the design to the size required. Cut out a template and place it in a plastic sleeve.

2 Create a flat black fondant cone for the body. Add a smaller white cone in the centre.

3 Make the head in the same way as the body, with smaller black and white cones.

4 Indent the eyes with a veiner and fill with black fondant. Indent again and add a little white fondant. Indent again.

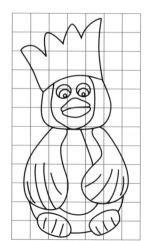

5 Add a yellow fondant beak, and slice the centre with the palette knife. Add orange fondant feet and mark claws with the veiner.

6 Make two cones of black fondant and flatten them onto the body for wings. Indent lines with the veiner.

7 Cut a party hat from rolled-out red fondant, and cut the top with a zigzag to create a crown. Position above the penguin's eyes.

8 Transfer the motif pieces to the cake in the order in which they were created.

Try making penguins of varying sizes.

# ßorse's head

Horseriding is a favourite hobby for many people – so make this striking horse's head motif to decorate a cake for their special day.

## Order of work

1 Adjust the design to the size required. Make a template and place in a plastic sleeve.

2 Take a ball of black fondant, and shape the head on the template, allowing extra thickness at the top. Mark a nostril with the veiner.

3 Shape a small ball of white fondant into a pointed oval for the eye. Add a tiny round ball of black fondant in the centre.

4 Make two teardrop-shaped ears of black fondant. Place them at the top of the horse's head.

5 Roll out some light brown fondant with a rolling pin, cut out a zigzag mane, and attach. Cut out the harness following the design. Insert a small, flattened teardrop of light brown fondant into the right ear.

6 Transfer the motif to the cake when dry.

Change the colours of the horse to suit the cake's recipient.

### Degree of difficulty

 Moderate

### Use for

◯ Cake top

### Mix and match

Lucky horseshoes, *page 170*

### Motif uses

 Low relief

◠ Flat

### Fondant colours

 Black

 White

 Light brown

### Tools

Plastic sleeve
Palette knife
Veiner
Rolling pin

*See also*
Making a template, *page 38*

77

# Leo the lion

**Degree of difficulty**

Moderate

This dramatic motif is especially suitable for someone born under the Zodiac sign Leo.

**Use for**

Cake top

## Order of work

1 Adjust the design to the size required. Make a template and place in a plastic sleeve.

**Mix and match**

Inscription banner, *page 206*

2 Mix a mid brown and a light brown fondant. Take a ball of mid brown fondant and flatten it to cover the whole of the teardrop shape, with the point at the base. Indent the mane and cut some triangles out to give it texture and shape, as shown in the picture.

**Motif uses**

Low relief

Flat

3 Roll a ball of light brown fondant and flatten it to form the face. Smooth the shape down at the edges and leave it deeper where the cheeks will be. Use a ball tool to indent the eye sockets one-third of the way down from the top.

**Fondant colours**

Mid brown

Light brown

Dark brown

Black

4 Now make the lion's ears. Take two small balls of light brown fondant and roll them to remove any cracks; place one ball at the top right of the face and one at the top left. Press the lower part of the ball into the face with the ball tool, allowing the top to curl over.

**Tools**

Plastic sleeve
Palette knife
Ball tool
Pointed tool
Veiner

5 Take a tiny ball of the light brown fondant, cut it in half and flatten it. Place these two balls below the lion's eyes to suggest the cheeks. Make a carrot shape from the darker fondant and add this to the centre, broad end at the base. Shape this into the nose. Indent two tiny dots for the nostrils with the pointed tool.

6 To complete the eyes, roll two tiny balls of dark brown fondant. Indent sockets with the veiner and add the brown balls. Indent the dark brown of the eyes and add black pupils.

7 Roll a tiny tube of dark brown fondant, roll each end to a point and place under the nose, between the cheeks. Divide the upper and lower lips by indenting with a knife.

8 Transfer the motif to the cake when dry.

*See also*

Using colour, *page 30*
Making a template, *page 38*
Working with fondant, *page 44*

Subtle shades of brown add character to the lion.

# Wise owl

The wise old owl is a favourite motif for many. Use for a birthday, a graduation, or a retirement celebration.

## Order of work

1 Adjust the design to the size required. Make a template and place in a plastic sleeve.

2 Roll a ball of light brown fondant, to remove any cracks. Place it onto the template and smooth it down to the edges, leaving some depth in the centre, for the body.

3 The owl's chest is made from mid brown fondant, rolled out with a rolling pin and cut into a trefoil shape with part of a large blossom cutter. Attach it to the owl. Use the end of a drinking straw to mark feathers. Divide a medium-sized ball of light brown fondant in half and shape two flattened cones. Add these for the owl's wings. Texture them with a veiner.

4 Take a small ball of light brown fondant, cut it in half, re-roll each into a ball and press into round shapes for the eyes. Attach these above the chest, indent the centre and add a tiny ball of dark brown to each. Texture radiating lines round the eyes with the veiner.

5 Make two tiny mid brown cones for the ears and add these above the eyes. Make a slightly larger cone for the beak, pressed into a triangle shape and placed between the eyes.

6 Use dark brown fondant to make a branch for the owl to perch on, and divide one end into two. Add tiny green leaves.

7 Position the branch for the owl to sit on. Roll two small balls of dark brown fondant, and flatten them into ovals. Add these to the owl's body and indent the claws using the veiner.

8 Transfer the motif to the cake when dry.

Use different texturing techniques to mark out the feathers.

79

**Degree of difficulty**

Moderate

**Use for**

Cake top

**Mix and match**

Rose leaves, *page 97*

**Motif uses**

Low relief

Flat

**Fondant colours**

Light brown

Mid brown

Dark brown

Green

**Tools**

Plastic sleeve
Rolling pin
Large blossom cutter
Drinking straw
Veiner

*See also*

Using colour, *page 30*
Making a template, *page 38*
Working with fondant, *page 44*

# Dapper dog

This cute, attentive little dog could convey all sorts of celebratory messages on a cake. Add an envelope to enhance the message.

**Degree of difficulty**

Moderate

**Use for**

Cake top

**Mix and match**
Sending a message,
*page 153*

**Motif uses**

Low relief

Flat

**Fondant colours**

Light brown

Dark brown ⬤

White ⬤

Pink ⬤

Green ⬤

**Tools**
Plastic sleeve
Veiner
Palette knife
Black food
colouring pen
Rolling pin

*See also*
Making a template,
*page 38*

## Order of work

1 Adjust the design to the size required. Make a template and place in a plastic sleeve.

2 Press a ball of light brown fondant into the shape of the head and mark lines round the edge with a veiner. Flatten a short tube of the same fondant and fit it under the chin to form a neck. Flatten two small teardrop shapes of light brown fondant and attach them to the head, bending them forwards, to form ears.

3 Indent the eyes halfway down the head with the veiner. Add a tiny sausage shape of light brown fondant below them for the snout. Flatten it out, and indent it with the veiner as shown. Add a nose made from dark brown fondant, and mark two nostrils with the veiner.

4 Roll a tiny ball of white fondant, then cut it in half and roll two cones. Drop the pointed ends into the eye sockets, and indent a small hole in each eye with the veiner. Fill with tiny balls of dark brown fondant, and mark the pupils with a black food colouring pen.

5 Indent a hole beneath the snout, using the point of the veiner. Roll a tiny teardrop of pink fondant, flatten it, and insert to make a tongue, allowing it to stick out a little.

6 Mould a flattened cone shape from light brown fondant for the body, and texture it with the veiner. Mould the paws from a ball of light brown fondant cut in half, and marked as shown with the veiner.

7 Roll out some green fondant for the bow tie. Cut a long strip, and bend each end in towards the centre. Position the bow tie over the dog's neck. Press a tiny ball of green fondant over the centre for the knot.

8 Transfer the motif to the cake when dry.

Colour co-ordinate the bow tie with other decorations.

# Frisky frog

This frog motif is three-dimensional and would work well on a cake top, with lilypads.

## Degree of difficulty

 Moderate

## Use for

Cake top

## Mix and match

Lilypads, *page 95*

## Motif uses

3-D

## Fondant colours

 Green

 White

 Black

 Red

## Tools

Plastic sleeve
Palette knife
Pointed tool
Veiner

## Order of work

1 Adjust the design to the size required. Make a template and place in a plastic sleeve.

2 Roll a chunky carrot shape of green fondant and then cut a line through the centre, from the pointed end to about one-quarter of the way along the carrot. Turn the cut edge of each of these segments outwards and fold the fondant into loops to make the back legs. Press the legs against the body.

3 Press in either side of the frog's body just in front of where the legs bend, to shape the head. Cut across the head to make a mouth. Insert a pointed tool and wriggle it up and down to open the mouth.

4 Insert the pointed tool into either side of the head, just above the mouth, and add two small cones of green fondant. Press the pointed tool again into these two 'eyes', and add a tiny ball of white fondant in each. Make a further hole in the white fondant and add a ball of black – ensure both eyes are looking at the same angle.

5 Roll four small cones of green fondant, and flatten them. Mark each twice with the veiner and place two under the back legs and two under the mouth.

6 Make a tiny, flattened cone of red fondant and pop it into the mouth to create a tongue. Vein the back of the frog with a few V-shaped lines to add texture.

7 Transfer the motif to the cake when dry.

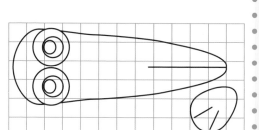

Sit the finished frog on a lilypad (see page 95).

*See also*
Using colour, *page 30*
Making a template, *page 38*
Working with fondant, *page 44*

# Pair of geese

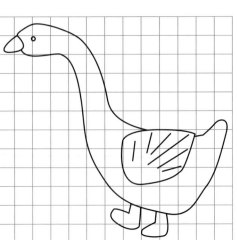

**Degree of difficulty**

Moderate

**Use for**

Cake top ⬭

**Mix and match**

Champagne glasses,
*page 150*
Inscription banner,
*page 206*

**Motif uses**

Low relief ⬭

Flat ⬭

**Fondant colours**

White

Yellow

**Tools**

Plastic sleeve
Veiner

*See also*
Using colour, *page 30*
Making a template,
*page 38*
Working with fondant,
*page 44*

A loving
pair of geese
make a cute cake
decoration to
celebrate news of
an engagement.

## Order of work

1 Adjust the design to
the size required. Make a
template and place in a
plastic sleeve.

2 Roll a carrot shape of
white fondant. Hold it against
the template, and keep
working and extending the
thin end until it is long
enough for the neck. Fold the
tip of the thin end underneath
itself to make a thicker part,
which forms the head. Make
a tiny indent for the eye.

3 Smooth the body into
shape on the template,
allowing the centre to remain
quite thick and thinning the
edges to form the back and
tail of the goose. Make a
small cone of white fondant,
flatten it and place it on the
side of the goose to form the
wing. Mark the feathers with
a veiner.

4 Make a tiny cone of
yellow fondant for the beak.
Make two small yellow cones
for the feet, fold them to a
right angle and pinch them
into shape. Add to the bottom
of the goose, with both facing
in the same direction.

5 Make a second goose
(the other way round) and
position them facing one
another. You could add a pink
bow (see page 204) round
the goose's neck, and a small
hat on the gander's head.

6 Transfer the motifs to the
cake when dry.

Reverse the template to create two geese facing each other.

82

# Pretty parrot

This fun motif would make a wonderfully colourful decoration on a child's birthday cake.

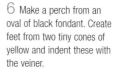

## Order of work

1 Adjust the design to the size required. Make a template and place in a plastic sleeve.

2 Roll a medium-sized ball of red fondant into a carrot shape and press it onto the template, smoothing down the sides to fit the outline of the body. Use the side of the palette knife to tap it into shape. Roll a small tube of yellow and a small tube of blue fondant and press them against the tail area to fit the template. Trim away any excess and vein the blue part of the tail.

3 Move the body of the bird to one side. Press small balls of red, yellow and blue together, make a smooth cone, and press down to make a wing shape using the template as the guide. Position over the body.

4 Make a small ball of yellow fondant. Cut it in half, and form the beak shape by allowing the top half to protrude beyond the bottom half; trim the other edge and fit the beak to the side of the parrot's head.

5 Indent a hole for the eye with the veiner. Add a ball of white fondant, indent again, and press in a tiny ball of yellow. Finally, indent this and add a tiny black pupil.

6 Make a perch from an oval of black fondant. Create feet from two tiny cones of yellow and indent these with the veiner.

7 Transfer the motif to the cake when dry.

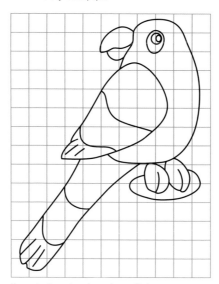

Use contrasting colours for maximum effect.

**Degree of difficulty**

🦪 Moderate

**Use for**

◯ Cake top

**Mix and match**

Balloons, *page 220*

**Motif uses**

🥚 Low relief

⬭ Flat

**Fondant colours**

⬤ Red

⬤ Yellow

⬤ Blue

◯ White

⬤ Black

**Tools**

Plastic sleeve
Palette knife
Veiner

*See also*

Using colour, *page 30*
Making a template, *page 38*
Working with fondant, *page 44*

83

# Lovebirds

**Degree of difficulty**

Moderate

These sweet little birds would be ideal on a cake for a special romantic occasion, such as an engagement or a wedding.

**Use for**

Cake top

**Mix and match**
Inscription banner,
*page 206*

**Motif uses**

Low relief

Flat ⬭

**Fondant colours**

Dark brown ●

Blue ●

Yellow ○

Light brown ●

Gold lustre

**Tools**
Plastic sleeve
Palette knife
Veiner
Tweezers
Drinking straw
Soft brush

*See also*
Making a template,
*page 38*

84

## Order of work

1 Adjust the design to the size required. Make a template and place in a plastic sleeve.

2 Roll two long, thin tubes of dark brown fondant, then twist them together and trim the ends.

3 Roll a ball of blue fondant, cut it in half, and re-roll, smoothing it down onto the template, for the birds' bodies. Use a veiner to texture all over their chests. Make the heads from a smaller ball of blue fondant, cut in half and re-rolled to form two balls. Smooth these into shape over the template.

4 Use tweezers to squeeze three little marks at the top of each bird's head. Mark the beaks and insert tiny yellow cones of fondant. Mark eyes on the birds with the veiner. Indent a curve above each eye, using the end of a drinking straw.

5 Roll a ball of blue fondant for the wings. Cut it in half, then in half again, and roll into four cones. Flatten the cones, and trim the pointed ends. Place the wings. Make three incisions in each wing, and separate the 'feathers'.

6 Cut a small ball of blue fondant in half and roll it into cones. Flatten them and make three incisions in each, then separate the 'feathers'. Trim the pointed ends, and ease the tails under the rope.

7 Make the feet from tiny balls of light brown fondant. Attach the feet to the rope, and indent with the veiner.

8 Finally, use a soft brush and a little gold lustre to add some highlights.

9 Transfer the motif to the cake when dry.

Tweak the wings and tails to a jaunty angle.

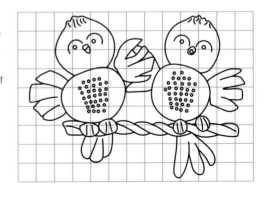

# *Puppy love*

Create a pair of loving puppies to celebrate an engagement party or bridal shower. Decorate with hearts, butterflies or flowers.

## Order of work

1 Adjust the design to the size required. Cut out a template and place in a plastic sleeve.

2 Make two cones of light brown fondant. Place these onto the template for bodies.

3 Cut three slices into each body with the palette knife. Add three small balls of light brown fondant for paws, and indent with the veiner.

4 Use four small carrot shapes of light brown fondant to make the ears. Flatten and indent; position as shown.

5 Form two flattened cones of light brown fondant for the heads and press onto the template.

6 Add conical noses of dark brown fondant, and indent the eyes and mouth.

7 Make a light brown collar for one puppy and a pink heart necklace for the other.

8 Transfer the motif to the cake when dry.

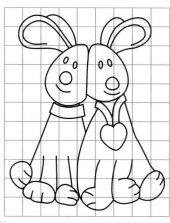

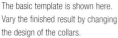

The basic template is shown here. Vary the finished result by changing the design of the collars.

**Degree of difficulty**

Moderate

**Use for**

Cake top

**Mix and match**

Sparkling butterfly, *page 62*

Bouquet, *page 102*

Hearts, *page 208*

**Motif uses**

Low relief

Flat

**Fondant colours**

Light brown

Dark brown

Pink

**Tools**

Plastic sleeve
Palette knife
Veiner

*See also*

Making a template, *page 38*

85

# Cock-a-doodle-doo

**Degree of difficulty**

Moderate

**Use for**

Cake top

**Mix and match**
Champagne glasses, *page 150*
Inscription banner, *page 206*

**Motif uses**

Low relief

Flat

**Fondant colours**

Green

Yellow

Red

Gold lustre

**Tools**
Plastic sleeve
Palette knife
Veiner
Soft brush

*See also*
Using colour, *page 30*
Making a template, *page 38*

This cockerel has something to crow about – perhaps a graduation or a new job!

## Order of work

1 Adjust the design to the size required. Cut out a template and place in a plastic sleeve.

2 Take a medium-sized ball of green fondant, and press it into shape on the template to form the body. Use the side of the palette knife to tap the edges into shape.

3 Model the tail feathers using yellow, red and green fondant rolled into fine tubes, pointed at one end. Curve them round on the template, and trim at the body end.

4 Make the head from a small, flattened cone of yellow fondant. Cut V shapes from the lower edge and fit the head onto the body. Curve it into shape with a point at the top.

5 Form the wing shape from a flattened ball of red fondant. Mark the feathers with a veiner and position it on the cockerel.

6 Model the feet from a single cone of yellow fondant, pinched into shape and attached to the bottom of the body. Roll a tiny piece of yellow fondant for the beak. Indent a tiny hole into the head to make the eye.

7 Use red fondant to make the comb and wattle – the comb is a chunky carrot shape with two cuts at the top, and the wattle is a tiny, flattened cone.

8 Apply gold lustre all over the cockerel with a soft brush.

9 Transfer the motif to the cake when dry.

Use bright, strong colours for maximum impact.

# Birdhouse

This motif is ideal for a gardener or country lover who enjoys feeding birds.

## Order of work

1 Adjust the design to the size required. Make a template and place in a plastic sleeve.

2 Roll a ball of light brown fondant into a cone, and place it onto the template. Flatten it down round the sides. Make two holes in the centre with a pointed tool. Mark vertical lines with the side of the palette knife to create the wood effect, and a curve over the tops of each hole. Roll a tube of the same fondant and shape it round the base of the birdhouse to make the platform.

3 Roll two tubes of dark brown fondant and place them against the sides of the birdhouse to form the roof. Add a small ball of dark brown fondant for the ridge, and a dark brown circle on top of this. Fill the two holes with a little of the dark brown fondant. Add three tubes of dark brown fondant for the perches.

4 Roll a small carrot shape of yellow fondant for each bird. Fold the fondant over at the thin end and press together – this creates the tail. At the broad end, pinch the fondant to form a tiny beak. Snip either side of the bird with scissors to create the wings. In front of this, indent a tiny dot for an eye. Carefully indent texture marks on the wings and tail with a veiner. Use a soft brush to lightly dust the wings, tail and beak with lustre. Repeat to make the other two birds.

5 Attach a bird on either side of the birdhouse, and one peeping out of the top hole.

6 Transfer the motif to the cake when dry.

### Degree of difficulty

Moderate

### Use for

Cake top

### Mix and match

Rubber boots, *page 163*

### Motif uses

Low relief

Flat

### Fondant colours

Light brown

Dark brown

Yellow

Gold lustre

### Tools

Plastic sleeve
Pointed tool
Palette knife
Scissors
Veiner
Soft brush

### See also

Making a template, *page 38*
Working with fondant, *page 44*

The birdhouse could be attached to a pole or the branch of a tree.

# Fishy friends

**Degree of difficulty**

Complex

**Use for**

Cake top

**Mix and match**
Inscription banner,
*page 206*

**Motif uses**

Low relief

**Fondant colours**

Yellow

Orange

Green

Dark brown

Gold lustre

**Tools**
Plastic sleeve
Veiner
Drinking straw
Soft brush

*See also*
Adding texture,
*pages 46–47*
Making a template,
*page 38*

This can be a continuous design round the side of a cake or a cake topper with a suitable message from one friend to another, such as 'Happy Birthday'.

## Order of work

1 Adjust the design to the size required. Cut out a template and place in a plastic sleeve.

2 Shape one oval each of yellow and orange fondant to fit the template. Mark off the fishes' faces with the veiner.

3 Indent the scales, using a drinking straw.

4 Roll out strips of green fondant and add the edge fins and tails to each fish, indenting with a veiner.

5 Roll three small carrot shapes of yellow fondant for each fish, and flatten them to form the side fins. Attach to the sides of the fish and mark with a veiner. Brush with gold lustre.

6 Mark the eyes and brows with a veiner and the drinking straw. Make small, flattened carrot shapes of yellow and orange fondant to form lips.

7 Make pebbles and grass from dark brown balls and strips of green fondant.

8 Transfer the motif to the cake when dry.

Reverse the pattern to make a second fish, facing the first.

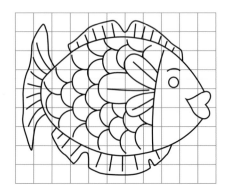

# *Prickly hedgehog*

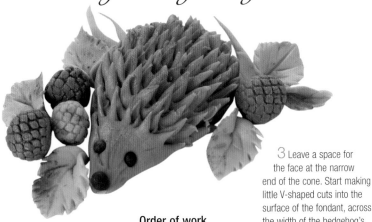

This little hedgehog would be suitable on a cake for a nature lover.

Make the berries in a range of colours; some ripen before others.

## Order of work

1 Adjust the design to the size required. Make a template and place in a plastic sleeve.

2 Shape a medium-sized ball of brown fondant into a cone, then flatten the base.

3 Leave a space for the face at the narrow end of the cone. Start making little V-shaped cuts into the surface of the fondant, across the width of the hedgehog's body. Make a second line of cuts behind the first, so that the 'V's fall between the previous ones. Continue making lines of cuts all over the body of the hedgehog, right to the very back.

4 Add a tiny black fondant nose and eyes on the face area.

5 For 'undergrowth', make some green leaves, grass and blackberries. The berries can be green or reddish purple and are made from small balls of fondant, textured by squashing them into a small piece of net. Add tiny amounts of red lustre to highlight the leaves and berries and surround the hedgehog.

6 Transfer the motif to the cake when dry.

**Degree of difficulty**

Complex

**Use for**

Cake top

**Mix and match**

Watering can,
*page 166*

**Motif uses**

3-D

**Fondant colours**

Brown

Black

Green

Reddish purple

Red lustre

**Tools**

Plastic sleeve
Sharp knife
Net fabric
Soft brush

*See also*

Using colour, *page 30*
Making a template,
*page 38*
Working with fondant,
*page 44*

89

# Bamboo canes

**Degree of difficulty**

Easy

**Use for**

Cake top

**Mix and match**
Playful panda,
*page 74*

**Motif uses**

Low relief

Flat

**Fondant colours**

Light brown

Green

**Tools**
Plastic sleeve
Tweezers
Palette knife

*See also*
Making a template,
*page 38*
Working with fondant,
*page 44*

Bamboo canes lend an Oriental theme to a cake. Try adding a panda peeping out from between them.

## Order of work

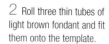

1 Make a template and place in a plastic sleeve. (If you make a panda, make it smaller than the canes.)

2 Roll three thin tubes of light brown fondant and fit them onto the template.

3 Take a pair of tweezers and create the bamboo markings by squeezing parallel lines across the fondant – about twice on each section of bamboo.

4 For leaves, roll a thin tube of green fondant, then cut it into around 12 sections. Roll each into a ball, then a thin carrot shape. Flatten into leaf shapes, and press the base of each leaf together. Arrange the leaves on the bamboo canes.

5 Transfer the motif to the cake when dry.

You could make any number of canes, and adjust the length to suit your design.

# *Blossom frame*

This smart arrangement of blossoms would add a finishing touch to all kinds of pretty celebratory cakes.

## Order of work

1 Adjust the design to the size required. This motif can be assembled directly on the cake.

2 Roll a long, thin tube of green fondant, and lay it down on the cake where the frame is required. This will not be seen when the frame is completed.

3 Roll a thin tube of green fondant, cut it into equal parts, and roll each piece into a cone. Flatten with the blade of the palette knife. Mark a central vein on each with the sharp

This trim can be attached to the top or sides of the cake.

edge of the knife. Assemble these leaves on the outline of the frame, at different angles, and allowing space to fit the flowers.

4 Roll a medium-sized tube of pink fondant, divide it into equal segments and roll each segment into a ball. Flatten each ball into a circle. Lay them on a foam pad and indent lines going right across, dividing each circle into six segments. Use a ball tool to press into each of the six segments.

5 Arrange the flowers in a straight line along the outline of the frame, between the leaves. Press the small ball tool down into the centre of each flower to anchor it to the frame, and then fill these indents with a tiny ball of orange fondant. Flatten the orange fondant and mark it with a pointed tool to texture. Continue until the whole frame is filled. Add extra leaves if necessary to balance the design.

### Degree of difficulty
⬦ Easy

### Use for
◯ Cake top

▭ Side design

### Mix and match
Inscription banner, *page 206*

### Motif uses
⬭ Low relief

### Fondant colours
⬤ Green

⬤ Pink

⬤ Orange

### Tools
Palette knife
Foam pad
Ball tool
Small ball tool
Pointed tool

### *See also*
Using colour, *page 30*
Making a template, *page 38*
Working with fondant, *page 44*

# Colourful cosmos

Cosmos are colourful flowers in a range of shades, from pink, white and red to deep purple.

**Degree of difficulty**

Easy

**Use for**

Cake top

Side design

**Mix and match**
Rose, *page 111*

**Motif uses**

Low relief

Flat

**Fondant colours**

Pink pastillage

Yellow

Dark green

**Tools**
Rolling pin
Sharp knife
Foam pad
Large ball tool
Veiner
Sieve

*See also*
Using colour, *page 30*
Making a template, *page 38*
Working with fondant, *page 44*

## Order of work

1 Adjust the design to the size required. Make a template of the flower and cut it out.

2 Mix pink fondant with a small amount of pastillage to help the flower hold its shape. Roll out the fondant quite thinly. Place the template on top and use a sharp knife to cut round the flower petals. Separate the petals a little, as shown. Turn over onto a foam pad and press a large ball tool into the edge of each petal to curve them. Turn the fondant back to the front and press the ball tool down in the centre. Mark each section of petal with radiating lines, using the veiner.

3 Flatten a small ball of yellow fondant and indent radiating lines close to one another all the way round the edge, using the veiner. Attach this to the centre of the flower and press down with the large ball tool. Take another small ball of yellow fondant and press it against a sieve to texture it. Attach this to the centre of the flower to finish it.

4 Roll a very fine tube of green fondant to make the stem. To make the leaves, roll a similar tube of green fondant and lay it across the flower stem. Make a few shorter lengths of green tube and arrange them into V shapes over this first 'leaf' to produce the finished effect.

5 Transfer the motif to the cake when dry.

Make several flowers and group them to create an attractive display.

92

# Spring daffodils

These bright, cheerful flowers make fabulous motifs for any springtime cake.

## Order of work

1 Adjust the design to the size required. Make a template and insert it into a plastic sleeve.

2 Roll some green fondant thinly, and cut some stems and leaves with the side of the palette knife to fit the pattern.

3 The petals are made individually and the trumpet sits in the centre. Roll a tube of yellow fondant and cut five equally sized pieces for each flower. Roll each into a ball, then into an oval, making it pointed at each end. Place the petals on the work surface and flatten them with the blade of the palette knife. Texture the veins with a veiner and assemble on the template, five per flower.

4 Make the trumpet from a chunky cone of yellow fondant. Use the bulbous tool to hollow out the centre of the broad end. Pinch the edges with your finger and thumb to make them finer and open out the trumpet. Use the veiner to mark the edges of the trumpet with some light indentations. Insert the small ball tool into the middle of the trumpet and press it onto the flower. Repeat for the other flower.

5 Transfer the motif to the cake when dry.

Alter the trumpet colour of the daffodil to orange for a variation.

### Degree of difficulty

 Easy

### Use for

⭕ Cake top

 Side design

### Mix and match

Rubber boots, *page 163*

Watering can, *page 166*

### Motif uses

⬭ Low relief

### Fondant colours

🟢 Green

🟡 Yellow

### Tools

Plastic sleeve
Palette knife
Veiner
Bulbous tool
Small ball tool

*See also*
Using colour, *page 30*
Making a template, *page 38*
Working with fondant, *page 44*

93

# *Ivy ring*

**Degree of difficulty**

Easy

**Use for**

Cake edging

Side design

**Mix and match**

Holly sprig,
*page 96*

**Motif uses**

Low relief

**Fondant colours**

Green

White

Gold lustre

**Tools**

Plastic sleeve
Rolling pin
Ivy-leaf cutter
Foam pad
Veiner
Green food colouring
Pointed tool
Soft brush

*See also*

Using colour, *page 30*
Making a template,
*page 38*

Fit this ring round the top or sides of a cake, or make it as a drape using half the circle.

## Order of work

1 Adjust the design to the size required. Make a template and place in a plastic sleeve.

2 Make a long tube of green fondant and fit it round the circle on the template. This will be hidden by the ivy leaves, while acting as a support.

3 Use an ivy-leaf cutter to cut out quantities of leaves from rolled-out green fondant. On a foam pad, vein each one through the middle with the veiner; this gives it a three-dimensional shape.

4 Arrange the leaves at a variety of angles, facing inward and outward, all round the circle. Paint green food colouring onto the ivy leaves in a ragged pattern to make the variegated ivy leaves. Leave to dry.

5 Make some small balls of white fondant for berries. On the ends that will be visible, indent crisscross lines with the veiner, then in the centre press a hole with a pointed tool.

6 At intervals round the circle, indent holes into the support ring and insert the berries.

7 Use a soft brush and a little gold lustre to add detail to the leaves and berries.

8 Transfer the motif to the cake when dry. If it is a large ring, cut it into sections between leaves and move a piece at a time.

Extend this template to form a larger drape or a ring round the cake.

# *Lilypads*

Float these pretty three-dimensional flowers and leaves on your cake top to create a watery theme.

## Order of work

1 Adjust the design to the size required. Cut out a template.

2 Use a mixture of pastillage and fondant to make the leaf. Place the template on top of the rolled-out green fondant mix, and cut out the leaf. Turn the leaf over and place on a foam pad. Run a ball tool round the edges to soften them and add curves. Turn the leaf back over and mark radiating lines with the veiner, as shown.

3 Use a soft brush and some gold lustre to emphasise the leaf details and edges.

4 Use white pastillage to make the lily. Cut out two six-pointed flowers with a cutter. Place them on a foam pad and use a ball tool to curve each petal, pressing down from the tip to the centre. Place one blossom on top of the other and press down the centre to join them.

5 Make the flower centre with a tiny ball of white fondant. Place it in the centre of the lily, and emboss a pattern with a small, round piping nozzle. Use a soft brush to add gold lustre to the centre and some of the petals. Place the flower on the leaf.

6 Transfer the motif to the cake when dry.

**Degree of difficulty**
⌓ Easy

**Use for**
◯ Cake top

**Mix and match**
Frisky frog, *page 81*

**Motif uses**
◯ Low relief

**Fondant colours**
● Green pastillage
◯ White
Gold lustre

**Tools**
Rolling pin
Palette knife
Foam pad
Ball tool
Veiner
Soft brush
Six-pointed flower cutter
Small piping nozzle

*See also*
Using colour, *page 30*
Making a template,
*page 38*
Working with fondant,
*page 44*

Use the motif at different sizes to create an arrangement.

95

# Holly sprig

**Degree of difficulty**

Easy

Scatter sprigs of holly on a Christmas cake, or use them as accents on other motifs.

**Use for**

Cake top

Side design

## Order of work

**Mix and match**

Christmas bells, *page 122*

Mistletoe, *page 123*

1 Adjust the design to the size required. (Don't make the holly leaves too big.) Make a template and place in a plastic sleeve.

2 Make a template of a single holly leaf, or use a holly-leaf cutter. Add pastillage to some green fondant to give it flexibility. Roll out the fondant; not too thin. Cut out some holly leaves; make five for each spray required.

**Motif uses**

Low relief

3 Set each leaf onto a foam pad and indent the veins as shown; a central one and several either side slanting towards the top.

4 Move the leaves to sit on the template, twisting them a little to shape them.

5 Add gold lustre to one side of the leaves with a soft brush.

**Fondant colours**

Green pastillage

Red

Gold lustre

6 Roll a tube of red fondant and divide it into equal tiny pieces. Roll each piece into a ball to make berries and arrange them in the centre of the leaves.

**Tools**

Plastic sleeve
Rolling pin
Holly-leaf cutter (optional)
Foam pad
Soft brush

7 Transfer the motif to the cake when dry.

*See also*

Making a template, *page 38*

Working with fondant, *page 44*

Vary the number of leaves and berries to create different arrangements.

# Rose leaves

Add these leaves to either of the two rose motifs for more detail on a cake top or side design.

## Order of work

1 Adjust the design to the size required. Make a template and cut it out.

2 Mix green fondant for the leaves. Add pastillage if a firm-setting leaf is required. The top leaf is bigger and the two side leaves match in size.

3 Roll out the fondant and cut out the leaf shapes, using the template as a guide. Add a central vein and slanted ones either side, with the veiner.

4 All round the leaf edges, slanted towards the top, press in the veiner and pull away to create a tiny tear.

5 Lay the leaves on a foam pad so they dry in curved shapes.

6 The stem is made from angel-hair spaghetti painted with green food colouring. (Alternatively, the stem could be piped directly onto the cake with icing before the leaves are arranged.)

7 Transfer the motif to the cake when dry.

For a five-leaf motif, place a pair of leaves, the same size as the top leaf, either side of it. Place two smaller leaves near the base.

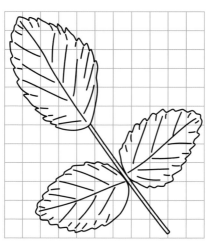

**Degree of difficulty**

⬦ Easy

**Use for**

◯ Cake top

▭ Side design

**Mix and match**

Wild rose, *page 110*
Rose, *page 111*

**Motif uses**

◯ Low relief

◯ Flat

**Fondant colours**

● Dark green

**Tools**

Plastic sleeve
Rolling pin
Veiner
Foam pad
Angel-hair spaghetti
Green food colouring

*See also*
*page 38*

97

# Rudbeckia

**Degree of difficulty**

Easy ○

**Use for**

Cake top ○

**Mix and match**
Daisy spray,
*page 114*

**Motif uses**

Low relief ○

Flat ○

**Fondant colours**

Yellow

Brown

Green

Bronze lustre

**Tools**
Plastic sleeve
Veiner
Palette knife
Small piping nozzle
Soft brush

*See also*
Making a template,
*page 38*
Working with fondant,
*page 44*

These handsome flowers can be used to decorate the sides of a cake, or grouped in a spray on the top.

## Order of work

1 Adjust the design to the size required. Make a template and place in a plastic sleeve.

2 Roll a long, thin sausage of yellow fondant. Cut it into seven equal pieces and shape them into long carrot shapes. Flatten these and assemble on the template for petals.

3 Roll a small ball of brown fondant and cut it in half. Mould the pieces onto the flower centres, and use a small piping nozzle to imprint a pattern all over them.

4 Use a soft brush to cover the flower centres with bronze lustre. Dust a little lustre onto the petals.

5 Roll out two long, thin tubes of green fondant to form a stem for each flower. Use the same fondant to make a leaf, from a flattened tube rolled to a point at one end and veined.

6 Assemble the finished motif on the cake.

Shape the stems with a slight curve.

# *Snazzy sunflowers*

Sunflowers make a big, bright decoration for a celebration cake.

## Order of work

1 Adjust the design to the size required. Make a template and place in a plastic sleeve.

2 Roll a medium-sized ball of light brown fondant and flatten it out on the template, leaving a small dome in the centre. Use a small piping nozzle to indent holes in concentric rings all over the fondant.

3 Roll a tube of yellow fondant and divide into 16 equal portions. Roll each portion into a ball, then a pointed cone. Flatten each one slightly with the blade of the palette knife, and then mark a vein through the centre. Place the petals close to each other round the flower centre, as shown.

4 Roll a thin tube of green fondant for the stalk. Make two leaves from flattened balls of green fondant. Vein the leaves and tease out the edges with the veiner to make them wrinkled.

5 Transfer the motif to the cake when dry.

Make several templates in different sizes for a stunning group arrangement.

### Degree of difficulty
Easy

### Use for
Cake top

### Mix and match
Poppy,
*page 105*
Watering can,
*page 166*

### Motif uses
Low relief

### Fondant colours
Light brown

Yellow

Green

### Tools
Plastic sleeve
Small piping nozzle
Palette knife
Veiner

*See also*
Making a template,
*page 38*
Working with fondant,
*page 44*

99

# Springtime tulips

Create a springtime display of tulips. Use a range of colours to suit your cake.

**Degree of difficulty**

Easy ◔

**Use for**

Cake top ◉

Side design

**Mix and match**
Watering can,
*page 166*

**Motif uses**

Low relief ⬭

Flat ⬭

**Fondant colours**

Light brown ⬤

Yellow ⬤

Green ⬤

Gold lustre

**Tools**
Plastic sleeve
Palette knife
Veiner
Soft brush

*See also*
Using colour, *page 30*
Making a template,
*page 38*

## Order of work

1 Adjust the design to the size required. Make a template and place in a plastic sleeve.

2 Roll some light brown fondant into very thin tubes, and cut to fit the stalks on the template.

3 Each flower is made from three petals. Roll a sausage of yellow fondant and cut into three equal sections. Roll each piece into a ball, then into a cone. Flatten each piece with the blade of the palette knife so that it looks like a teardrop. Mark a vein on each.

4 Place the central petal, then one on either side, with the points towards the top of the flowerhead.

5 Roll several thin tubes of green fondant. Cut them into sections of different lengths and roll the ends into points to make leaves. Flatten the leaves with the blade of a palette knife, then assemble them on the template. Mark a vein down the centre of each leaf.

6 Use a soft brush to apply gold lustre onto the leaves and the outside petals of the tulips.

7 Assemble the finished motif on the cake.

Use single flowerheads for a slightly different effect.

# *With love*

The heart-shaped petals of this plant convey a special message of love.

## Order of work

1 Adjust the design to the size required. Make a template and place in a plastic sleeve.

2 Prepare a flowerpot as shown on page 166, using light brown fondant.

3 Roll out a tube of green fondant and cut it into three pieces. Roll one of these pieces into a thin tube and trim it to make the stem. Make leaves from the other two pieces by rolling them into balls, then cones, and flattening with the blade of the palette knife. Indent a central vein on each with the side of the palette knife.

4 Roll a small ball of pink fondant and divide into six equal pieces. Roll each piece into a ball, then a cone. Make an indent in the broad end of each cone with the veiner. Flatten them with the blade of the palette knife to produce heart shapes.

5 Take a little pink fondant and a tiny amount of light brown fondant and roll them together to create a tiny round ball for the flower centre. Emboss a circle with a large drinking straw. Imprint round dots inside the embossed circle with a small piping nozzle.

6 Assemble the pieces on the cake to form the motif.

One plant plus a suitable greeting makes a quick and easy cake top.

## Degree of difficulty

⬠ Easy

## Use for

◯ Cake top

▱ Side design

## Mix and match

Watering can,
*page 166*

## Motif uses

◯ Low relief

◯ Flat

## Fondant colours

● Light brown

● Green

● Pink

## Tools

Plastic sleeve
Palette knife
Veiner
Large drinking straw
Small piping nozzle

*See also*
Using colour, *page 30*
Making a template,
*page 38*
Working with fondant,
*page 44*

# *Bouquet*

**Degree of difficulty**

Easy

**Use for**

Cake top

**Mix and match**
Gift box, *page 204*
Message labels,
*page 207*

**Motif uses**

Low relief

Flat

**Fondant colours**

White

Red

Green

**Tools**
Plastic sleeve
Rolling pin
Veiner
Sharp knife

*See also*
Using colour, *page 30*
Making a template,
*page 38*
Working with fondant,
*page 44*

A wrapped bouquet of flowers with a message label is a charming addition to a cake top.

## Order of work

1 Adjust the design to the size required. Make a template and place in a plastic sleeve.

2 Roll a carrot-shaped piece of white fondant to form the inside of the bouquet. Take another piece of white fondant, and roll it out thinly, until it is large enough to wrap round the bouquet.

3 Texture the fondant sheet with swirls, using the veiner. Turn over so the decorated side is face down and wrap the sheet round the carrot-shaped piece. Trim the sheet so that a V-shaped join is left at the front, and the wrapping ends just above the broad end of the carrot.

4 Roll a sausage of red fondant and cut into eight equal portions for the flowerbuds. Mould each into a ball, then a cone, and slightly flatten them. Use the veiner to mark a Y shape on each to define the petals.

5 Assemble the red flowerbuds in the top of the bouquet at different angles, starting at the back and filling up the whole space.

6 Use green fondant to make several small leaves. For each, roll a ball and then a cone, flatten it, and imprint with the veiner to give a three-dimensional shape. Arrange these in any available spaces to complete the bouquet.

6 Transfer the motif to the cake when dry.

Add a message label to the bouquet (see page 207).

# $\mathcal{P}$retty parasol

Make a jaunty parasol trimmed with blossom to decorate a special celebration cake.

## Order of work

1 Adjust the design to the size required. Make a template and place in a plastic sleeve.

2 Follow the instructions for the umbrella (page 187) but make it with a pink canopy and a pale brown handle.

3 Roll out a length of pink fondant with the rolling pin, and cut two parallel lines to make a strip of 'ribbon' for the bow. From this strip, cut two ribbon 'tails' with forked ends, and two diamond shapes. Bend the diamonds in half to form the bow loops. Assemble the loops and the tails on the handle in a bow shape, and finish with a small ball of pink fondant for the knot.

4 Mix equal quantities of white pastillage and fondant. Cut out 20 small blossoms with a small blossom cutter. Place these on a foam pad and roll round the edges of each one with a ball tool. Turn each one over on the foam pad, and press down in the centre to cup the blossom.

5 Make a long sausage of pink fondant and spread it along the edge of the parasol, where it will act as a base on which to place the blossoms. Dampen the fondant and arrange the blossoms to cover it.

6 Transfer the motif to the cake when dry.

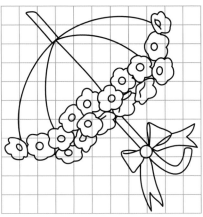

You could attach a message label to the handle.

103

### Degree of difficulty

◇ Easy

### Use for

○ Cake top

### Mix and match

Message labels, *page 207*

### Motif uses

▱ Low relief

▱ Flat

### Fondant colours

● Pink

● Pale brown

○ White pastillage

### Tools

Plastic sleeve
Rolling pin
Palette knife
Small blossom cutter
Foam pad
Ball tool

### *See also*

Using colour, *page 30*
Making a template, *page 38*

# Blossom basket

**Degree of difficulty**

Easy

**Use for**

Cake top

**Mix and match**
Bouquet, *page 102*

**Motif uses**

Low relief

Flat

**Fondant colours**

Brown

Orange

Yellow

Green

**Tools**
Plastic sleeve
Rolling pin
Round cutter
Veiner
Small blossom cutter
Ball tool
Foam pad
Vegetable shortening
Garlic press

A basket of flowers used alone or combined with other motifs is perfect for all sorts of occasions.

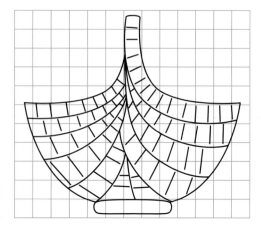

## Order of work

1 Adjust the design to the size required. Make a template and place in a plastic sleeve.

2 The basket and handle are made as one piece. Roll out some brown fondant and cut out a circle with a cutter. Use the same round cutter to trim away two curves from the top of the basket, leaving a central column for the handle.

3 Use the veiner to mark the basketwork. Mark a straight line from the top of the handle to the bottom of the basket. Then mark curved lines on either side as shown on the template. To mark the weave add short lines between the curved lines, alternating their position on each strip, like brickwork.

4 Add a small sausage of brown fondant to form the base of the basket.

5 Cut out some small blossoms from orange fondant. Lay them on a foam pad, and use the small end of a ball tool to press into each of the petals and indent the centre so that the blossoms curve upwards. Add tiny yellow fondant centres to each flower.

6 Soften some green fondant with a little vegetable shortening, and push it through a garlic press to form stands of foliage. Place these on the basket, then add the flowers, pressing them into the soft fondant of the greenery.

7 Transfer the motif to the cake when dry.

Any extra flowers can be strewn round the base of the basket or used to decorate the cake sides.

# *Poppy*

Poppies are bright,
vibrant flowers that
make striking motifs
on a cake.

## Order of work

1 Adjust the design to the size required. Make a template and place in a plastic sleeve.

2 Use red fondant and pastillage mixed half and half for the petals. Roll the fondant into a tube and cut it into four equal pieces. Roll each into a ball then flatten into a circle. Place each circle onto a foam pad and run the large ball tool round the edge to thin it and give some movement. Add a little texture by lightly marking with the veiner, in a radiating pattern from a point at one edge.

3 Place two petals as shown on the template, meeting in the centre. Position some tiny scraps of foam pad under sections of the petals to give them movement.

4 Make a small ball of white fondant and flatten it in the centre of the flower. Use a cocktail stick to scratch short lines outward all round this white circle to tear the fondant. Make a similar size ball of black fondant, flattened but not as thin, and place this in the centre of the white fondant. Use the cocktail stick to prick holes all over the black fondant to texture it. Finally, make a tiny ball of black fondant and add this to the centre of the flower.

5 Colour a length of angel-hair spaghetti with green food colouring for the stem. Roll and cut some spiky leaves from green fondant to attach to the stem.

6 When dry, remove the foam supports and transfer the motif to the cake.

Poppies grow in a variety of colours,
including pale blue.

## Degree of difficulty
◇ Easy

## Use for
○ Cake top

## Mix and match
Exotic orchid,
*page 115*

## Motif uses
◯ Low relief

## Fondant colours
● Red pastillage
○ White
● Black
● Green

## Tools
Plastic sleeve
Palette knife
Foam pad
Large ball tool
Veiner
Cocktail stick
Angel-hair spaghetti
Green food colouring

## *See also*
Making a template,
*page 38*
Working with fondant,
*page 44*

# *Arum lily*

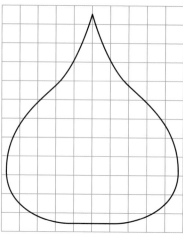

**Degree of difficulty**

Easy ○

**Use for**

Cake top ◎

**Mix and match**

Exotic orchid,
*page 115*

**Motif uses**

Low relief ⬭

**Fondant colours**

Orange ●

Pink pastillage ●

Green ●

**Tools**

Plastic sleeve
Cocktail stick
Vegetable shortening
Egg white
Sugar
Foam pad
Veiner
Green food colouring
Soft brush

*See also*

Making a template,
*page 38*

Working with fondant,
*page 44*

This sophisticated flower motif can be made in many colours.

## Order of work

1 Adjust the design to the size required. Make a template and place in a plastic sleeve.

2 The flower is formed round a cocktail stick for ease of handling. Grease the cocktail stick with vegetable shortening – this will enable it to be removed more easily.

3 Roll a long, thin tube of orange fondant, and place it onto the cocktail stick. Brush it with egg white and roll in some sugar. Set aside to dry.

4 Roll out some pink pastillage, and cut one large petal from it, using the template as a guide. Wrap the petal, pointed end upwards, round the yellow centre, and overlap the edges. Stick the base together. Curve the point of the petal backwards and support the flower on a foam pad until it has set.

5 Make two leaves from long tubes of green fondant, flattened and pointed at one end. Vein them down the centre. Brush green food colouring onto the base of the flower and add the leaves. Remove the cocktail stick.

6 Transfer the motif to the cake when dry.

You could colour the petal white, red or yellow.

# Fancy fuchsias

Use this elegant fuchsia motif to create a graceful hanging arrangement. Combine with draping designs for maximum effect.

## Order of work

1 Adjust the design to the size required. Make a template for reference but assemble the motif directly on the cake.

2 Use a mixture of pink pastillage and fondant for both the bud and the flower.

3 To make the bud, take a small ball of the pink fondant mix and roll it into a cone. Press the veiner into the side of the cone, working from top to bottom to make a petal edge. Make a tiny ball and attach it to the bulbous part of the bud. Use dark green fondant to roll a very fine tube for the stem, and add some very tiny pointed carrot shapes for the calyx where it joins the flower.

4 To make the flower, roll a medium-sized ball of the pink fondant mix into an oval, and mark the line of the petal on this using a veiner. Cut out petal shapes from rolled-out pink fondant. Mark these with long veins, and add them to the flower, curling upward and curving as shown. Make some very tiny balls of pink fondant for the stamens that hang down from the centre of the flower.

Fuchsias hang, so place the stems above the flowers.

107

### Degree of difficulty

◇ Easy

### Use for

◯ Cake top

▭ Side design

### Mix and match

Pleated drape,
*page 221*
Draped braid,
*page 222*

### Motif uses

⬭ Low relief

### Fondant colours

● Bright pink pastillage

● Dark green

### Tools

Veiner
Rolling pin
Sharp knife

*See also*
Making a template,
*page 38*

# Oak leaves and acorns

**Degree of difficulty**

Easy

**Use for**

Cake top

Side design

**Mix and match**
Wise owl, *page 79*
Pine cones,
*page 109*

**Motif uses**

Low relief

**Fondant colours**

Light brown

Green

Gold lustre

**Tools**
Plastic sleeve
Veiner
Small piping nozzle
Ball tool
Soft brush

*See also*
Making a template,
*page 38*
Working with fondant,
*page 44*

108

'Great oaks from little acorns grow!' Use this motif on a cake intended to wish someone well on a new venture.

## Order of work

1 Adjust the design to the size required. Make a template and place in a plastic sleeve.

2 Roll a small section of branch from light brown fondant. Texture it with the veiner to give the impression of bark.

3 Roll two small light brown ovals of fondant, and press the round end of the piping nozzle into the top to make the acorns. Set the acorns aside.

4 Use little balls of green fondant to form cups in which to sit each acorn. Press a ball tool into each ball to make the socket, place the acorn inside, and then press round it for a cosy fit. Use the piping nozzle to press round indents all round the outside of the cup. Repeat this step to make a cup for the other acorn. Use a soft brush to apply a little gold lustre to the acorns, and set them aside.

5 Press out two leaves from balls of green fondant, using the template as a guide. Add a central vein with the veiner. To make the shape of the leaf, pull the veiner from the outside into the leaf to form the indentations, three along each side. Make a second leaf in the same way.

6 Assemble the leaves and acorns on the branch and allow to dry before transferring to the cake.

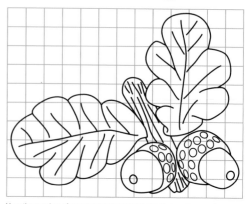

Vary the number of acorns and leaves to fit the design of your cake.

# $\mathcal{P}$*ine cones*

Try these lovely pine
cones as an addition
to a countryside
theme on a cake.

## Order of work

1 Adjust the design to the size required.
Make a template and place in a plastic sleeve.
Add a small amount of pastillage to give extra
firmness to the fondant for this motif.

2 Roll a tube of dark brown fondant, place
it on the pattern, and mark it with the veiner
to resemble bark.

3 Roll a ball of dark brown fondant. Press a
cocktail stick into one end to hold while you
are working. Use the pointed scissors to cut
tiny snips at an angle into the fondant. Keep
working round the fondant in circles until
the cone is snipped all
round, and down to the
base. Place the points of the
scissors on either side of the
cocktail stick to lift the cone
off the stick and place it
down on the template. Make
two more pine cones in the
same way.

4 Make the
needles by
rolling tiny pieces of
green fondant into small,
thin tubes. Roll the ends of
the tubes until they are pointed.
Fold each needle into a V shape and press
onto the twig between the cones. Make a
few of these double sprigs, allowing them
to stick out in different directions.

5 Transfer the motif to the cake when dry.

Add more pine cones on the sprig
to suit your design.

### Degree of difficulty

 Easy

### Use for

○ Cake top

▭ Side design

### Mix and match
Wise owl, *page 79*
Oak leaves and
acorns, *page 108*

### Motif uses

◁ Low relief

### Fondant colours

● Dark brown
pastillage

● Green

### Tools
Plastic sleeve
Veiner
Cocktail stick
Small, pointed
scissors

*See also*
Making a template,
*page 38*
Working with fondant,
*page 44*

# Wild rose

This easy rose motif can be assembled singly or in clustres.

**Degree of difficulty**
Easy

**Use for**
Cake top ◯

**Mix and match**
Rose leaves,
*page 97*

**Motif uses**
Low relief ◠

Flat ◠

**Fondant colours**

Pink pastillage

Yellow ◯

Green ●

Gold lustre

**Tools**
Plastic sleeve
Rolling pin
Five-petal cutter
Foam pad
Large ball tool
Veiner
Soft brush

*See also*
Working with fondant,
*page 44*

## Order of work

1 Adjust the design to the size required. Make a template and place in a plastic sleeve.

2 Use pink pastillage to help this flower hold its shape. Roll out the paste thinly and cut out a five-petal blossom with the cutter. Place the flower on a foam pad and use a large ball tool to press round the edges in a continuous movement. Press into the centre of each of the segments to cup the blossom. Turn the fondant over. Press the ball tool into the centre of the flower to indent.

3 Roll a small ball of yellow fondant for the centre of the flower. Flatten it, and texture it with the veiner, adding little marks all over the top and round the edges. Place a tiny ball of green fondant in the centre and texture it in the same way.

4 Use a soft brush to brush gold lustre over the flower, and set it aside to dry. Support the petals with pieces of foam pad so that they dry in a curved shape.

5 Make rose leaves (see page 97). Brush a little gold lustre over them and assemble the arrangement.

6 Transfer the motif to the cake when dry.

The petals can be tinted different colours to suit the colour scheme of the cake.

# *Rose*

Roses grow in many colours. Make buds and open blooms to beautifully enhance any celebration cake.

## Order of work

1 Make a template of the rose cone, petal and calyx and place in a plastic sleeve. (If the cake is large, increase the number of flowers rather than making the blooms too big.)

2 Try out the rosebud first. Use all pastillage or two parts pastillage to one part fondant. Make a yellow cone, then pinch out one side of the cone to make a very thin flap. Wrap this round the cone to look like a furled petal. Add the calyx cut from rolled-out green fondant. Roll a ball of green fondant for the rose-hip to fit at the base of the rose.

3 For the rose, roll a cone of the pastillage mix and let it set hard. To provide something to hold on to while making the rose, push a cocktail stick into the broad end of the cone before it dries. (This will be removed when the flower is complete.)

4 Cut out petals round the template. Work on one petal at a time, and cover any spare petals with a plastic sheet to stop them from drying out.

5 Place a petal onto a foam pad, and press the ball tool lightly all round the edge, moving from the point to the broad end and back. The tool needs to be half on the petal and half on the foam. Wrap the petal, broad end up, tightly round the cone. Work two more petals in the same way. Wrap them round the rose cone, but curl the top edges of the petals over slightly; one to the right and one to the left.

6 Add seven more petals, laying each one across the join of the previous one and curling their edges. Add a calyx cut from green fondant, and a green rose-hip. Set aside to dry.

7 Use a soft brush and some pink lustre to tint the edges of the petals.

8 Transfer the motifs to the cake when dry.

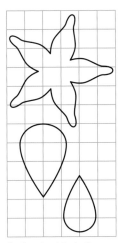

Use these templates for (from top): calyx, cone, and petal.

**Degree of difficulty**

Moderate

**Use for**

Cake top

**Mix and match**
Rose leaves,
*page 97*

**Motif uses**

Low relief

**Fondant colours**

Yellow pastillage

Green

Pink lustre

**Tools**
Plastic sleeve
Cocktail stick
Palette knife
Foam pad
Ball tool
Soft brush

*See also*
Using colour, *page 30*
Making a template,
*page 38*

# Dogwood branch

Add a spray of dogwood or make it into a garland round a cake to create a very quick floral design.

**Degree of difficulty**

Moderate

**Use for**

Cake top

Side design

**Mix and match**
Sparkling butterfly,
*page 62*

**Motif uses**

Low relief

**Fondant colours**

Dark brown

Green

White

Yellow

Gold lustre

**Tools**
Plastic sleeve
Veiner
Rolling pin
Palette knife
Soft brush
Red food colouring

*See also*
Making a template,
*page 38*

## Order of work

1 Adjust the design to the size required. Cut out a template and place in a plastic sleeve.

2 Roll a twig of dark brown fondant. Curve it and indent a texture with the veiner.

3 Roll out the green fondant and cut out leaves. Mark the veins with a veiner and brush them with gold lustre.

4 Roll out the white fondant and cut four heart-shaped petals. Thin the top edges and postion them as shown. Support the petals with small balls of white fondant to raise them from the surface.

5 Fill the centre with tiny yellow fondant balls for stamens.

6 Brush the petal edges with red food colouring.

7 Transfer the motif to the cake when dry.

Extend the basic motif to create a garland or a border.

# Bunch of grapes

Add some grapes to a wine lover's cake for any celebration.

## Order of work

1 Adjust the design to the size required. Make a template and place in a plastic sleeve.

2 Mix a dark bluish purple fondant colour. To create the bunch of grapes, first model a teardrop-shaped mound of this fondant for a base support. Roll a chunky tube of the same fondant and cut it into equal pieces. Roll each of the pieces into a round ball and then into an oval. Starting at the broad end of the teardop, place the 'grapes', allowing them to overlap.

3 Add some pastillage to the green fondant to give it extra flexibility. Roll out the green fondant and cut out some leaves. Vein the leaves, then ease them into position just under the grapes at the top of the bunch.

4 Use a soft brush dipped into melted vegetable shortening to brush over the grapes to give them a bloom.

5 Transfer the motif to the cake when dry.

White miniature grapes look good as decorative accents on a wedding cake.

### Degree of difficulty

Moderate

### Use for

◯ Cake top

▭ Side design

### Mix and match

Champagne glasses, *page 150*

### Motif uses

◯ Low relief

### Fondant colours

● Bluish purple

● Green pastillage

### Tools

Plastic sleeve
Palette knife
Veiner
Soft brush
Vegetable shortening

*See also*
Making a template,
*page 38*

113

# Daisy spray
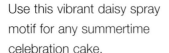

Use this vibrant daisy spray motif for any summertime celebration cake.

**Degree of difficulty**
Moderate

**Use for**
Cake top ⬭

**Mix and match**
Fluttering butterfly,
*page 63*

**Motif uses**
Low relief ⬭

**Fondant colours**

Green ●

White ●

Yellow ●

Bright blue ●

**Tools**
Net fabric
Veiner
Cocktail stick

## Order of work

1 Adjust the design to the size required. Cut out a template.

2 Make strips of green fondant and position them directly onto the cake for the stalk and leaves.

3 Use the pattern as a guide to mould daisy petals from white fondant.

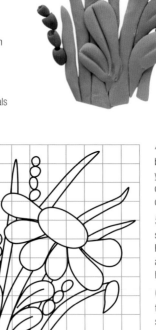

A single, large flowerhead makes a good decorative centrepiece.

4 Create the daisy centre by pressing an oval ball of yellow fondant onto a piece of net fabric. Add this to the centre of the flower.

5 Form four small carrot shapes of green fondant. Flatten and curve them, and add to the daisy stem for leaves. Add a vein on each.

6 On a cocktail stick, form tiny individual teardrop shapes of bright blue, stacking them in rows. Add these to the motif, as shown.

*See also*
Making a template,
*page 38*

# Exotic orchid

There are many orchid varieties, so vary the colours you use to suit the theme of your cake.

## Order of work

1 Adjust the design to the size required. Some orchids are quite big and spectacular, while others are tiny. Make a template of the whole bloom and insert into a plastic sleeve. Make separate templates of the 'wing' petals and the 'throat'.

2 Use white fondant and pastillage mixed half and half. Roll out the fondant mix and use the template to help you cut out the outer petals in one piece. Lightly vein them, then place them onto the orchid template in the plastic sleeve. Place a cocktail stick beneath each of the petals, towards the tip, to give them a little movement.

3 Cut out two individual 'wing' petals from the white fondant. Place them on the foam pad, and roll the ball tool round the edges half on the fondant and half on the foam; this stretches and curls the fondant. Move the petals to the template and position against one another. Press each one down in the centre with the large ball tool.

4 The 'throat' needs to be frilled round the broad end. Dust the work surface with cornflour, place the throat on this and use a bulbous tool to roll backwards and forwards along the broad edge of the fondant so it curls up. Move the throat onto a foam pad, and press a ball tool into the centre, stroking it along to the point. This makes the central indent. Position the throat between the wing petals.

5 For the 'nose', make a small cone and flatten the base. Use tweezers to squeeze two lines along the top of the nose. Position it at the top of the throat, protruding from the flower.

6 When the orchid is dry, lightly brush sections of the flower with gold lustre to give it depth and movement. Transfer the finished motif to the cake.

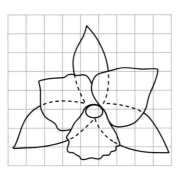

The top left and top right petals are the 'wings', the bottom centre petal is the 'throat' and the centre is the 'nose'.

115

## Degree of difficulty

 Moderate

## Use for

Cake top

## Mix and match
Rose, *page 111*

## Motif uses

Low relief

## Fondant colours

 White pastillage

Gold lustre

## Tools
Plastic sleeve
Rolling pin
Palette knife
Veiner
Cocktail sticks
Foam pad
Large ball tool
Cornflour
Bulbous tool
Ball tool
Tweezers
Soft brush

## See also
Making a template, *page 38*
Working with fondant, *page 44*

# Pretty pansy

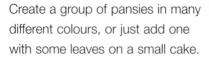

Create a group of pansies in many different colours, or just add one with some leaves on a small cake.

## Degree of difficulty

Moderate

## Use for

Cake top ○

Side design ▭

## Mix and match

Colourful cosmos,
*page 92*

## Motif uses

Low relief

## Fondant colours

Yellow pastillage

Dark brown ●

Black ●

Green ●

## Tools

Plastic sleeve
Ball tool
Veiner
Five-petal cutter
Palette knife

*See also*
Making a template,
*page 38*
Working with fondant,
*page 44*

## Order of work

1 Make a template and place in a plastic sleeve. (For a large cake, increase the number of flowers rather than making the blooms too big.)

2 Mix some pastillage with yellow fondant for the petals. The pansy has a large lower petal and four smaller ones. Roll a small sausage of yellow fondant, and divide it into six. Roll two bits together to form a ball, make a short, chunky carrot shape, flatten it, and shape this to fit the lower petal on the template. Soften the edges with a ball tool and indent radiating lines with the veiner, as shown.

3 Roll the four remaining pieces into balls, then cones. Flatten them to form petal shapes. Add the two top petals to the template, and then lay the two side petals on either side, so that all the petals meet in the centre.

4 Roll out a small piece of dark brown fondant, and cut out a small blossom with a five-petal cutter. Trim off one petal and place the resulting shape over the side and base petals in the centre of the pansy. Use the ball tool to press the brown fondant into the petals to incorporate it into the centre.

5 Mould a small ball of yellow fondant and place it on the top of the dark brown patch. Use the side of a palette knife to divide it in half vertically, and press the segments to either side. Mould a tiny piece of black fondant and place this at the top of this divided shape to complete the flower.

6 Make leaves for each flower. Form long oval shapes, and vein them as shown.

7 Assemble the finished design on the cake when the motifs are dry.

Pansies grow in a wide variety of vibrant colours, so make a selection of these and arrange them in a garland.

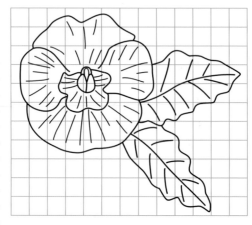

# Fan with roses

Make this stylish motif in the
shape of a fan decorated
with tiny pink rosebuds.

## Order of work

1 Adjust the
design to the size
required. Make a
template and
place in a plastic
sleeve. Make an extra
template for the fan.

2 Roll out some white
fondant and cut out the fan
round the template. Indent
straight lines on the fan with
the veiner. Use piping nozzles
or small cutters to indent a
pattern. Use a soft brush to
dust ivory lustre all over the
fan. Place onto the template
in the plastic sleeve.

3 Make some leaves
(see page 97).

4 Roll out some pink and
red fondant and cut it into
strips. Soften the top of a
strip by running your thumb
along it. Roll the strip up into
a curl to form a rosebud and
trim away any surplus from
the base. Repeat to make as
many roses as you need.

5 Place the rosebuds on the
base of the fan and tuck the
leaves in round them.

6 Make a ribbon bow from
red fondant (see page 204)
to add to the base of the fan.

7 Transfer the motif to
the cake when dry.

Textured patterns can be imprinted with piping nozzles.

### Degree of difficulty

Moderate

### Use for

Cake top

### Mix and match

Inscription banner,
*page 206*

### Motif uses

Low relief

### Fondant colours

White

Green

Pink

Red

Ivory lustre

### Tools

Plastic sleeve
Rolling pin
Palette knife
Veiner
Piping nozzle(s)
Small cutter(s)
Soft brush

*See also*
Working with fondant,
*page 44*

117

# Seasonal sleigh

Packed with mysterious gifts, this sleigh motif is a fun addition to a children's cake at Christmas.

**Degree of difficulty**

Easy

**Use for**

Cake top

**Mix and match**

Santa Claus, *page 128*
Gift box, *page 204*

**Motif uses**

Low relief

Flat

**Fondant colours**

Grey

Light blue

Dark blue

White

Silver lustre

**Tools**

Plastic sleeve
Rolling pin
Palette knife
Soft brush

*See also*

Making a template,
*page 38*
Working with fondant,
*page 44*

## Order of work

1 Adjust the design to the size required. Make a template and place in a plastic sleeve.

2 Roll out some grey fondant and cut out the body of the sleigh. Mark lines with the side of the palette knife – three together in the centre and three at the base.

3 Roll a long, thin tube of grey fondant and curl it round at the ends to form the runner. Join the runner to the sleigh with short tubes of grey fondant, flattened and indented. Use a soft brush to coat all this with silver lustre.

4 Cut out presents from rolled-out light blue, dark blue and grey fondant. Mark the string with the side of the palette knife and add simple bow shapes, as shown.

5 Roll a tube of white fondant for the sleigh's rim. Attach a star to the sleigh.

6 Transfer the motif to the cake when dry.

Pile other gifts round the sleigh ready to be loaded.

118

# Sugar cane

Make this simple sugar cane from twists of brightly coloured fondant.

## Order of work

1 Adjust the design to the size required. Make a template and place in a plastic sleeve.

2 Roll long tubes of red, green and white fondant and twist together. Place them on the template.

3 Roll out some green fondant and cut a strip. Attach two lengths of twisted ribbon to the sugar cane.

4 Roll out some red fondant, and cut out two calyx shapes. Place one on top of the other. Place them over the sugar cane and press down in the centre. Add a small ball of yellow fondant, textured by pressing it against a sieve, in the centre. Use a soft brush to dust the flower with gold lustre.

5 Transfer the motif to the cake when dry.

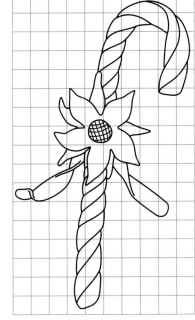

Add a holly sprig for a larger motif.

### Degree of difficulty

○ Easy

### Use for

○ Cake top

▭ Side design

### Mix and match
Holly sprig, *page 96*

### Motif uses

◇ Low relief

◇ Flat

### Fondant colours

● Red

● Green

○ White

○ Yellow

Gold lustre

### Tools
Plastic sleeve
Rolling pin
Palette knife
Sieve
Soft brush

*See also*
Making a template, *page 38*

# Red-nosed reindeer

**Degree of difficulty**

Easy

**Use for**

Cake top

**Mix and match**
Seasonal sleigh,
*page 118*
Santa Claus,
*page 128*

**Motif uses**

Low relief ⌒

Flat ⌒

**Fondant colours**

Light brown ⬤

Black ⬤

Red ⬤

White ⬤

**Tools**
Plastic sleeve
Veiner
Drinking straw

*See also*
Making a template,
*page 38*

This cheerful reindeer face is a fabulous motif to use on a children's Christmas party cake.

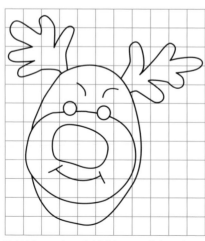

## Order of work

1 Adjust the design to the size required. Make a template and place in a plastic sleeve.

2 Roll a good-sized ball of light brown fondant and smooth it out into an oval on the template. Roll a smaller light brown ball and smooth it out into an oval on top of the head, to make the cheeks.

3 Use the veiner to indent the eyes and fill with tiny balls of black fondant. Indent the pupils. Above the eyes, indent two curves with the end of a drinking straw. Use the veiner to press in a curve for the smiling mouth, and indent a crease on either side of the mouth.

4 Roll a ball of red fondant for the nose, and flatten it into shape.

5 Add some white fondant to the light brown and roll out some tiny tubes. Shape them into V shapes and build up the antlers to fit the pattern.

6 Transfer the motif to the cake when dry.

Rudolph has a red nose, but dark brown would also work.

# Christmas tree

This simple, stylized Christmas tree is easy to make. Choose a striking colour scheme and make an array of different sizes for a festive display.

## Order of work

1 Adjust the design to the size required. Make a template and cut it out.

2 Thinly roll out some green fondant and place the template on top of it. Cut out the triangular outline of the tree round it.

3 Remove alternate sections of the tree as shown by cutting straight, parallel lines across the triangle.

4 Attach the tree trunk to fit right up to the top of the tree, with a portion extending at the base.

5 Cut a star from white fondant, place it on a piece of paper, and dust with gold lustre using a soft brush.

6 Assemble the tree on the cake and attach the star to the top.

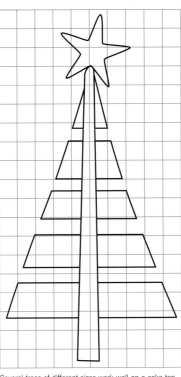

Several trees of different sizes work well on a cake top.

## Degree of difficulty

◇ Easy

## Use for

◯ Cake top

▭ Side design

## Mix and match

Mistletoe, *page 123*
Gift box, *page 204*

## Motif uses

◯ Flat

## Fondant colours

● Green

◯ White

Gold lustre

## Tools

Rolling pin
Palette knife
Soft brush

## See also

Using colour, *page 30*
Making a template, *page 38*

# Christmas bells

Use this Christmas motif as a main feature for a cake top or at the tops of swags on the sides of a cake.

**Degree of difficulty**

Easy

**Use for**

Cake top

Side design

**Mix and match**

Holly sprig, *page 96*
Draped braid,
*page 222*

**Motif uses**

Low relief

Flat

**Fondant colours**

White

Red

Gold lustre

**Tools**

Plastic sleeve
Palette knife
Soft brush

*See also*

Using colour, *page 30*
Making a template,
*page 38*
Working with fondant,
*page 44*

## Order of work

1 Adjust the design to the size required. Make a template and place in a plastic sleeve.

2 Roll a ball of white fondant slightly smaller in diameter than the size of the bell. Cut this in half. Mould each piece into a cone, flatten the sides, and stretch the bottom of the cone to fit the template. Make the shape thicker in the centre and at the base, and thinner round the other edges. Use the side of the palette knife to indent two parallel lines towards the base of the bells.

3 Mould two small white balls to form the bell clappers. Place the bells and clappers on a piece of paper and, using a soft brush, dust with gold lustre. Move them back to the template.

4 Make the bow from red fondant (see page 204), with long, trailing ribbon tails, and position this at the top of the bells, twirling the tails.

5 Transfer the motif to the cake when dry. If you are using it as part of a side design with swags, first place the swags and then the decorative bell motif.

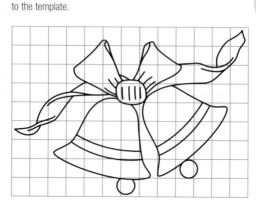

This motif would also look good with a sprig of holly round the top of the bells.

122

# Mistletoe

A sprig of mistletoe tied up with a red bow adds a festive and romantic note to a Christmas cake.

## Order of work

1 Adjust the design to the size required. Make a template and place in a plastic sleeve.

2 Roll three long, thin tubes of green fondant and place them along the lines of the stems on the mistletoe template.

3 Roll a tube of green fondant and cut it into 10 equal sections, each of which will make a leaf. Roll each one into a ball, then a cone, and flatten the cone into a leaf shape using the veiner. Assemble the leaves on the stems.

4 Make a tube of white fondant, divide into seven equal pieces, and roll each one into a small ball, to make the berries. Position these with the leaves and press the end of a pointed tool into each one.

5 Use red fondant to make the bow (see page 204).

6 Arrange all the pieces in sections on the cake when dry.

Vary the number of stems, leaves and berries for a different arrangement.

### Degree of difficulty

⬭ Easy

### Use for

◯ Cake top

▥ Side design

### Mix and match

Holly sprig, *page 96*
Sugar cane,
*page 119*

### Motif uses

⬭ Low relief

⬭ Flat

### Fondant colours

● Green

◯ White

● Red

### Tools

Plastic sleeve
Palette knife
Veiner
Pointed tool

### *See also*

Making a template,
*page 38*
Working with fondant,
*page 44*

123

# Peace dove

## Degree of difficulty

Easy

## Use for

Cake top

## Mix and match

Inscription banner,
*page 206*

## Motif uses

Low relief

Flat

## Fondant colours

White

Orange

Green

Red

## Tools

Plastic sleeve
Palette knife
Veiner
Angel-hair spaghetti
Green food colouring

*See also*
Using colour, *page 30*
Making a template,
*page 38*

Make a snow-white dove – or two facing each other – to symbolize a time of peace and happiness at Christmas.

Reverse the template to make two doves facing each other.

## Order of work

1 Adjust the design to the size required. Make a template and place in a plastic sleeve. (Make another template and reverse it if you are making two doves facing each other, as shown here.)

2 Smooth out a medium-sized ball of white fondant to a flat shape, allowing a little depth at the centre, for the body and head of the bird. Use the palette knife to trim away V shapes to create the tail. Mark a small indent for the eye with the veiner.

3 Roll a smaller ball of white fondant and shape it over the wing. Indent lines with the veiner.

4 Add an orange beak.

5 Fit a length of angel-hair spaghetti coloured green under the beak, and mould some tiny leaves and berries from green and red fondant to sit against this stem.

6 Transfer the motif to the cake when dry.

# Party crackers

Party crackers
are fun at
any time of
the year, but
are used especially
at Christmas.

## Order of work

1 Adjust the design to the size required. Make a template and place in a plastic sleeve.

2 Roll a medium-sized tube of grey fondant and make an indent in either end. Take another ball of grey fondant, cut it into two equal parts and shape each into a cone. Press a bulbous tool into the broad end of each cone and, while the tool is still in position, vein all round it to mark frills. Position the cones into the indents at either end of the cracker tube.

3 To decorate the cracker, roll out a strip of red fondant, cut it to size, and fit it round the body of the cracker. Roll out some green fondant and cut narrow strips of this to fit round either end of the red trim. Cut out tiny green stars and add these to the cracker. Mark both the red trim and the centres of the stars with a small, round piping nozzle.

4 Use a soft brush to add a little gold lustre.

5 Transfer the motif to the cake when dry.

### Degree of difficulty
△ Easy

### Use for
○ Cake top

### Mix and match
Balloons, *page 220*

### Motif uses
○ 3-D

### Fondant colours
● Grey
● Red
● Green
Gold lustre

### Tools
Plastic sleeve
sharp knife
Bulbous tool
Veiner
Rolling pin
Small piping nozzle
Soft brush

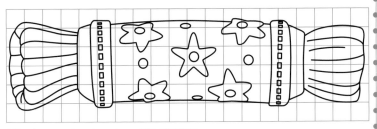

Add crackers – one for each guest – round the cake's base.

*See also*
Making a template,
*page 38*

125

# *Plum pudding*

This round plum pudding motif makes a fun addition to a cake for Christmas.

**Degree of difficulty**

Easy ⌣

**Use for**

Cake top ⬭

**Mix and match**

Christmas candle, *page 140*

**Motif uses**

Low relief ⬭

Flat ⬭

**Fondant colours**

Brown ●

White ◔

Green ●

Red ●

**Tools**

Plastic sleeve
Piping nozzle
Sharp knife
Rolling pin
Drinking straw
Small brush
Black food colouring

*See also*

Making a template, *page 38*

## Order of work

1 Adjust the design to the size required. Make a template and place in a plastic sleeve.

2 Roll a ball of brown fondant and flatten it onto the template, leaving some depth at the centre. Press a piping nozzle into the fondant to mark the currants.

3 Roll a sausage shape of white fondant and place this over the top of the pudding. Trim it into a curvy shape to represent the sauce dripping down the sides of the pudding.

4 Roll out some green fondant and use the end of a drinking straw to cut out the curves of small holly leaves – three on each side of a leaf.

5 Add the leaves and some tiny red berries to the top of the pudding. Use a small brush to paint the currants with black food colouring.

6 Transfer the motif to the cake when dry.

Add lots of juicy 'currants' to the pudding.

# Christmas stocking

A stocking that hangs at the end of a bed, waiting to be filled with gifts, is a great motif on a children's cake.

## Order of work

1 Adjust the design to the size required. Make a template and place in a plastic sleeve.

2 Take a large ball of red fondant, roll to get rid of any creases, then shape into a tube. Bend the tube to form the foot and leg of the stocking, pressing it onto the pattern and smoothing the edges. Use the side of a palette knife to tap the stocking into shape with a flat base and back edge. Indent lines for the heel and toe of the stocking.

3 Roll a small tube of white fondant, flatten it, and place it across the top. Trim to size. Texture the edge with the small piping nozzle.

4 Make holly-leaf shapes from flattened cones of green fondant. Mark the veins and press out the points of each leaf with the veiner. Assemble the leaves on the stocking and add some tiny red berries.

5 Transfer the motif to the cake when dry.

Make some small gifts to sit in the top of the stocking.

### Degree of difficulty
Easy

### Use for
Cake top

### Mix and match
Seasonal sleigh,
*page 118*
Santa Claus,
*page 128*

### Motif uses
Low relief

Flat

### Fondant colours
Red

White

Green

### Tools
Plastic sleeve
Palette knife
Small piping nozzle
Veiner

### See also
Making a template,
*page 38*
Working with fondant,
*page 44*

127

# Santa Claus

**Degree of difficulty**

Easy

**Use for**

Cake top ◎

**Mix and match**

Christmas candle,
*page 140*
Gift box, *page 204*

**Motif uses**

Low relief ◠

Flat ⬭

**Fondant colours**

Red 🔴

Pink 🌙

Black ⚫

White ⚪

**Tools**

Plastic sleeve
Palette knife
Veiner

*See also*

Making a template,
*page 38*
Working with fondant,
*page 44*

128

A jolly Santa waving to everyone is a great motif to add to a cake to celebrate a very merry Christmas.

## Order of work

1 Adjust the design to the size required. Make a template and place in a plastic sleeve.

2 Roll two short tubes of red fondant and press them together to make the legs. Trim to size. Roll a ball of red fondant and press it out over the body area, smoothing it at the sides and leaving it domed in the centre. Add two smaller balls at the sides and shape them into arms.

3 Roll a ball of pink fondant for the face. Add a red carrot shape, and smooth to fit the hat. Indent a hole for the nose with the veiner and insert a cone of pink fondant.

4 Make two mittens from flattened cones of black fondant. Make two cones of black fondant for feet. Use the side of the palette knife to straighten the base. Add two tiny black buttons.

5 Roll thin tubes of white fondant, flatten them and indent the top and bottom edges with the veiner to make 'fur'. Add strips to the coat, legs, arms and hat. Make a small, double-ended white cone, flatten and press into place for the beard. Add two tiny cones of white fondant for the mustache. Finally, add the bobble on the hat.

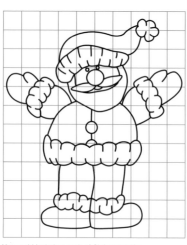

You could include a sack of Christmas gifts.

6 Transfer the motif to the cake when dry.

# Jolly snowman

Add this festive snowman to any winter celebration cake.

## Order of work

1 Adjust the design to the size required. Make a template and place in a plastic sleeve.

2 Press a ball of white fondant into a dome to cover the snowman's face on the template. Use the veiner to make an indent in the centre. Use a tiny ball of red fondant, rolled first into a ball and then into a cone, to make the nose, inserting the pointed end into the indent. Use a large blossom cutter to press a curve into the white fondant below the nose to make a 'smiley' mouth. Indent eye sockets and use a tiny piece of black fondant, cut in half and made into cone shapes, to form each eye.

3 Cut off the top of the head. Replace with a sausage of black fondant, pointed at both ends and shaped to form the brim of the hat. Roll a tube of red fondant and place above the hat brim. To form the top hat, take a small ball of black fondant, flatten it and smooth down each side. Cut off the top and bottom with the palette knife and shape to fit above the red fondant. Finally, tap into shape on the template with the edge of the palette knife.

4 To make the scarf, roll one long tube of red fondant and one of blue, and twirl them round each other. Press the twisted fondant down to flatten it. Cut a length and place it round the snowman's neck, then cut and place two more lengths for the scarf ends. Indent fringes on the ends. Brush the motif with a little gold lustre.

5 Transfer the motif to the cake when dry.

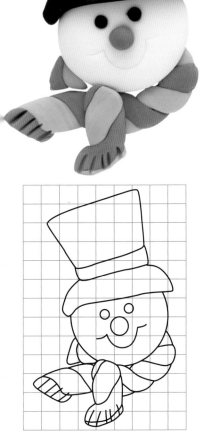

Change the scarf colours to suit the cake design.

## Degree of difficulty

⌂ Easy

## Use for

◯ Cake top

## Mix and match

Seasonal sleigh, *page 118*

## Motif uses

⬡ Low relief

⬡ Flat

## Fondant colours

⬤ White

⬤ Red

⬤ Black

⬤ Blue

Gold lustre

## Tools

Plastic sleeve
Veiner
Large blossom cutter
Palette knife
Soft brush

## See also

Making a template, *page 38*

129

# Robin redbreast

**Degree of difficulty**

Easy

**Use for**

Cake top

**Mix and match**

Balloons, *page 220*

**Motif uses**

Low relief

Flat

**Fondant colours**

Light brown

Red

Black

Yellow

**Tools**

Plastic sleeve
Palette knife
Cocktail stick
Black food colouring

*See also*
Making a template,
*page 38*

Perch this cute little robin motif among bunches of tulips or other springtime flowers.

## Order of work

1 Adjust the design to the size required, but do not make this motif too big. Make a template and place in a plastic sleeve.

2 Roll a ball of light brown fondant into an oval shape, and squash it down all round the edge to fit the template – the centre is the highest point in this design.

3 Roll out a circle of red fondant, the diameter of the bird's body. Cut this in half, then cut a V shape in the centre of the flat side. Attach to the body, with the V upside down.

4 Roll two long, thin carrot shapes of light brown fondant. Flatten and curve them to form the wings before attaching them on either side of the bird. The wings should just cross over at the bottom.

5 Roll a thin tube of black fondant and place at the base of the bird. Mark a line with the palette knife to divide it into two legs, then place a very tiny ball of black fondant on either side.

6 Add a pointed yellow beak just above the robin's red breast. Use a cocktail stick to make two tiny eye sockets. Dip the cocktail stick into some black food colouring and touch it into the eye sockets.

7 Use black fondant to make a tiny sausage and place it across the top of the bird's head for the hat brim. Then make a black fondant rectangle and place it above the brim to complete the bowler hat.

8 Transfer the motif to the cake when dry.

Try arranging some leaves and twigs round the bird's feet.

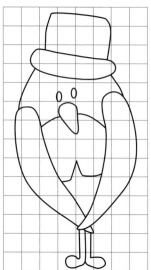

# *Prayer book*

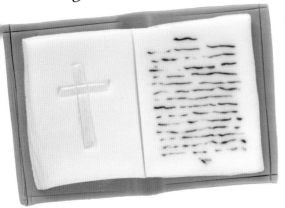

Make a book with text and an appropriate symbol to represent scripture relating to a festival such as Easter.

**Degree of difficulty**

△ Easy

**Use for**

○ Cake top

**Mix and match**
Easter egg, *page 132*
Easter chick, *page 133*

**Motif uses**

▱ Low relief

**Fondant colours**

⬤ Green

◯ White

Gold lustre

## Order of work

1 Adjust the design to the size required. Make a template and place in a plastic sleeve.

2 Roll out some green fondant into a rectangle and trim to size. Use the side of a palette knife to indent line markings round the outside. Press a round dowel into the centre of the oblong to mark the open spine of the book.

3 Roll out a rectangle of white fondant for the book pages. Place on the book cover. Tap the edges of the fondant to 'age' the pages. Mark a line for the centre fold of the book.

4 On the left-hand 'page' draw a cross shape with the palette knife.

5 Use a black food colouring pen to add lines of 'writing' across the opposite page, as shown.

6 Use a small, soft brush dampened with water to add gold lustre to the cross and to the edges of the pages.

7 Transfer the motif to the cake when dry.

**Tools**
Plastic sleeve
Rolling pin
Palette knife
Round dowel
Black food colouring pen
Soft brush

*The basic book template could be adapted for other festivals or celebrations.*

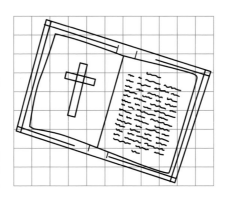

*See also*
Making a template, *page 38*

# *Easter egg*

**Degree of difficulty**

Easy

**Use for**

Cake top

**Mix and match**

Spring daffodils,
*page 93*

**Motif uses**

Low relief

Flat

**Fondant colours**

Light brown

Yellow

Orange

**Tools**

Plastic sleeve
Palette knife
Tweezers
Veiner

This Easter egg has just cracked to reveal a sweet little chick!

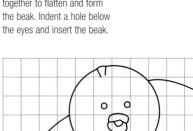

## Order of work

1 Adjust the design to the size required. Make a template and place in a plastic sleeve.

2 Roll out a sizeable ball of light brown fondant and mould it over the egg shape, leaving some depth in the centre and making it very shallow round the edge. Use a palette knife to cut a zigzag break in the egg. Move the two pieces off the template while you make the chick.

3 Roll a ball of yellow fondant, and smooth it down onto the body area. Replace the cracked egg pieces.

4 Roll a smaller yellow ball, and press it down onto the head area. Use tweezers to crimp a little pattern at the top of the head.

5 Indent two eyes with the veiner, forming a triangular shape. Make two tiny, pointed orange cones. Press them together to flatten and form the beak. Indent a hole below the eyes and insert the beak.

6 Transfer the motif to the cake when dry.

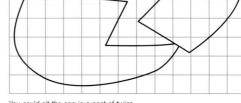

You could sit the egg in a nest of twigs.

*See also*

Making a template,
*page 38*

# *Easter chick*

This Easter chick is just about
to flap its wings and jump
out of the egg.

## Order of work

1 Adjust the design to the size
required. Make a template and
place in a plastic sleeve.

2 Roll a ball of light brown fondant,
smooth it onto the egg, and use a
palette knife to cut cracks at the top.

3 Mould a ball of yellow fondant to
make the head. Place a strip of yellow
under the cracked section of the egg
for the top of the body. Roll and cut
out two yellow heart shapes for
wings. Place these on either side of
the head with the curved edges
outward. Indent with lines using the
palette knife.

4 Make two round holes with the
pointed tool for the eyes, and insert
tiny balls of black fondant. Mark
curves above the eyes using the
end of a drinking straw.

5 Use tiny balls of red fondant to
add a comb (divided into three with
the veiner) and a wattle. Mix red and
yellow fondant to make a tiny orange
ball and shape this into a cone. Indent
a hole beneath the eyes and put the
beak in place. Mark the division.

6 Transfer the motif to the
cake when dry.

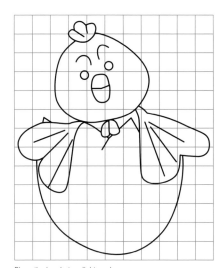

Place the head at a slight angle.

## Degree of difficulty

◇ Easy

## Use for

◯ Cake top

## Mix and match

Easter bunny,
*page 143*

## Motif uses

⬭ Low relief

⬭ Flat

## Fondant colours

⬤ Light brown

⬤ Yellow

⬤ Black

⬤ Red

## Tools

Plastic sleeve
Palette knife
Rolling pin
Pointed tool
Drinking straw
Veiner

*See also*
Making a template,
*page 38*

# Menorab

**Degree of difficulty**

Easy

**Use for**

Cake top

**Mix and match**

Star of David,
*page 135*
Torah scroll,
*page 164*

**Motif uses**

Low relief

Flat

**Fondant colours**

Yellow

Blue

**Tools**

Plastic sleeve
Rolling pin
Palette knife
Six-pointed
star cutter

A menorah is a seven-branched candlestick, and is a symbol of the Jewish faith.

## Order of work

1 Adjust the design to the size required. Make a template and place in a plastic sleeve.

2 Make the menorah from yellow fondant; it is easiest to make it in sections. Roll out some yellow fondant (it needs to be fairly thick as the candles must sit on the top). Cut and trim each section, and assemble it on the template. Indent a star into the main area with a cutter or the palette knife. Add the base strip – curve it a little before trimming it to size.

3 Roll a long, thin tube of blue fondant, and trim it into seven equal-sized candles. Sit them on top of the menorah.

4 Roll some tiny cones of yellow fondant and place one above each candle, for flames.

5 Transfer the motif to the cake when dry. Move the flames separately.

For a Hanukkah celebration motif, use the basic menorah template, but add nine candles.

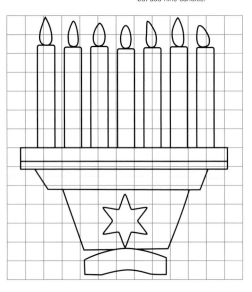

*See also*
Making a template,
*page 38*

# Star of David

The Star of David is one of the most widely recognized symbols of the Jewish world. These exceptionally simple but effective stars can be made as cake-top or side decorations for Jewish festivals.

## Order of work

1 Adjust the design to the size required. Make a template and place in a plastic sleeve.

2 Mix some blue fondant and finely roll it out.

3 Use a sharp knife or rolling cutter to cut out some strips of fondant. Lay the fondant onto the design, arranging the strips under and over each other as shown.

4 When the star is assembled, trim off all the angles with a sharp knife.

5 Transfer the motif to the cake when dry.

Remember that the cake and decorations should all be kosher.

**Degree of difficulty**

Easy

**Use for**

Cake top

Side design

**Mix and match**
Menorah, *page 134*
Torah scroll, *page 164*

**Motif uses**

Low relief

Flat

**Fondant colour**

Blue

**Tools**
Plastic sleeve
Rolling pin
Sharp knife/
rolling cutter

*See also*
Making a template, *page 38*

135

# *Top hat and shamrock*

St Patrick's Day in the month of March is celebrated all over the world, not just in the Emerald Isle. Use this motif to decorate your cake for the celebrations.

**Degree of difficulty**

Easy

**Use for**

Cake top

**Mix and match**

Wishing on a star, *page 213*

**Motif uses**

Low relief

Flat

**Fondant colours**

Bright green

White

**Tools**

Plastic sleeve
Palette knife
Icing smoother
Veiner

## Order of work

1 Adjust the design to the size required. Make a template and place in a plastic sleeve.

2 Roll thin tubes of green and white fondant, cut into lengths and set alternate colours side by side across the hat template, starting and ending with green.

3 Place an icing smoother on top of the tubes of fondant and press down so that the tubes fuse together to give a striped fondant.

4 Use the blade of the palette knife to squash the sides in towards the bottom.

5 Trim the bottom end flat, then trim the top of the hat to a slight curve.

6 Make a tube of white fondant and flatten it slightly. Place at the base of the hat, allowing it to extend either side. Trim the ends to create the brim.

7 Roll three small balls of green fondant. Shape them into cones and press into the broad end of each with a veiner. Flatten the cones with the blade of the palette knife to form heart shapes. Assemble the three heart shapes onto the hat, and then add a fine, flattened tube of green for the stalk.

8 Transfer the motif to the cake when dry.

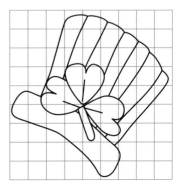

*See also*
Making a template, *page 38*

You could team this motif with stars (see page 213) and tie a green ribbon round your cake.

# *Pumpkin witch*

Dress up this decorated pumpkin with a witch's hat to create a fun motif for Halloween.

## Order of work

1 Adjust the design to the size required. Make a template and place in a plastic sleeve.

2 Roll a ball of orange fondant, smooth it down onto the face area, and indent the lines with a veiner, working from bottom to top. Make holes with the veiner for the nose, eyes and mouth. Fill them with black fondant.

3 Make a cone of black fondant for the hat and press it into shape. Make the brim of the hat from a tube of black fondant, pressed out to fit the pattern.

4 Roll out some green fondant and cut a strip for the hat band. Fit it onto the hat and trim away any surplus.

5 Transfer the motif to the cake when dry.

Enlarge the motif enough to cover most of the cake top or use small for single cupcakes.

### Degree of difficulty

⌣ Easy

### Use for

◯ Cake top

### Mix and match

Halloween ghosts, *page 138*

### Motif uses

⬭ Low relief

⬭ Flat

### Fondant colours

◯ Orange

● Black

◯ Green

### Tools

Plastic sleeve
Veiner
Rolling pin
Palette knife

*See also*
Making a template, *page 38*

# Halloween ghosts

Simple but scary ghost motifs
are perfect for Halloween cakes.

**Degree of difficulty**

Easy

**Use for**

Cake top

**Mix and match**
Wishing on a star,
*page 213*

**Motif uses**

Low relief

Flat

**Fondant colours**

White

Black

**Tools**
Plastic sleeve
Veiner
Drinking straw

## Order of work

1 Adjust the design to the size
required. Make a template and
place in a plastic sleeve.

2 Roll a medium-sized ball of white
fondant, elongate it into a tube, and place
it on the pattern. Smooth out the fondant
until it fills the shape, leaving a bit of
depth in the centre.

3 Use the veiner to make holes for the
eyes, and half-fill these with black fondant.

4 Add an oval indentation for the nose
beneath the eyes, and indent a semicircle
for the mouth underneath this with a
drinking straw.

5 Transfer the motif to the cake when dry.

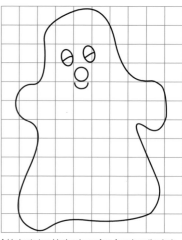

Add ghosts to a black cake surface for a haunting look.

*See also*
Making a template,
*page 38*

# Pumpkin family

Make these pumpkin motifs in several sizes to decorate a Halloween cake.

## Order of work

1 Adjust the design to the size required. Make a template and place in a plastic sleeve.

2 Roll a medium-sized ball of orange fondant, and press it down onto the pattern. Turn the template round. Make the base indents by indenting the fondant with the veiner and pulling the veiner through the fondant from bottom to top. (It is much easier to pull the veiner towards you.)

3 Turn the template the right way round again. Use the side of a sharp knife to cut a curve for a mouth, and carefully open out the shape. Cut out triangles above this for the eyes and a pointed oval for the nose.

4 Insert two black fondant 'teeth' into the mouth.

5 Make a small, flattened cone of green fondant. Place it at the top of the pumpkin for the stalk, and indent lines in it with the knife. Make two tiny green curly tubes for tendrils, and attach them to the stalk.

6 Transfer the motif to the cake when dry.

Make a row of several pumpkins in a range of sizes.

## Degree of difficulty
△ Easy

## Use for
🎂 Side design

## Mix and match
Halloween ghosts, *page 138*
Wishing on a star, *page 213*

## Motif uses
⬭ Low relief

⬭ Flat

## Fondant colours
● Orange

● Black

● Green

## Tools
Plastic sleeve
Veiner
Sharp knife

*See also*
Making a template, *page 38*

# Christmas candle

**Degree of difficulty**

Moderate

**Use for**

Cake top ⬭

**Mix and match**
Holly sprig, *page 96*

**Motif uses**

Low relief ⬭

Flat ⬭

**Fondant colours**

Light brown ⬤

Red ⬤

Green pastillage ⬤

Gold lustre

**Tools**
Plastic sleeve
Rolling pin
Palette knife
Soft brush

*See also*
Using colour, *page 30*
Making a template,
*page 38*
Working with fondant,
*page 44*

Add a gentle glow to your seasonal celebratory cake with this candle motif, decorated with holly leaves.

## Order of work

1 Adjust the design to the size required. Make a template and place in a plastic sleeve.

2 Make the candleholder using light brown fondant. Create the base by rolling out some fondant to a 0.5 cm (¼ inch) thickness and cutting it out using the template as a guide. Roll a tube of the same fondant and curve it to form the handle. Use a soft brush to cover the candle holder with gold lustre.

3 Roll two long, thin tubes of red fondant. Place them side by side, and twist them several times to make the candle. Press down slightly to flatten and connect them together. Trim the top and bottom to fit to the template.

4 Make a candle flame from a double layer of fondant, one small ball each of red and light brown. Roll the colours individually into cones, place one on top of the other, and squash them to form a flame shape. Brush half of the flame with gold lustre to make it glimmer.

5 Make the holly leaves and berries (see page 96), and attach them to the candle holder to complete the motif.

6 Transfer the motif to the cake when dry.

Make the flame gleam with lustre.

# Christmas angel

This angel will waft her special seasonal sparkle over the Christmas festivities from your cake top.

## Order of work

1 Adjust the design to the size required. Make a template and place in a plastic sleeve. Make a second template and cut out the pieces to use as guides.

2 Roll out a small amount of white fondant. Cut out the dress and sleeves and place them on the template in the plastic sleeve. Indent a pattern round the dress using a serrated piping nozzle.

3 Roll out a small amount of yellow fondant, and cut out the wings, the headdress and a small star. Emboss the wings with the veiner. Put these components onto a piece of paper and brush them with gold lustre.

4 Use pale pink fondant to form a round head, and trim the top where the headdress will sit. Roll a small ball of pale pink fondant, cut it in half and mould each half into a cone. Flatten each cone slightly and use the veiner to indent a thumb. Take another small ball of pink fondant and divide it in half. Roll each half into a ball, then a cone, and elongate the thin end to form the angel's legs. Position them on the template.

5 Roll some light brown fondant into tiny strands between your finger and thumb, and place different lengths on either side of the angel's head, for hair. Place the headdress and the wings. Roll a wand from light brown fondant, position it in the angel's left hand, and attach the gold star.

6 Add a little gold lustre with a soft brush to enhance the angel, then transfer the motif to the cake top when dry.

Make a few extra stars to scatter round the motif.

**Degree of difficulty**

Moderate

**Use for**

Cake top

**Mix and match**
Mistletoe, *page 123*

**Motif uses**

Low relief

Flat

**Fondant colours**

White

Pale yellow

Pale pink

Light brown

Gold lustre

**Tools**
Plastic sleeve
Rolling pin
Serrated piping nozzle
Sharp knife
Veiner
Soft brush

*See also*
Making a template, *page 38*

# Christmas rose

This soft, waxy Christmas flower is seen here with some ivy leaves, but a sprig of holly would work well too.

**Degree of difficulty**

Moderate

**Use for**

Cake top

**Mix and match**

Holly sprig, *page 96*

**Motif uses**

Low relief

Flat

**Fondant colours**

White

Yellow

Pale green

Gold lustre

**Tools**

Plastic sleeve
Palette knife
Sheet of plastic
Net fabric or a
small sieve
Soft brush
Foam pad

*See also*

Making a template,
*page 38*

## Order of work

1 Adjust the design to the size required. Make a template and place in a plastic sleeve.

2 Roll out a thin tube of white fondant and slice it into five equal sections. Roll each piece of white fondant into a small ball and place onto the template, allowing space round each one.

3 Cover with the other sheet of plastic and flatten each ball with your thumb. Smooth each petal round three parts of its edge to make it finer, leaving one part thicker. Release the petals from the plastic and fold each into a V-shape where the edge is thickest.

4 Arrange the petals in a circle, with the V-shaped edges pushed together,

overlapping as required. Roll a small ball of yellow fondant, and press it against some net fabric or a small sieve to texture it. Place this at the centre of the flower, textured edge upwards.

5 Make the buds from cones of white fondant with lines cut into the broad end to show petals. Brush a little gold lustre onto the thin end.

6 Cut out a selection of ivy leaves from green fondant. Vein and twist them, and set them aside to dry on a foam pad.

7 Assemble the motif on the cake with the main flower in the centre, surrounded by buds and ivy leaves.

Vary the number of flowers and buds to suit your design.

# *Easter bunny*

This bunny
delivering a bunch
of spring flowers
is a fun Easter motif.

## Order of work

1 Adjust the design to the size
required. Make a template and
place in a plastic sleeve.

2 Make the body from a stubby carrot shape
of light brown fondant. Press it down on either
side, with more bulk in the centre. Roll a small
ball of the same fondant and cut it in half,
then roll each piece into a cone and place
with the broad ends outward, to form feet.

3 With another small ball of light brown
fondant, smooth the face into position. Indent
a line horizontally across the centre. Press the

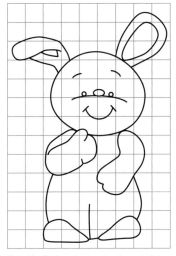

Reposition the bunny's arms to suit your design.

fondant down a little just above this line. Mark
the mouth with a drinking straw and indent
'smile' lines on either side. Use the veiner to
lightly indent two eye sockets and insert tiny
pieces of black fondant into each. Make an
indent for the nose, and insert a tiny cone of
black fondant, pointed end into the hole.

4 The ears are made from two flattened
cones of light brown fondant. Add a smaller
flattened cone of white fondant to each, and
press the colours together. Insert the ears
beneath the head and bend one over,
as shown.

5 The arms are moulded from a ball of light
brown fondant, cut in half. Roll each half into
a ball, then a sausage; flatten one end and
indent the paw with the veiner. Curve into
shape and position on the body.

6 Make flowers and stems (see page 104).
Add these to the bunny so that he is holding
them in one arm.

7 Transfer the motif to the cake when dry.

**Degree of difficulty**

Moderate

**Use for**

Cake top

**Mix and match**
Blossom basket,
*page 104*

**Motif uses**

Low relief

Flat

**Fondant colours**

Light brown

Black

White

Green

Orange

**Tools**
Plastic sleeve
Palette knife
Veiner
Drinking straw

*See also*
Making a template,
*page 38*

143

# Fourth of July

Add this fun character to a cake for Fourth of July celebrations.

**Degree of difficulty**

Moderate

**Use for**

Cake top

**Mix and match**

American heart,
*page 174*

**Motif uses**

Low relief

Flat

**Fondant colours**

Light brown

Red

White

Blue

Yellow

**Tools**

Plastic sleeve
Veiner
Drinking straw
Rolling pin
Soft brush
Red food colouring

*See also*

Making a template,
*page 38*

Keep the colours bright and strong.

## Order of work

1 Adjust the design to the size required. Make a template and place in a plastic sleeve.

2 Roll a ball of light brown fondant, place on the template, and smooth down the edges, to make the face. In the centre, indent a hole with the veiner and add a small cone of light brown fondant to make the nose. Indent two eyes and use a drinking straw to mark the mouth. Indent two marks with the drinking straw for ears.

3 Roll tubes of red and white fondant, cut lengths to fit the crown of the hat, and press together alternate colours. Trim the top and base. Roll a white tube of fondant for the brim, and add a blue strip of fondant as a hat band. To finish, tuck a few pieces of yellow fondant under the brim of the hat to suggest hair.

4 Roll a small blue ball into an oval, and position it below the chin for the body. Make two blue tubes for arms, and position them on the template, bending them to meet at the base of the motif. Add a white star to cover the join.

5 The red bow tie is made from two tiny, flattened cones of fondant, creased in the middle and positioned facing one another. Roll a tiny red ball and attach this to the centre. To complete the face, use a soft brush, dampened with red food colouring, to give a blush to the cheeks and definition to the mouth.

6 Transfer the motif to the cake when dry.

# Thanksgiving turkey

This is a fun
motif to use on a
Thanksgiving cake.

## Order of work

1 Adjust the design to
the size required. Make a
template and place in a
plastic sleeve. Make another
template as a pattern guide.

2 Roll out some yellow
fondant and use the template to
help you cut out the tail. Place it onto the
template in the plastic sleeve, then mark it
into segments with the veiner and texture it
with shapes and dots. Indent the eyes.

3 Roll a ball and then a cone of light yellow
fondant. Squeeze the thin end to form the
head and body and shape it onto the pattern.

4 Make two wings from red fondant
and two from light yellow. For each
wing, flatten a cone and trim away
V shapes for the feathers. Texture with
the veiner. Position first the red and
then the yellow wings. Add a yellow
beak and red wattle to the face.

5 Mould small brown cones for the
feet, flatten them and divide the broad
end into three. Insert into indents in
the base of the body. Press green
fondant into shape for the hat, then
add a brim using a tiny tube of green
fondant. Add a brown trim, and a
buckle in the centre using a small ball
pressed down with the veiner.

6 Transfer the motif to the
cake when dry.

Use bright colours for a striking effect.

### Degree of difficulty

Moderate

### Use for

Cake top

### Mix and match

Star on flag,
*page 212*

### Motif uses

Low relief

Flat

### Fondant colours

Yellow

Light yellow

Red

Brown

Green

### Tools

Plastic sleeve
Veiner
Small cutter
Palette knife

### *See also*

Making a template,
*page 38*
Working with fondant,
*page 44*

# Flower basket

**Degree of difficulty**

Easy

**Use for**

Cake top ◯

**Mix and match**
Message labels,
*page 207*

Celebrate a special occasion with this delightful floral motif; change the flower colours to suit the design of your cake.

**Motif uses**

Low relief ⬭

Flat ⬭

**Fondant colours**

Light brown ⬤

Dark green ⬤

Light blue ⬤

Yellow ⬤

**Tools**
Plastic sleeve
Palette knife
Veiner
Soft brush
Blossom cutter
Foam pad
Small ball tool

*See also*
Making a template,
*page 38*

## Order of work

1 Adjust the design to the size required. Make a template and place in a plastic sleeve.

2 Roll six carrot shapes of light brown fondant, and arrange them on the basket template. Trim the edge, and add a short tube for the base.

3 Add a carrot shape of light brown fondant to form a lip for the basket. Use a veiner to add some lines to indicate the basket weave. Roll a thin tube of light brown fondant and curve it onto the template to form the handle of the basket.

4 Make green leaves from flattened ovals of fondant. Mark a vein down the centre of each. Brush the back of the leaves with a damp brush, and place them on the edge of the basket.

5 Cut blossoms from light blue fondant with a blossom cutter. Place them on a foam pad, and press the centres with a small ball tool to cup each flower. Roll tiny balls of yellow fondant and press into the centre of each blossom with the small ball tool.

6 Arrange the blossoms around the top edge of the basket. Brush the back of each blossom with a damp brush to attach them.

7 Transfer the motif to the cake when dry.

You could add a special message by combining this motif with a label.

146

# *Baby's bib*

This motif is perfect for a baptism cake. Make a blue version for a baby boy, or a pink one for a baby girl.

## Order of work

1 Adjust the design to the size required. Make one template and place in a plastic sleeve. Make another template to cut around.

2 Roll out some light blue fondant and cut out the shape of the bib using the template as a guide. Cut out a smaller shape from the top of the bib for the neck hole, and gently ease the fondant into shape.

3 Use a small piping nozzle to imprint a pattern all around the edge of the bib and around the neck hole.

4 Take a drinking straw and squash it slightly to make a crease. Emboss a pattern of leaves into the base of the bib, marking each leaf with the veiner.

5 Roll out some yellow fondant and cut out two blossoms using a small blossom cutter. Position these over the leaf decoration. Add tiny balls of green fondant to the centre of each flower.

6 Roll four fine tubes of dark blue fondant for the bow. Fold two tubes to make the loops, and add two straight tubes for the tails. Add a tiny ball of dark blue fondant for the knot.

7 Transfer the motif to the cake when dry.

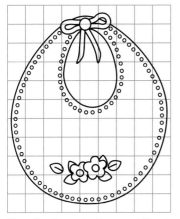

This motif could be made with a range of different colour combinations.

### Degree of difficulty

👌 Easy

### Use for

⭕ Cake top

### Mix and match

Baby bootees, *page 148*

Rattle, *page 158*

### Motif uses

🥟 Flat

### Fondant colours

🔵 Light blue

🟡 Yellow

🟢 Green

🔵 Dark blue

### Tools

Plastic sleeve
Rolling pin
Palette knife
Small piping nozzle
Drinking straw
Veiner
Small blossom cutter

### *See also*

Making a template, *page 38*

Working with fondant, *page 44*

# Baby bootees

**Degree of difficulty**

Easy

**Use for**

Cake top

**Mix and match**

Baby's bib, *page 147*

Rattle, *page 158*

**Motif uses**

Low relief

Flat

**Fondant colour**

Pink

**Tools**

Plastic sleeve

Palette knife

Veiner

These tiny bootee motifs are just the thing to welcome a new baby. Change the colour of the bootees to make them suitable for a baby boy or girl.

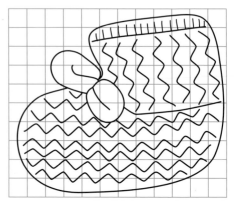

## Order of work

1 Adjust the design to the size required. Make a template and place in a plastic sleeve.

2 Roll a ball of pink fondant. Roll the ball into a tube and bend it at right angles. Smooth it down over the pattern. Use the side of a palette knife to tap the fondant into shape. Make a second bootee using a reversed template.

3 Mark zigzag indents on the bootee with the veiner to give a knitted look – the foot part is marked with horizontal zigzags, and the leg is marked with vertical zigzags. At the top of the leg, mark the cuff with a line and some tiny vertical indents. Repeat the process for the second bootee.

4 Roll two tiny cones for each bootee, and indent the centre to flatten, then assemble them on the bootees as shown.

5 Transfer the motifs to the cake when dry.

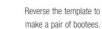

Reverse the template to make a pair of bootees.

**See also**

Making a template, *page 38*

Working with fondant, *page 44*

# *Champagne bottle*

Champagne is a symbol of celebration all over the world. Add this motif to a party or special occasion cake to wish someone all the best.

## Order of work

1 Adjust the design to the size required. Make a template and place in a plastic sleeve.

2 Roll a carrot shape of green fondant. Thin it out and flatten it at the narrow end to create the neck of the bottle. Trim the base of the bottle straight with a palette knife and adjust the neck of the bottle. Mark a ridge around the top with the veiner.

3 Roll out some white fondant and cut out the label. Mark a line along each edge with the sharp edge of a palette knife. Use a pair of tweezers to make a row of tiny indentations in the label to suggest a line of writing. Use a soft brush to add gold lustre to the label, and attach it to the bottle.

4 Roll a small tube of light brown fondant to fit the neck of the bottle for the cork. Mould a ridge in it, and mark indentations with the veiner. Flatten the top of the cork, and set it to one side.

5 Transfer the motif to the cake when dry. Place the cork above the bottle as if it has just popped out.

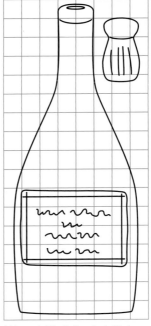

Add some bubbles to the cake, 'spilling' around the top of the bottle.

### Degree of difficulty

△ Easy

### Use for

○ Cake top

### Mix and match

Bouquet, *page 102*
Champagne glasses, *page 150*

### Motif uses

Low relief

Flat

### Fondant colours

● Green

○ White

● Light brown

Gold lustre

### Tools

Plastic sleeve
Palette knife
Veiner
Rolling pin
Tweezers
Soft brush

### *See also*

Making a template, *page 38*

149

# Champagne glasses

Celebrate any special occasion in style with an elegant pair of champagne glasses sparkling with fizz!

## Degree of difficulty

Easy

## Use for

Cake top

## Mix and match

Bouquet, *page 102*
Champagne bottle,
*page 149*

## Motif uses

Low relief

Flat

## Fondant colours

White

Gold lustre

## Tools

Plastic sleeve
Palette knife
Soft brush
Small piping nozzle

*See also*
Using colour, *page 30*
Making a template,
*page 38*
Working with fondant,
*page 44*

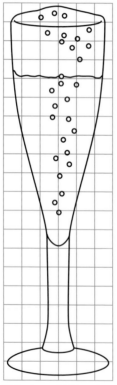

Tilt the glasses slightly towards one another.

## Order of work

1 Adjust the design to the size required. Make a template and place in a plastic sleeve.

2 Roll a ball of white fondant into a long, thin carrot shape. Smooth it down onto the template, doubling over the pointed end, to provide more fondant to spread out for the base of the glass. Tap the sides of the glass with the flat of the palette knife to fit the pattern. Indent a line at the top of the glass so it appears to be tilted slightly forwards. Repeat the process to make another glass, and position the pair tilted towards each other and slightly overlapping at the top, as shown.

3 Moisten the lower section of the glasses where the champagne will show through, and paint this with gold lustre using a soft brush. Indent holes in the glass with the piping nozzle to give a bubble effect, right up to the rim. Use the dampened brush to add gold lustre to all of the bubbles.

4 Transfer the motif to the cake when dry.

150

# Baby in a cradle

Celebrate a new arrival with this motif – changing the colour scheme from blue to pink as appropriate.

## Order of work

1 Adjust the design to the size required. Make a template and place in a plastic sleeve.

2 Roll out some light blue fondant and cut out a rectangle. Roll out some white fondant, and cut a slightly smaller rectangle to fit within the blue shape. Press a ball tool around the edges of the blue fondant for a decorative edging. Make a pillow from white fondant to fit on the top half of the cradle. Texture with the piping nozzle.

3 Roll a tiny tube of light pink fondant, and place on the base of the pillow in a V shape to suggest the arms. Press lightly at each end to cup the hands. To make the head, roll a small ball of the same fondant. Use tweezers to give a little texture, indent a mouth and, above this, add a really tiny ball of the same fondant for the nose. Use a soft brush to dust the hair area with lustre to match the new baby's hair colour.

4 Roll out some deep blue fondant, and cut a rectangle to fit the lower half of the cradle, for the blanket. At the same time, model the head and one paw of the rabbit from scraps.

Mix and match with other baby motifs.

5 Make a decorative band for the blanket using white fondant. Indent a pattern with the piping nozzle. Add a bow to the coverlet, made from two flattened cone shapes with a tiny ball in the centre for the knot.

6 Transfer the motif to the cake when dry.

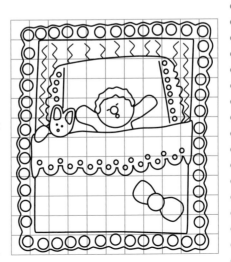

**Degree of difficulty**

◌ Easy

**Use for**

◯ Cake top

**Mix and match**
Bootees, *page 148*

**Motif uses**

⬡ Low relief

⬭ Flat

**Fondant colours**

◯ Light blue

◯ White

◯ Light pink

◯ Deep blue

Lustre

**Tools**
Plastic sleeve
Rolling pin
Palette knife
Ball tool
Small piping nozzle
Tweezers
Soft brush

*See also*
Making a template,
*page 38*

# Mortarboard and diploma

**Degree of difficulty**

Easy

**Use for**

Cake top

Side design

**Mix and match**
Inscription banner,
*page 206*

**Motif uses**

Low relief

Flat

**Fondant colours**

Black

White

Green

**Tools**
Plastic sleeve
Rolling pin
Palette knife
Cornflour
Cocktail stick

*See also*
Making a template,
*page 38*

Add this motif to a celebratory cake to mark a special academic achievement.

## Order of work

1 Adjust the design to the size required. Make two templates and place one in a plastic sleeve. Cut the other one into its various components.

2 Roll out enough black fondant to cut out the pieces of the hat. First cut out the piece that fits around the head, and place on the template. Now cut out the diamond shape for the top, and position that. Cut five tiny strips from some of the remaining rolled-out fondant. Place one strip from the centre almost to the edge of the board, then place the other four strips together at the end of the first strip, hanging over the board. At the junction, place a tiny ball of black fondant and press down to complete the tassle.

Add to other party motifs.

3 Roll out a rectangle of white fondant. Dust it with cornflour and trim the edges. Place a cocktail stick along one of the shorter sides and roll the fondant up to form the diploma. Remove the cocktail stick.

4 Roll out some green fondant. Cut it into five strips. Drape one strip around the diploma, and use the others to create tiny bow loops and tails on the top of the rolled-up fondant. Add a tiny knot.

5 Transfer the motif to the cake when dry.

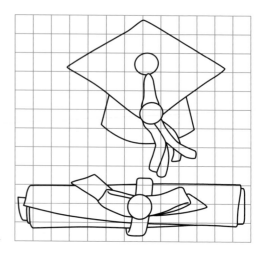

# Sending a message

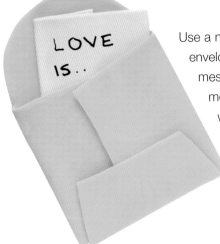

Use a note inside an envelope to contain a message. This versatile motif can be used with many others to convey a special sentiment.

**Degree of difficulty**

⬠ Easy

**Use for**

⬡ Cake top

**Mix and match**

Little dog, *page 65*

Cool kitten, *page 73*

Blossom basket, *page 104*

**Motif uses**

⬡ Low relief

⬡ Flat

**Fondant colours**

⬤ Dark pink pastillage

◯ Light pink

**Tools**

Rolling pin

Palette knife

Black food colouring pen

## Order of work

1 Adjust the design to the size required. Make a template and cut it out.

2 Mix together equal quantities of pastillage and dark pink fondant. Roll the mixture out and cut around the template.

3 Fold the two sides inward to line up with the base of the curve. Fold the base upward, and press down lightly to attach it. Leave the top of the envelope open.

4 Make a small folded 'letter' of rolled-out light pink fondant to fit inside the envelope. Make sure you do this before the envelope has dried.

5 Once the fondant has dried, a message or name can be written on the letter with a black food colouring pen.

6 Transfer the motif to the cake when dry.

Adjust the colour of the motif to suit the design of your cake.

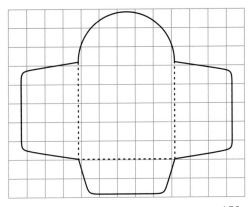

*See also*

Using colour, *page 30*

Making a template, *page 38*

# Golf bag

Create this motif to decorate a cake for an avid golfer.

**Degree of difficulty**

Easy

**Use for**

Cake top ◯

**Mix and match**

Golf ball and club, *page 167*

**Motif uses**

Low relief ◯

Flat ◯

**Fondant colours**

Blue ●

Light brown ●

Gold lustre

**Tools**

Plastic sleeve
Small, pointed knife
Rolling pin
Palette knife
Angel-hair spaghetti
Brown food colouring
Soft brush

*See also*
Making a template,
*page 38*
Working with fondant,
*page 44*

## Order of work

1 Adjust the design to the size required. Make a template and place in a plastic sleeve.

2 Mould a ball of blue fondant into a tube, and flatten it to cover the main area of the bag. Add more flattened pieces of blue fondant to create the smaller side bags, and mark the 'stitching' with a small, pointed knife. Roll a thin tube and add as the handle in a curvy shape.

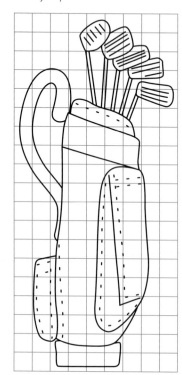

3 Use two rolled-out strips of light brown fondant to add the trim at the top and bottom of the bag. Trim to size with the palette knife.

4 Brush short lengths of angel-hair spaghetti with brown food colouring. Press them into the top of the bag for golf club handles.

5 Make various shaped ends for the clubs from flattened balls of light brown fondant, and arrange them on the handles.

6 Transfer the motif to the cake when dry.

Make the head of each golf club different.

154

# *Mailbox*

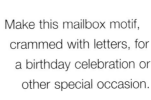

Make this mailbox motif, crammed with letters, for a birthday celebration or other special occasion.

## Order of work

1 Adjust the design to the size required. Make a template and place in a plastic sleeve.

2 Roll a tube of brown fondant and smooth it onto the pattern for the post. Trim the ends to size. Use a soft brush to add a little gold lustre.

3 Make the container fairly deep to give a 3-D effect. Use white fondant to mould the main shape onto the pattern, making it thicker at the bottom. Fit two strips of white fondant over the container. Add a flattened piece of white fondant as the flap – this should hang open to display the envelopes. Brush the container with a little gold lustre.

4 Cut some small rectangles from rolled-out white fondant for envelopes. Mark postage stamps with food colouring pens, and slot the letters into the mailbox. At the same time, make a small rectangle for the sign. Write 'MAIL' on it using a black food colouring pen, and add a black 'nail'. Attach the sign to the post.

5 Add some green fondant grass at the base of the post, textured with the veiner. The longer blades are formed by thin tubes of green fondant, tapered at either end and folded into a V shape. Roll some tiny balls of red fondant for flowers, and press them into the grass with the pointed tool.

6 Transfer the motif to the cake when dry.

Add some letters that stick out.

### Degree of difficulty

◇ Easy

### Use for

○ Cake top

### Mix and match

Sending a message, *page 153*

### Motif uses

⬭ Low relief

⬭ Flat

### Fondant colours

● Brown

○ White

● Green

● Red

Gold lustre

### Tools

Plastic sleeve
Palette knife
Soft brush
Food colouring pens
Veiner
Pointed tool

*See also*
Working with fondant, *page 44*

155

# Cup of love

Send a message of love with this delightful motif, which would be perfect for a Mother's Day cake.

### Degree of difficulty

Easy 🖐

### Use for

Cake top ⬭

### Mix and match

Blossom basket,
*page 104*

### Motif uses

Low relief ⬭

Flat ⬭

### Fondant colours

Light yellow ●

Pink ●

Gold lustre
Pink lustre

### Tools

Plastic sleeve
Veiner
Serrated piping
nozzle
Palette knife
Soft brush

*See also*
Making a template,
*page 38*
Working with fondant,
*page 44*

## Order of work

1 Adjust the design to the size required. Make a template and place in a plastic sleeve.

2 Flatten out an oval of light yellow fondant onto the template for the saucer, and impress lines around the edge using the veiner.

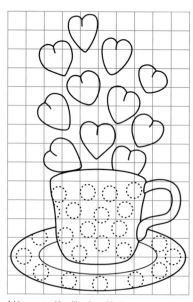

Add some sparkle with coloured lustre.

3 Smooth a ball of light yellow fondant over the cup pattern. Make it thicker in the centre and thinner at the sides and bottom to give the appearance of a rounded cup shape. Roll a tiny tube of light yellow fondant, and attach it as the handle. Create a pattern on the cup by lightly pressing a serrated piping nozzle into the surface.

4 Make 10 or 11 small cones of pink fondant. Divide them at the broad ends with the veiner. Press them flat with the blade of a palette knife to create hearts. Arrange the hearts randomly above the teacup – like steam rising.

5 Use a soft brush to dust the cup and saucer with gold lustre. Dust pink lustre onto the hearts.

6 Transfer the motif to the cake when dry.

# *Pram*

This traditional pram motif would work well on a cake to celebrate the arrival of a new baby.

**Degree of difficulty**

⬭ Easy

**Use for**

◯ Cake top

**Mix and match**
Baby's bib, *page 147*
Rattle, *page 158*

**Motif uses**

⬭ Low relief

⬭ Flat

**Fondant colours**

◯ Yellow

◯ Light grey

◯ White

Gold lustre

**Tools**
Plastic sleeve
Rolling pin
Palette knife
Veiner
Calyx cutter
Soft brush

*See also*
Making a template,
*page 38*
Working with fondant,
*page 44*

## Order of work

1 Adjust the design to the size required. Make a template and place in a plastic sleeve.

2 Roll out some yellow fondant, and cut out a semicircle and a quarter circle. Place the semicircle with the flat side up, and mark a line along the edge with a veiner. Place the quarter circle above it, slightly overlapping the carriage. Mark radiating lines on the quarter circle for the canopy.

3 Roll out some light grey fondant and cut out two wheels. Mark radiating lines with the calyx cutter for the spokes.

4 Create a blanket from rolled-out white fondant and use a soft brush to dust it with gold lustre. Attach it to

Add some little blossoms around the base of the wheels.

the top of the carriage. Make a yellow bow with curly tails (see the bow motif on page 204) to fit where the carriage and the canopy join.

5 Position the wheels with the centres just below the curved line of the carriage. Roll two tiny balls of grey

fondant for the wheel centres and brush them with gold lustre. Add a tiny curved tube of grey fondant for the handle, and finish it with a tiny grey ball.

6 Transfer the motif to the cake when dry.

# Rattle

This sweet little rattle is an ideal motif to use on a baby's cake. Change the colour to suit a baby girl or boy.

**Degree of difficulty**

Easy

**Use for**

Cake top

**Mix and match**
Baby's bib, *page 147*
Baby bootees, *page 148*

**Motif uses**

Low relief

Flat

**Fondant colours**

Light blue

Medium blue

**Tools**
Plastic sleeve
Blossom cutter
Serrated piping nozzle
Ball tool
Palette knife

*See also*
Making a template, *page 38*
Working with fondant, *page 44*

## Order of work

1 Adjust the design to the size required. Make a template and place in a plastic sleeve.

2 Roll a medium-sized ball of light blue fondant, and flatten it onto the round shape of the rattle on the template. Indent this with any pattern you wish – here, a small blossom shape and a serrated piping nozzle have been used, with a tiny dot impressed in the centre.

3 Make two long, thin tubes of light blue fondant and create the stem and handle of the rattle on the template. Use the side of a palette knife to tap the fondant into shape.

4 Roll out some medium blue fondant, and cut two ribbon tails. Roll two flattened cones from the same fondant and indent them along the centres to make bow loops. Position the bow on the rattle. Add a tiny ball of medium blue fondant for a knot.

5 Transfer the motif to the cake when dry.

A miniature rattle would look good on a cupcake for a baby shower.

# Shirt and tie

A smart shirt and
tie motif is ideal to
celebrate Father's Day,
a new job or perhaps
a promotion.

## Order of work

1 Adjust the design to
the size required. Make a
template and place in a
plastic sleeve. The whole
cake could form the fabric of
the shirt, or a smaller motif
could sit on the cake top.

2 Roll out a rectangle of
light blue fondant and trim to
size. Place it on the template.
Mark two parallel lines down
the centre of the shirt with
the side of the palette knife.
Add the buttons with a small
round piping nozzle.

3 Roll out more blue
fondant and cut out two
collar pieces. Attach these to
the top of the shirt and indent
two buttons. Cut a pocket
from a scrap of the same
fondant. Indent lines with the
side of the palette knife, then
add a button and position the
pocket on the shirt.

4 Roll out some light green
fondant. Cut a tie shape
about two-thirds of the length
of the shirt. Position the tie
and neaten the edges by
tapping them with the palette
knife. Cut a triangle for the
knot and place it in the space
between the collar ends.

Add stripes or another
pattern to the tie.

5 Transfer the motif to
the cake when dry.

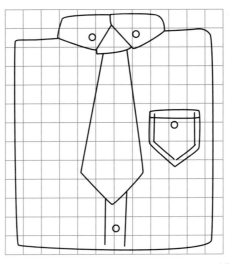

### Degree of difficulty

△ Easy

### Use for

◯ Cake top

▥ Whole cake

### Mix and match
Inscription banner,
*page 206*

### Motif uses

▭ Flat

### Fondant colours

⬤ Light blue

⬤ Light green

### Tools
Plastic sleeve
Rolling pin
Palette knife
Small piping nozzle

### *See also*
Using colour, *page 30*
Making a template,
*page 38*
Working with fondant,
*page 44*

# *Signpost*

## Degree of difficulty

Easy

## Use for

Cake top

Side design

## Mix and match

Champagne bottle,
*page 149*

## Motif uses

Low relief

Flat

## Fondant colours

Light brown

Green

Yellow

## Tools

Plastic sleeve
Palette knife
Veiner
Small blossom cutter
Foam pad
Ball tool
Food colouring pen
(optional)

*See also*
Working with fondant,
*page 44*

Use this motif to signify a new life experience – such as moving house or starting a new job.

## Order of work

1 Adjust the design to the size required. Make a template and place in a plastic sleeve.

2 Roll a tube of light brown fondant to make a post for the sign. Flatten this onto the template and mark a vertical line through the centre almost to the top with the palette knife. Mark two lines at the top to make the pole appear square.

3 Roll out a rectangle of light brown fondant for the sign. Cut one end to a point and remove several V-shaped 'nicks' from the edges. Mark the wood grain with a veiner. To support the sign so that it lies flat across the post, add two pieces of scrap fondant behind the sign on either side of the post. The sign can point in either direction to suit the design of your cake.

4 Roll several tiny tubes of green fondant and taper them to points at either end, then fold each into two and position with the pointed end up around the base of the signpost, for grass. Cut out some small yellow flowers and press them into a foam pad with a ball tool to cup and curve them. Add them to the base of the signpost. Add tiny balls of green fondant to the centres.

5 When the signpost is dry, a message can be written on it with a food colouring pen if desired.

6 Transfer the motif to the cake when dry.

Write a message on the signpost with food colouring pens.

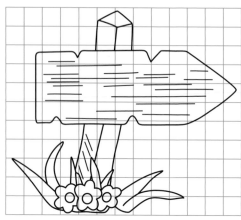

# $\mathcal{D}$o-it-yourself

This motif is just right for a person who can always be relied upon to take care of any tricky little jobs around the house.

## Degree of difficulty

⬦ Easy

## Use for

◯ Cake top

## Mix and match

Inscription banner,
*page 206*

## Motif uses

▱ Low relief

▱ Flat

## Fondant colours

⚪ White

🔵 Light brown

🔵 Medium brown

Ivory lustre

## Tools

Plastic sleeve
Rolling pin
Palette knife
Small piping nozzle
Soft brush

## Order of work

1 Adjust the design to the size required. Make a template and place in a plastic sleeve. Make another to cut around.

2 Roll out some white fondant, and cut out the apron shape around the template. At the same time, cut out a rectangle to form the apron pocket. Attach the pocket to the apron and add a trim of rolled-out light brown fondant across the top of the pocket.

3 Make holes in the apron with a small piping nozzle. Roll three thin tubes of light brown fondant to make the apron ties and neck strap.

4 Shape a screwdriver, pliers and hammer using scraps of white, light brown and medium brown fondant. Use a soft brush to lightly dust them with ivory lustre. Tuck the tools into the pocket.

5 Transfer the motif to the cake when dry.

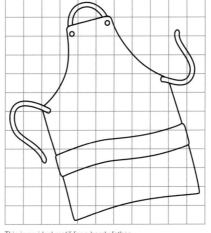

This is an ideal motif for a handy father.

161

*See also*
Making a template,
*page 38*

# Wedding bells

**Degree of difficulty**

Easy ✍

**Use for**

Cake top

Side design

**Mix and match**
Hearts, *page 208*

**Motif uses**

Low relief

Flat

**Fondant colours**

White

Apricot

Ivory lustre

Gold lustre

**Tools**
Plastic sleeve
Rolling pin
Palette knife
Soft brush
Veiner
Blossom cutter
Foam pad
Ball tool

*See also*
Making a template,
*page 38*

Add these ringing bells to a wedding cake to celebrate the happy occasion.

## Order of work

1 Adjust the design to the size required. Make a template and place in a plastic sleeve.

2 Roll out some white fondant, and cut out two bells. Lay them on the pattern, overlapping one another. Use a soft brush to dust the bells with ivory lustre.

3 The bows are made from two pairs of heart shapes – make a template of each size to cut around. Roll out the apricot fondant, and cut two large and two small hearts. Add lines with the veiner. Cut out two ribbon tails from the same fondant, and vein them as shown. Assemble the tails with the hearts over them on the pattern to form the bow. Use a small ball of apricot fondant to make the knot of the bow. Add texture using the veiner. Use a soft brush to dust the bow with gold lustre before assembling it over the overlapping bell shapes.

4 Roll out more apricot fondant and cut out two blossoms with the cutter. Place these on a foam pad. Press in the centre with the ball tool to cup the blossom. Add a tiny ball of white fondant in the centres and add the finished blossoms to the lowest point of each bell as clappers.

5 Assemble the motif on the cake. If the bells are to curve over the top and sides of the cake, they need to be transferred to the cake before the fondant dries.

Colour co-ordinate the ribbons with the cake design.

# *Rubber boots*

Make this motif to
adorn a cake for
an avid gardener,
and mix and
match it with
other gardening
paraphernalia.

**Degree of difficulty**

○ Easy

**Use for**

○ Cake top

**Mix and match**
Watering can,
*page 166*

**Motif uses**

▷ Low relief

▽ Flat

○ 3-D

**Fondant colours**

● Green

● Light brown

**Tools**
Plastic sleeve
Palette knife

## Order of work

1 Adjust the design to
the size required. Make
a template and place
in a plastic sleeve.

2 Roll a ball of green
fondant and smooth out any
creases. Cut the ball in half
to make the two boots.

3 Roll each piece of green
fondant into a tube and bend
into a right angle. Remember
that one boot needs to be
right-footed, and the other
left-footed. Shape the boots a
little, flattening the top of the
boot with the side of the
palette knife and rounding
the toe cap.

4 Use the palette knife to
mark a line across the top
of each boot.

5 Roll two thin tubes of light
brown fondant to make the
soles of the boots. Flatten the
tubes and attach to the base
of each boot.

6 Make the arch of the sole,
then add some indents with
the side of the palette knife
on the front sole of the boots.
Shape and trim off any
surplus from either end of
the sole.

7 Transfer the motif to
the cake when dry.

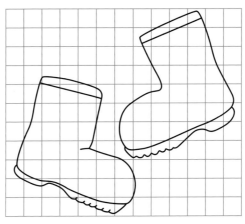

Place the boots in
a patch of mud!

*See also*
Making a template,
*page 38*

# *Torah scroll*

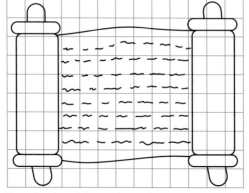

**Degree of difficulty**

Easy

**Use for**

Cake top

**Mix and match**

Inscription banner,
*page 206*

**Motif uses**

Low relief

Flat

**Fondant colours**

White

Green

**Tools**

Plastic sleeve
Palette knife
Pointed tool
Black food
colouring pen

This motif represents the Torah, and would make a suitable decoration for a cake to celebrate a Bar Mitzvah or Bat Mitzvah.

## Order of work

1 Adjust the design to the size required. Make a template and place in a plastic sleeve.

2 Roll two tubes of white fondant for either end of the scroll.

3 Roll a tube of green fondant. Cut it into six equal parts. Roll four of the parts into balls and flatten them with the blade of a palette knife. Indent a hole in one side of each flattened ball with the pointed tool. Take the two remaining parts, divide them in two, and roll four tiny tubes. Insert one tube into each of the holes in the flattened balls. Attach these onto each end of the white cylinders.

4 Roll out a thin piece of white fondant, and trim it to fit between the cylinders with the palette knife. Mark writing on the scroll with the black food colouring pen. Fit the cylinders at each end of this scroll.

5 Transfer the motif to the cake when dry.

The scroll can be made longer or shorter to fit the cake.

*See also*
Making a template,
*page 38*
Working with fondant,
*page 44*

# Book

This book motif will appeal to anyone who enjoys reading, such as a student, someone who has just graduated, a librarian or simply an enthusiastic bookworm!

## Order of work

1 Adjust the design to the size required. Make a template and place in a plastic sleeve.

2 Make a rectangular block of white fondant for the book pages, and use the side of a palette knife to mark horizontal lines for pages on three sides.

3 Roll out a rectangle of yellow fondant for the book cover, allowing for a slight overhang around the pages, and including the depth of the spine. Trim to size. Place the pages near one edge of the cover, and fold the yellow fondant over them. Trim away any excess. Mark the spine of the book with the veiner.

4 Press some decorative shapes into the book cover.

Mark some indents underneath them with the veiner to represent the title of the book.

5 Transfer the motif to the cake when dry.

Change the motif imprinted on the book cover.

**Degree of difficulty**

⌂ Easy

**Use for**

◯ Cake top

**Mix and match**
Champagne glasses, *page 150*
Shirt and tie, *page 159*

**Motif uses**

⬭ Low relief

**Fondant colours**

◯ White

◯ Yellow

**Tools**
Plastic sleeve
Palette knife
Rolling pin
Veiner
Cutters or other indenting tools

*See also*
Making a template, *page 38*

# Watering can

This bold, bright watering can would make a great decoration on any special occasion cake for an avid gardener.

**Degree of difficulty**

Easy ◌

**Use for**

Cake top ◯

Side design ▱

**Mix and match**

Blossom basket,
*page 104*
Rubber boots,
*page 163*

**Motif uses**

Low relief ◠

Flat ◯

**Fondant colours**

Light green ●

Light brown ●

Gold lustre

**Tools**

Plastic sleeve
Palette knife
Veiner
Ball tool
Soft brush
Piping nozzle

## Order of work

1 Adjust the design to the size required. Make a template and place in a plastic sleeve.

2 Smooth a ball of light green fondant over the watering can template. Cut the base straight with the palette knife. Mark an indent with the veiner across the top of the can. Roll a thin tube of light green fondant to make a seam above the base. Roll a tube for the spout and position it, then trim the end. Make a short tube slightly wider than the spout for the sprinkler. Indent the end of the sprinkler with the veiner.

3 Roll a tube of green fondant for the handle and attach it to the can as shown. Add a small ball of fondant beneath this and indent with a ball tool. Brush the whole can with gold lustre.

4 Roll a cone of light brown fondant, and press it into the broad end of a piping nozzle, allowing some fondant to overflow. Turn upside-down and flatten the pot top on the work surface. Remove the fondant from the piping nozzle and cut the pot in half vertically to make two identical pots. Make as many pots as you need and stack them in a pile. Dust them lightly with gold lustre.

5 Transfer the motif to the cake when dry.

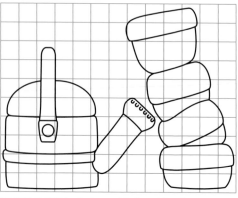

You could stand stacks of pots around the base of the cake.

# Golf ball and club

What better motif to make for
an avid golfer's celebration
cake than some tools of the
trade – a golf ball and club?

## Order of work

1 Adjust the design to
the size required. Make a
template and place in a
plastic sleeve.

2 Roll a ball of white
fondant for the golf ball, and
press it down onto the
template to create a dome.
Indent a pattern all over the
dome with the ball tool. Use
the side of a palette knife to
tap the edges back into a
round shape if the ball
becomes distorted.

3 Roll a thin carrot shape of
white fondant for the tee,
spread the broad end out a
little, and flatten it. Now,
shape the broad end to fit the
bottom of the golf ball, then
move the tee to a piece of
paper and use a soft brush
to coat it with gold lustre.
Move the gold tee back onto
the template.

4 Roll out some
white fondant, not too
thin, and shape it onto
the club template. Indent
lines horizontally with a
veiner as shown. Roll a thin
tube of white fondant for the
handle, and place it against
the side of the club. Move the
club to a piece of paper and
use a soft brush to dust the
golf club with gold lustre.

5 Transfer the motifs
to the cake when dry.

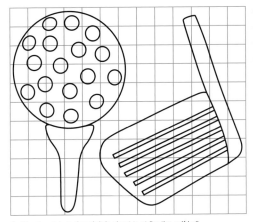

Position the club as though it is about to strike the golf ball.

167

### Degree of difficulty
○ Easy

### Use for
◯ Cake top

### Mix and match
Golf bag,
*page 154*

### Motif uses
◡ Low relief
◡ Flat

### Fondant colour
◯ White
Gold lustre

### Tools
Plastic sleeve
Ball tool
Palette knife
Piece of paper
Soft brush
Veiner

### *See also*
Using colour, *page 30*
Making a template,
*page 38*
Working with fondant,
*page 44*

# Little girl

**Degree of difficulty**

Easy

**Use for**

Cake top

**Mix and match**

Hearts, *page 208*

**Motif uses**

Low relief

Flat

Linework

**Fondant colours**

Violet

Pink

Yellow

White

**Tools**

Plastic sleeve
Palette knife
Cocktail stick
Piping nozzle
Small blossom cutter
Black food colouring

*See also*

Making a template,
*page 38*

This pretty motif can be used for all kinds of celebrations – birthdays, passing an exam, winning a prize or going to a new school.

## Order of work

1 Adjust the design to the size required. Make a template and place in a plastic sleeve.

The piped details can be added on the template and left to dry, or piped directly onto the cake.

2 Roll a carrot shape of violet fondant and smooth it onto the template for the dress, making it thicker down the centre to the hemline.

3 Roll small tubes of pink fondant for the neck, arms and legs. Cut these to size and position on the template.

Roll a small ball of pink fondant and flatten it to a slight dome for the head. Mark the eyes with a cocktail stick and the mouth with the base of a piping nozzle.

4 Roll some long, thin tubes of yellow fondant. Use these to add strands of hair.

5 Use the blossom cutter to cut out some small white flowers. Shape a pair of small shoes from tiny balls of white fondant, rolled into cones and flattened.

6 Roll some long, thin tubes of violet fondant. Use this to add bows to the shoes and hair. Place the blossoms.

7 Dip a cocktail stick into black food colouring and mark the eyes.

8 Transfer the motif to the cake when dry.

# *Ocean liner*

This could be just the motif to use on a celebration cake for anyone venturing off on their travels.

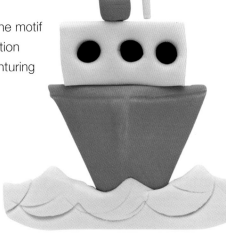

## Order of work

1 Adjust the design to the size required. Make a template and place in a plastic sleeve.

2 Roll a carrot shape of red fondant for the ship. Squash the sides of the carrot to fit the edges of the template, forming a ridge in the centre for the ship's bow.

3 Roll out some light brown fondant and cut out a rectangle for the bridge. Cut out three round holes for the portholes – this can be done with a large drinking straw or a piping nozzle. Fill these with small balls of black fondant.

4 Roll a short tube of red fondant for the funnel. Roll a short thin tube of light brown fondant for the mast. Add a tiny triangle of light blue for the flag. Roll the same light blue fondant into a thick tube and flatten it. Pinch some wave shapes into the top edge. Use the veiner to indent more waves into the fondant.

5 Transfer the motif to the cake when dry.

Vary the colours to suit the design of the cake.

### Degree of difficulty

◁ Easy

### Use for

○ Cake top

### Mix and match

Anchor, *page 175*
Rope and shells, *page 205*

### Motif uses

◁ Low relief

◁ Flat

### Fondant colours

● Red

○ Light brown

● Black

○ Light blue

### Tools

Plastic sleeve
Palette knife
Large drinking straw
or piping nozzle
Veiner

### *See also*

Making a template, *page 38*
Working with fondant, *page 44*

# Lucky horseshoes

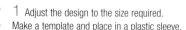

This pair of horseshoes would look great on a wedding or engagement cake as a symbol of good luck.

**Degree of difficulty**

Easy

**Use for**

Cake top

**Mix and match**

Wedding bells,
*page 162*
Inscription banner,
*page 206*

**Motif uses**

Low relief

Flat

**Fondant colour**

White

Ivory lustre

**Tools**

Plastic sleeve
Palette knife
Veiner
Small piping nozzle
Small ball tool
Soft brush

## Order of work

1 Adjust the design to the size required. Make a template and place in a plastic sleeve.

2 To make the horseshoes, roll two tubes of fondant, and curve them into the shape of the horseshoes on the template. Trim the ends with the palette knife. Use the veiner to mark a line inside the inner and outer edges of the horseshoes. Press a small piping nozzle into the horseshoes to mark nail holes.

3 Fit the horseshoes onto the template, one overlapping the other.

4 Roll a tube of white fondant and cut it into 16 equal pieces. Roll each piece into a short cone, and flatten into petal shapes. Assemble two six-petal flowers and a pair of two-petal buds. Make two tiny balls for the bud centres. Place the flowers and buds on the horseshoe, and press with a small ball tool to indent.

5 Roll very thin tubes of white fondant and shape into curves to make the bows. Make two ribbon tails by flattening some of the tubing and cutting a V shape into one end. Assemble the ribbons as shown on the picture – there are four loops and three tails. Roll a tiny ball of fondant to flatten onto the centre as a knot.

6 With a soft brush, dust ivory lustre all over the motif.

7 Transfer the motif to the cake when dry.

Make extra flowers to scatter around the motif.

*See also*
Making a template,
*page 38*

# *Pink rabbit*

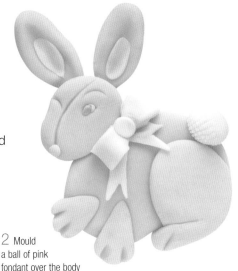

This cute motif would be great for Easter and many other special occasions too.

## Order of work

1 Adjust the design to the size required. Make a template and place in a plastic sleeve.

Change the bow to pink or blue if you prefer.

2 Mould a ball of pink fondant over the body of the rabbit, leaving some depth in the centre and thinning it out at the edges.

3 Roll an oval of pink fondant for the head and smooth it onto the pattern. Indent the eyes and mouth, and vein lines from the mouth to the top of the head and over the eyes.

4 Make two long, flat cones of pink fondant for the ears. Press a ball tool down the centres, and add teardrops of white fondant. Insert the ears behind the head.

5 Model the back leg and front paws from balls of pink fondant and indent the paws with the veiner. Add a tail made from a ball of white fondant pressed against some net fabric to texture it.

6 Make a bow of white fondant (see page 204).

7 Transfer the motif to the cake when dry.

### Degree of difficulty
Easy

### Use for
Cake top

### Mix and match
Blossom basket, *page 104*

### Motif uses
Low relief

Flat

### Fondant colours
Pink

White

### Tools
Plastic sleeve
Veiner
Ball tool
Net fabric
Palette knife

*See also*
Making a template, *page 38*

# Holding the key

**Degree of difficulty**

Easy ◌

**Use for**

Cake top ◯

**Mix and match**

Champagne glasses,
*page 150*
Sending a message,
*page 153*

**Motif uses**

Low relief ◠

Flat ◠

**Fondant colour**

Light brown ●

Gold lustre

**Tools**

Plastic sleeve
Rolling pin
Palette knife
Piping nozzle
Soft brush
Vegetable shortening

*See also*
Making a template,
*page 38*
Working with fondant,
*page 44*

A key is a great motif for many celebrations – coming of age, getting a promotion or buying a house.

## Order of work

1 Adjust the design to the size required. Make a template and place in a plastic sleeve.

2 Roll out some light brown fondant, not too thin. Cut a long strip for the shaft of the key. Cut a second, shorter strip, then cut it in two unequal pieces at an angle. Use these pieces to make the key shape at the end of the shaft, as shown.

3 Roll three small balls of fondant, flatten them and press them together at the end of the shaft to make the handle. Indent each of the circles with a piping nozzle.

4 Use a soft brush to cover the whole key with a little vegetable shortening. Wash and dry the brush, then use it again to dust over the key with gold lustre.

5 Transfer the motif to the cake when dry.

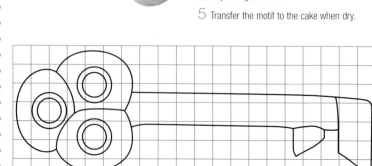

This motif would also work in grey and silver.

172

# Candle power

Candles are highly symbolic of light, life, energy – all the necessary ingredients for a bright and successful future.

## Order of work

1 Adjust the design to the size required. Make a template and place in a plastic sleeve.

2 Roll two long, thin tubes of white fondant. Twirl them together, and cut into five equal lengths for the candles.

3 Roll a tube of white fondant and flatten it to form a base for the candles. Use a soft brush to coat this with gold lustre, and attach it to the base of the candles.

4 Roll a small tube of yellow fondant and cut it into five equal pieces for the flames. Roll each into a ball, and then a flattened cone. Place a flame above each candle.

5 Transfer the motif to the cake when dry.

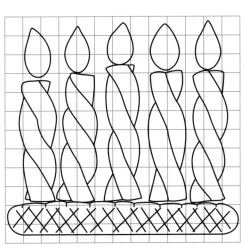

Change the number of candles to suit the occasion.

### Degree of difficulty
◇ Easy

### Use for
◯ Cake top

### Mix and match
Inscription banner, *page 206*

### Motif uses
◠ Low relief

◡ Flat

### Fondant colours
◯ White

● Yellow

Gold lustre

### Tools
Plastic sleeve
Palette knife
Soft brush

### *See also*
Making a template, *page 38*
Working with fondant, *page 44*

# *American heart*

## Degree of difficulty

Easy

## Use for

Cake top ◯

Side design

## Mix and match

Fourth of July,
*page 144*

## Motif uses

Low relief ⬭

Flat ⬭

## Fondant colours

Red ●

White ○

Blue ●

## Tools

Plastic sleeve
Rolling pin
Palette knife
Star cutter

*See also*
Making a template,
*page 38*

Celebrate in a truly patriotic manner with a heart decorated in the stars and stripes of the American flag.

## Order of work

1 Adjust the design to the size required. Make a template and place in a plastic sleeve.

2 Roll out some red fondant and use the template to help you cut out the heart shape. Smooth the edges of the shape with your fingers.

3 Roll out some white fondant, fairly thin, and cut some stripes to the width required. Lay these across the red heart and tuck them over the sides, then trim to size. Gently tap the sides with the side of the palette knife to secure.

4 Roll out some blue fondant, and cut out a rectangle. Place this on the pattern and smooth down the outer edge of the heart shape before trimming it with the palette knife.

5 Roll out some white fondant and use a tiny star cutter to cut out stars. Assemble these on the blue fondant; if you are making a relatively large motif, more stars might fit into this area than are shown here. If no star cutter is available, use the template on page 213.

6 Transfer the motif to the cake when dry.

Multiple hearts would make a good side decoration.

# Anchor

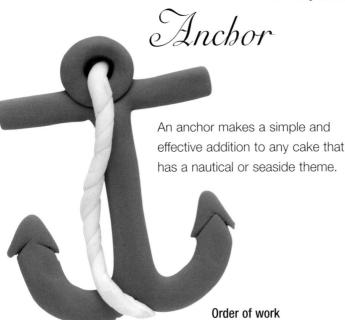

An anchor makes a simple and effective addition to any cake that has a nautical or seaside theme.

**Degree of difficulty**

⬨ Easy

**Use for**

◯ Cake top

**Mix and match**
Fishy friends,
*page 88*
Ocean liner,
*page 169*

**Motif uses**

⬭ Low relief

⬭ Flat

◯ 3-D

**Fondant colours**

● Blue

○ White

**Tools**
Plastic sleeve
Palette knife
Scissors

## Order of work

1 Adjust the design to the size required. Make a template and place in a plastic sleeve. If you want the anchor to stand away from the cake, add some pastillage to the fondant to give it added strength.

2 Roll out some long tubes of blue fondant. Arrange these over the anchor template. Tap into shape with the side of the palette knife. Use scissors to snip an arrow shape at each end of the anchor's arms to make the flukes.

3 Roll a smaller tube of blue fondant. Shape it into a circle for the top.

4 Roll two long, thin tubes of white fondant. Gently twist them together to form the rope. Position the rope from top to bottom, using it to hide the joins in the anchor and the ring at the top.

5 Transfer the motif to the cake when dry.

The rope covers any joins needed to model the anchor.

175

*See also*
Making a template,
*page 38*

# Ballet slippers

**Degree of difficulty**

Easy

**Use for**

Cake top

Side design

**Mix and match**
Bouquet, *page 102*
Sending a message,
*page 153*

**Motif uses**

Low relief

Flat

**Fondant colours**

Pink

Gold lustre

**Tools**
Plastic sleeve
Ball tool
Soft brush
Pointed tool

*See also*
Making a template,
*page 38*

Children who enjoy dancing will love these ballet slippers, poised delicately on their special cake.

## Order of work

1 Adjust the design to the size required. Make a template and place in a plastic sleeve.

2 Roll two balls of pink fondant. Roll the balls into elongated ovals and then flatten them slightly to form the slipper shape. Press the ball tool into the slipper and work a hole for the foot. Use a soft brush to dust the insides with gold lustre.

3 Roll some very fine tubes of pink fondant for the ties and add a crisscross shape over each shoe. Use the pointed tool to indent the front of each shoe.

4 Arrange the slippers on the cake. The long ends of the ties should be arranged directly on the cake while the fondant is fresh so that they do not break during transfer.

Ballet slippers make an effective repeat pattern for a side design.

# Baseball mitt

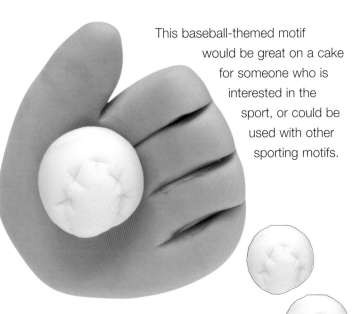

This baseball-themed motif would be great on a cake for someone who is interested in the sport, or could be used with other sporting motifs.

## Order of work

1 Adjust the design to the size required. Make a template and place in a plastic sleeve.

2 Roll a ball of light brown fondant and flatten it gently, pressing down more in the centre.

3 Use a veiner to mark the fingers of the mitt, and cut away a section between the thumb and fingers. To finish, smooth all the edges with your fingers to round them, and curl the finger section upwards.

4 Roll a ball of white fondant. Use the veiner to mark the stitch lines and the stitching. Place the ball in the centre of the mitt.

5 Transfer the motif to the cake when dry.

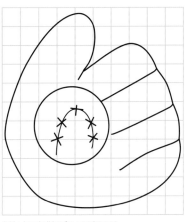

Add a baseball bat for extra interest.

### Degree of difficulty

◇ Easy

### Use for

◯ Cake top

### Mix and match

Golf bag,
*page 154*
Tennis racquet,
*page 188*

### Motif uses

⬭ Low relief

⬭ Flat

### Fondant colours

⬤ Brown

◯ White

### Tools

Plastic sleeve
Veiner

*See also*
Making a template,
*page 38*

177

# Beer mug

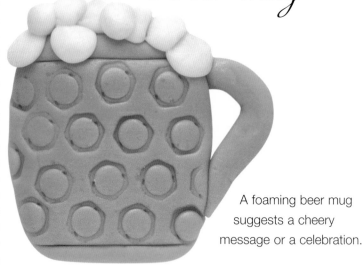

A foaming beer mug suggests a cheery message or a celebration.

**Degree of difficulty**

Easy

**Use for**

Cake top

**Mix and match**

Golf bag,
*page 154*
Baseball mitt,
*page 177*

**Motif uses**

Low relief

Flat

**Fondant colours**

Brown

White

Gold lustre

**Tools**

Plastic sleeve
Palette knife
Ballpoint pen with
hexagon-shaped
barrel
Soft brush

*See also*
Using colour, *page 30*
Making a template,
*page 38*

## Order of work

1 Adjust the design to the size required. Make a template and place in a plastic sleeve.

2 Roll a ball of brown fondant, then flatten it out over the mug shape, leaving some depth in the centre. Trim the mug flat at the top and bottom, and indent lines adjacent to these edges. Roll a small tube of the same fondant to make the handle.

3 Find a ballpoint pen that has a hexagon-shaped barrel, take the stud out of the end, and use the barrel to imprint a pattern on the body of the mug. Use a soft brush to dust gold lustre over the glass and make it shine.

4 Roll some small balls of white fondant for the foam.

5 Transfer the motif to the cake when dry.

Lustre makes the beer sparkle.

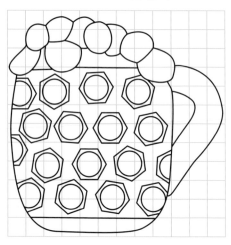

178

# *Bucket and spade*

This motif is evocative of days spent building sandcastles on the beach. Use it with other seaside motifs.

## Order of work

1 Adjust the design to the size required. Make a template and place in a plastic sleeve.

2 To make the bucket, roll a ball of red fondant and flatten it onto the template, leaving the centre slightly higher and smoothing it down on either side. Trim the top and the bottom. Indent a line adjacent to the bottom.

3 Roll a long, thin tube of red fondant and drape it over the bucket for the handle. Cut off any surplus and indent each end with the small piping nozzle.

4 Roll out a small piece of light brown fondant, and cut out the shape of the spade. Indent a line along the pointed end.

5 Roll a thin tube of yellow fondant. Cut one end into a point and position this over the spade. Trim the top and place a short yellow tube at right angles for the handle.

6 Roll out some light brown fondant for shells. Cut them out and indent as shown.

7 Transfer the motifs to the cake when dry.

Add some sandcastles for extra interest.

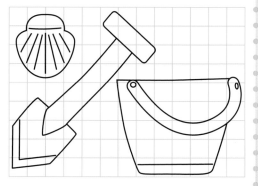

### Degree of difficulty
⬯ Easy

### Use for
◯ Cake top

### Mix and match
Rope and shells, *page 205*

### Motif uses
⬭ Low relief
⬯ Flat

### Fondant colours
🔴 Red
🟤 Light brown
🟡 Yellow

### Tools
Plastic sleeve
Palette knife
Small piping nozzle
Rolling pin
Veiner

*See also*
Using colour, *page 30*
Making a template, *page 38*
Working with fondant, *page 44*

# Convertible car

**Degree of difficulty**

Easy

**Use for**

Cake top

Side design

This stylish convertible would be great for a new driver, or to celebrate a new venture of some kind.

**Mix and match**
Signpost, *page 160*
Inscription banner,
*page 206*

## Order of work

1 Adjust the design to the size required. Make a template and place in a plastic sleeve.

2 Roll out some bright pink fondant and cut out the car shape — use a round dish or plate to help you cut a smooth curve. Scoop out a smaller curve for the driver's door. Use a veiner to mark the position of the door.

3 Cut out the wheel arches. Add a small, curved piece of pink fondant for the seat. Make the folded hood from three thin carrot shapes of pink fondant pressed together, and attach it to the top of the car.

4 Roll a ball of black fondant, cut it in half, and flatten to fit the wheel shapes on the pattern. Then press a round piping nozzle into these for the hubcaps.

5 Make a tiny black exhaust pipe, set at the back of the car, and add a steering wheel of brown fondant. Scoop out two small disks from the front and back of the car, and replace with yellow fondant to represent the headlights and the tail lights.

6 Transfer the motif to the cake when dry.

Make multiple cars racing around the sides of a cake.

**Motif uses**

Low relief

Flat

**Fondant colours**

Bright pink

Black

Brown

Yellow

**Tools**
Plastic sleeve
Palette knife
Round dish or plate
Veiner
Round piping nozzle

*See also*
Making a template,
*page 38*

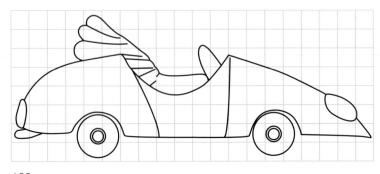

# *Footsteps in the sand*

Paddling at the ocean's edge is one of life's great joys. Use this fun motif on a holiday cake.

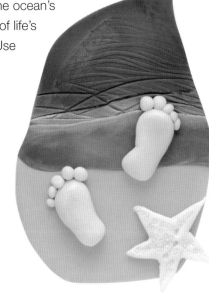

## Order of work

1 Adjust the design to the size required. Make a template and place in a plastic sleeve.

2 Roll out some blue fondant and cut out a shape for the sea. Roll out some sand-coloured fondant and add it below the sea. Mark ripples at the water's edge with the pallete knife. Use a soft brush to dust the ripples with gold lustre.

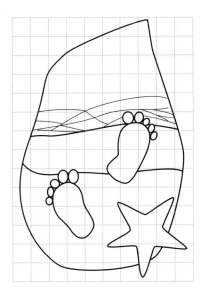

3 Roll two small sausages of light pink fondant, making one end of each a little thinner than the other. Flatten slightly to create a foot shape. Make toes by rolling a tiny carrot shape of light pink fondant. Cut into five pieces, roll each into a ball, and place on the foot in size order, starting with the big toe. Repeat for the other foot. Add a little gold lustre.

4 Cut a star shape from white fondant and texture it with a small piping nozzle, to make the starfish.

5 Transfer the motif to the cake when dry.

This motif could also be used for a baby cake, to signify the patter of tiny feet. Replace the beach with a pink or blue rug.

## Degree of difficulty

⬠ Easy

## Use for

◯ Cake top

## Mix and match

Rope and shells, *page 205*

## Motif uses

⬭ Low relief

⬭ Flat

## Fondant colours

⬤ Blue

⬤ Sand

⬤ Light pink

◯ White

Gold lustre

## Tools

Plastic sleeve
Palette knife
Soft brush
Veiner
Small piping nozzle

## *See also*

Using colour, *page 30*
Making a template,
*page 38*

181

# Acoustic guitar

Celebrate a special birthday singalong or a campfire party with this guitar and a few well-chosen musical notes.

**Degree of difficulty**

Easy

**Use for**

Cake top

**Mix and match**
Drum, *page 193*

**Motif uses**

Low relief

Flat ⬯

**Fondant colours**

Light brown ⬤

Black ⬤

**Tools**
Plastic sleeve
Palette knife
Piping nozzles
Veiner

## Order of work

1 Adjust the design to the size required. Make a template and place in a plastic sleeve.

2 Roll a long, thin carrot shape of light brown fondant, and smooth it onto the guitar template, being careful not to let any parts of the guitar get too thin.

3 Indent a curved rectangle with the palette knife and two concentric circles with piping nozzles. Use the side of the palette knife to indent the strings along the length of the guitar. Use the veiner to indent several holes in the end of the neck to represent keys.

4 Use black fondant to make a few black musical notes that can sit wherever you choose around the guitar.

5 Transfer the motif to the cake when dry.

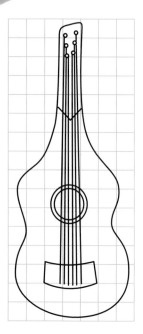

For a woodgrain surface, do not mix the colour completely into the fondant.

*See also*
Making a template,
*page 38*

# *Flying high*

A fluttering kite with brightly
coloured ribbons makes a
versatile decoration for
a child's cake.

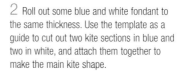

## Order of work

1 Adjust the design to the size required.
Make a template and place in a plastic sleeve.

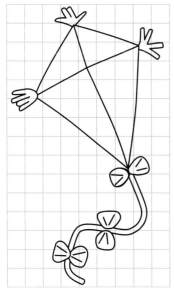

You could pipe the kite's tail directly onto the cake.

2 Roll out some blue and white fondant to
the same thickness. Use the template as a
guide to cut out two kite sections in blue and
two in white, and attach them together to
make the main kite shape.

3 Roll a long, thin tube of white fondant and
attach it to the base of the kite for the tail. Add
three bows, made from six small red cones.
Flatten the cones and vein them, and place
pairs on either side of the tail, at intervals.

4 Roll out a fine strip of white fondant. Make
cuts across the fondant, leaving one long edge
uncut. Cut the strip into three sections, and
squeeze the uncut edges of each section
together to make three mini tassels. Add a
tassel to the three top corners of the kite.

5 Allow the motif to dry before moving it in
two sections: the kite itself and then the tail.

### Degree of difficulty

⌂ Easy

### Use for

◯ Cake top

### Mix and match
Clown, *page 200*

### Motif uses

⬭ Low relief

⬭ Flat

### Fondant colours

● Blue

○ White

● Red

### Tools

Plastic sleeve
Rolling pin
Palette knife
Veiner

*See also*
Making a template,
*page 38*

# Top hat and gloves

## Degree of difficulty

Easy

## Use for

Cake top

## Mix and match

Bouquet, *page 102*
Champagne bottle,
*page 149*

## Motif uses

Low relief

Flat

## Fondant colours

Black ●

Cream

Gold lustre

## Tools

Plastic sleeve
Veiner
Palette knife
Soft brush

Add these motifs to a themed wedding cake, with a bottle of champagne or a bride's bouquet.

## Order of work

1 Adjust the design to the size required. Make a template and place in a plastic sleeve.

2 Roll a ball of black fondant to make the crown of the hat. Roll the ball into a tube and smooth down the edges to fit the template.

3 Flatten an oval of black fondant onto the template for the hat brim — it should protrude beyond the crown.

4 Indent a slot into the centre of the brim with the veiner. Roll a tiny tube of

cream fondant and place it in the slot. Press down and vein a line through the centre.

5 Press cream fondant onto the glove template. Trim away any surplus around the fingers and thumb, and gently smooth the cut edges to round them. Indent lines at the wrist. Make a second glove, remembering to reverse the template.

6 Use a soft brush to add gold lustre highlights.

7 Transfer the motif to the cake when dry.

This motif is a good addition to a formal wedding cake.

*See also*
Making a template,
*page 38*

# Toy steam train

This simple
motif of a toy
train is suitable
for a very young
child's cake.

**Degree of difficulty**

 Easy

**Use for**

◯ Cake top

**Mix and match**
Balloons, *page 220*

**Motif uses**

⬭ Low relief

⬭ Flat

**Fondant colours**

🔴 Red

🟢 Green

⚫ Black

**Tools**
Plastic sleeve
Rolling pin
Palette knife
Piping nozzle

## Order of work

1 Adjust the design to the size required. Make a template and place in a plastic sleeve. Make another template, and cut it into separate components.

2 Roll out some red fondant and cut out all the relevant pieces. Assemble them on the template in the plastic sleeve. Indent the diamond shape with the palette knife.

3 Use green fondant to make the front of the engine. Roll thin tubes of green and black fondant to fit across the engine. Mould a green funnel and top it with a small tube of red fondant, trimmed to fit.

4 Roll three small balls of black fondant and flatten them. Place them at the bottom of the train for wheels. Indent each with the piping nozzle.

5 Transfer the motif to the cake when dry.

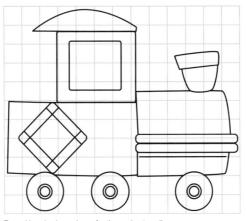

Try making simple carriages for the engine to pull.

*See also*
Making a template,
*page 38*

# Racing car

**Degree of difficulty**

Easy

**Use for**

Cake top

**Mix and match**

Champagne bottle,
*page 149*

**Motif uses**

Low relief

Flat

**Fondant colours**

Red

Black

Green

**Tools**

Plastic sleeve
Palette knife
Wooden spoon
Cocktail stick

Make a few of these 3-D motifs
to zoom across the top of a cake.
It's fun to make several of these in
different 'racing' colours.

## Order of work

1 Adjust the design to the size required.
Make a template and place in a plastic sleeve.

2 Roll a ball of red fondant into a flattened
oval and tap it into shape with the side of a
palette knife — one end should be slightly
narrower. Press the handle of a wooden spoon
into the broader end to form the
driver's seating area. Texture the
back and bonnet of the car with
the palette knife.

3 Roll a tube of black fondant
and cut it into four slices to make
the wheels. Use the palette knife
to add a hatched texture to the
wheels, then position them
around the car. Roll a tiny black
cone and position it at the back
of the car to make the exhaust.
Roll a small ball of black fondant
and flatten it to make the
steering wheel.

4 The driver is made from a tiny tube and a
ball of green fondant (for the shoulders and
head). Press a cocktail stick horizontally into
the front of the helmet to mark the visor.

5 Transfer the motif to the cake when dry.

Change the numbers on different cars.

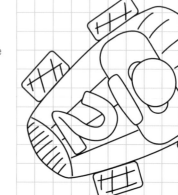

*See also*
Making a template,
*page 38*

# *Umbrella*

This umbrella is a versatile motif. Combine it with flowers for a pretty floral tribute, or add a duck to continue the watery theme.

## Order of work

1 Adjust the design to the size required. Make a template and place in a plastic sleeve.

2 The umbrella's canopy is made in one piece. To construct in low relief, the top of the umbrella must curve down and the base should stand out from the cake surface.

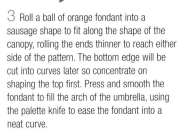

You could add a decorative bow to the handle (see page 204).

3 Roll a ball of orange fondant into a sausage shape to fit along the shape of the canopy, rolling the ends thinner to reach either side of the pattern. The bottom edge will be cut into curves later so concentrate on shaping the top first. Press and smooth the fondant to fill the arch of the umbrella, using the palette knife to ease the fondant into a neat curve.

4 Use the veiner to mark a central spoke, then curved spokes on either side. With a sharp knife or a small round cutter trim the base of the umbrella into curves to fit the template.

5 Roll a long, thin tube of light brown fondant. Place it on the template with a curve at the base and trim to size. Add a tiny ball of light brown fondant to the top of the umbrella.

6 Transfer the motif to the cake when dry.

### Degree of difficulty

◇ Easy

### Use for

◯ Cake top

### Mix and match

Lovely duck, *page 68*
Colourful cosmos, *page 92*
Gift box, *page 204*

### Motif uses

⬯ Low relief

⬯ Flat

### Fondant colours

● Orange

● Light brown

### Tools

Plastic sleeve
Palette knife
Veiner
Sharp knife or small round cutter

*See also*
Making a template, *page 38*

187

# Tennis racquet

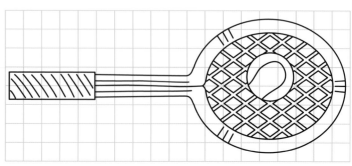

Anyone for tennis? Many people enjoy this game, so a racquet could be suitable for a variety of occasions.

**Degree of difficulty**

Easy

**Use for**

Cake top

**Mix and match**
Golf ball and club,
*page 167*
Baseball mitt,
*page 177*

**Motif uses**

Low relief

Flat

**Fondant colours**

Light brown

Black

Yellow

**Tools**
Plastic sleeve
Ice-cream wafer
Scissors
Palette knife
Veiner
Thin wire

*See also*
Making a template,
*page 38*

## Order of work

1 Adjust the design to the size required. Make a template and place in a plastic sleeve.

2 The racquet is made from an ice-cream wafer. Use scissors to cut out an oval shape from the wafer.

3 Roll a long, thin tube of light brown fondant. Drape it around the wafer and then bring the two long ends together to form the handle. Trim the handle where the grip will start. Use the side of the palette knife to tap the fondant into shape and straighten the sides of the handle. Flatten the racquet by pressing down on it with the blade of the palette knife. Indent some decorative lines.

4 Make the grip from black fondant rolled into a tube a little thicker than the handle. Use the palette knife to indent it with diagonal lines and trim it to size. Add to the end of the handle.

5 Roll a ball of yellow fondant. Bend a piece of thin wire into a U shape, and use this to imprint the distinctive surface markings of the tennis ball. Place the ball on the racquet.

6 Transfer the motif to the cake when dry.

Make extra tennis balls to add to the cake if required.

# Helicopter

This helicopter motif is sure to satisfy a future chopper pilot!

## Degree of difficulty
 Easy

## Use for
◯ Cake top

## Mix and match
Toy steam train, *page 185*

## Motif uses
⬭ Flat

## Fondant colours
 Yellow

 Grey

Gold lustre

## Tools
Plastic sleeve
Palette knife
Soft brush
Veiner

## Order of work

1 Adjust the design to the size required. Make a template and place in a plastic sleeve.

2 Roll out some yellow fondant and cut a semicircle to fit the template. With the side of a palette knife mark the surface as shown. Use a soft brush to dust a line of gold lustre along the bottom of the helicopter. Add a tiny yellow tube at the top.

3 Roll two long, thin carrot shapes of yellow fondant for the blades, flatten them with the veiner and attach to the tube at the top of the helicopter. Add a tiny yellow ball at the join.

4 Cut a short strip of yellow fondant to make the tail. Roll a tiny spiral of yellow fondant and attach this at the end. Make two tiny yellow legs and then add a thin, pointed and slightly curved tube of fondant for the ski. With a damp brush, colour these pieces with gold lustre to give a metallic look, using the picture as a guide.

5 Mould tiny pieces of grey fondant to make a helmet, shoulders and waving arm. Add these to the cockpit.

6 Transfer the motif to the cake when dry.

Add landscape features beneath the helicopter.

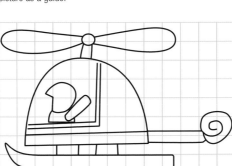

*See also*
Making a template, *page 38*

189

# *Sailing boat*

This sailing boat motif is suitable for an avid sailor. Mix and match with other nautical motifs.

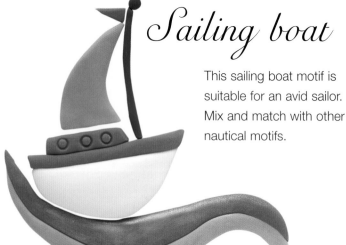

**Degree of difficulty**

Easy

**Use for**

Cake top

**Mix and match**

Anchor, *page 175*

**Motif uses**

Low relief

Flat

**Fondant colours**

Light blue

Mid-blue

White

Dark blue

Gold lustre

**Tools**

Plastic sleeve
Soft brush
Palette knife
Piping nozzle or
drinking straw

 *See also*
 Making a template,
 *page 38*

## Order of work

1 Adjust the design to the size required. Make a template and place in a plastic sleeve.

2 Roll a tube of light blue fondant and a similar sized tube of mid-blue, with points at both ends. Curve them onto the template together to make the waves. Use a soft brush to dust the top wave with gold lustre.

3 Flatten a ball of white fondant onto the main part of the hull. Use the side of the palette knife to tap the fondant into shape.

4 Roll a long, thin tube of mid-blue fondant and press it along the top of the hull. Trim the ends with the palette

knife. The superstructure is made from another tube of mid-blue fondant, pressed down and trimmed to size. Use a round piping nozzle or a small drinking straw to mark the portholes. Roll a long, thin tube of dark blue fondant for the mast, and add a small ball of dark blue fondant on the top.

5 Make a sail from the light blue fondant, and a pennant from the mid-blue. Tap the fondant to fit the template shape so the sail has a bulge in the centre.

6 Transfer the motif to the cake when dry.

Lustre adds shine to the water.

190

# *Mobile phone*

One of today's must-have items provides the ability to send messages to people wherever they may be! Add a mobile phone motif to a truly modern cake to pass on your message.

**Degree of difficulty**

👌 Easy

**Use for**

⭕ Cake top

**Mix and match**

Cup of love, *page 156*
Shirt and tie, *page 159*

**Motif uses**

🫓 Low relief

⬭ Flat

**Fondant colours**

🔴 Silver-grey

🟣 Lilac

🔵 Light blue

## Order of work

1 Adjust the design to the size required. Make a template and place in a plastic sleeve.

2 Shape some silver-grey fondant into a chunky sausage shape. Flatten it out to form a 'phone' shape.

3 Mark a square for the screen using a veiner. Beneath this, indent rows of buttons as shown, using a variety of piping nozzles or other indenting tools.

4 Roll some equal-sized tiny balls of lilac fondant and press these into the indentations to make the buttons.

5 Roll out a piece of light blue fondant and cut it to the size of the screen. Add the screen to the phone. Leave to set before writing on a message with a food colouring pen.

6 Transfer the motif to the cake when dry.

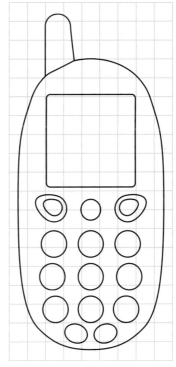

**Tools**

Plastic sleeve
Veiner
Piping nozzles or other indenting tools
Palette knife
Black food colouring pen

Use abbreviations where appropriate, just as if you were sending a text message.

*See also*
Making a template, *page 38*

# Dashing Stetson

**Degree of difficulty**

Easy

**Use for**

Cake top

This simple Stetson motif would add a western or cowboy flavour to a cake.

**Mix and match**

Horse's head,
*page 77*

**Motif uses**

Low relief

Flat

**Fondant colours**

Light brown

Dark brown

**Tools**

Plastic sleeve
Veiner

## Order of work

1 Adjust the design to the size required. Make a template and place in a plastic sleeve.

2 The hat is made in two pieces – the crown and the brim – joined together with the hat band. First, roll a ball of light brown fondant for the crown. Flatten and shape it onto the pattern. Use the veiner to make a deep crease in the top.

3 Roll a tube of light brown fondant for the brim and set it around the base of the crown, moulding it into shape and smoothing the edges into a curve.

4 Roll a long tube of dark brown fondant and place it above the brim to form the hat band. Add a V-shaped piece of the same fondant to one side to indicate the ends of the band fluttering behind the hat.

5 Transfer the motif to the cake when dry.

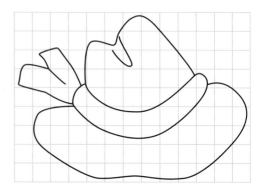

A buckle or decorative accent could be added to the hat band.

*See also*

Making a template,
*page 38*

192

# Drum

Announce some good news with a strident drum roll suggested by this colourful motif. Or mix and match with motifs for a music lover.

## Order of work

1 Adjust the design to the size required. Make a template and place in a plastic sleeve.

2 Flatten some yellow fondant for the shell and head of the drum. Use the palette knife to trim the sides straight and to trim the top and bottom into matching curves.

3 Roll a very thin tube of red fondant and shape it around the top edge. Trim it to fit with the palette knife.

4 Roll more red fondant into a thicker tube, and flatten it to the same depth as the shell of the drum. Cut along its length to make two strips. Place one strip along the curved base of the drum. Add the other strip to the front top edge of the drum, curving as shown. Trim the strips to fit.

5 Colour some angel-hair spaghetti with green food colouring. Cut it into short lengths to make the zigzag decorations between the two red strips.

6 Add tiny, flattened balls of blue fondant to the drum as shown. Roll two long, thin tubes of blue fondant for drumsticks.

7 Transfer the motif to the cake when dry.

Add some musical notes to the cake.

### Degree of difficulty

 Easy

### Use for

Cake top

### Mix and match

Acoustic guitar, *page 182*

### Motif uses

 Low relief

 Flat

### Fondant colours

 Yellow

Red

Blue

### Tools

Plastic sleeve
Palette knife
Angel-hair spaghetti
Green food colouring

*See also*

Making a template, *page 38*

# Over the moon

This sweet teddy motif neatly illustrates that special feeling of being over the moon, perfect for decorating a celebration cake.

**Degree of difficulty**

Moderate

**Use for**

Cake top

**Mix and match**
Wishing on a star,
page 213

**Motif uses**

Low relief

Flat

**Fondant colours**

Purple

Light brown

Black

Yellow

**Tools**
Plastic sleeve
Palette knife
Ball tool
Veiner

*See also*
Making a template,
page 38

## Order of work

1 Adjust the design to the size required. Make a template and place in a plastic sleeve. Make a separate template for the moon.

2 Roll out some purple fondant and use the template to help you cut out the moon. Place it on the template.

3 Roll two small sausages of light brown fondant for the teddy's legs. Bend them to make the feet, and tap the bases with the blade of the palette knife to flatten them. Mark the pads beneath one foot with a ball tool.

4 Roll a ball of light brown fondant and flatten it onto the template for the head. Add a smaller, flattened ball for the muzzle. Indent two holes for eyes with the veiner and fill with tiny balls of black fondant. Indent the muzzle and add a nose of black fondant. Use the veiner to mark the forehead and the mouth as shown.

5 Roll two tiny balls of light brown fondant. Place on either side of the top of the head, and press down with a ball tool to create the ears.

6 Roll two small sausages of light brown fondant,

thinner at one end. Place them on either side of the head and drape over the moon to make the arms.

7 Transfer the motif to the cake when dry. Add some yellow stars (see page 213).

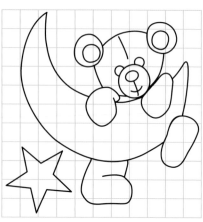

Dust the moon with lustre to add sparkle.

194

# Teddy bear in a box

A teddy bear jumping out of a box is perfect for a celebration cake. Put a message on the label for the cake's lucky recipient.

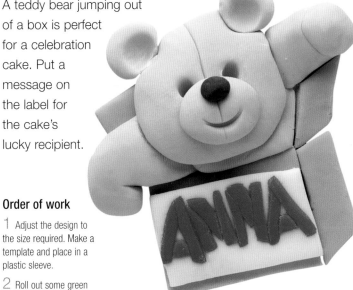

## Order of work

1 Adjust the design to the size required. Make a template and place in a plastic sleeve.

2 Roll out some green fondant and cut out the elements of the box shape.

3 Shape the body from a ball of light brown fondant. Mould arms from two smaller balls of the same fondant.

4 Roll a ball of light brown fondant for the head. Add two smaller balls for ears and press into them with the ball tool. Indent the features with the veiner and add a dark brown nose.

5 Make a white label and add a message in red.

6 Place the box around the bear and attach the label.

7 Transfer the motif to the cake when dry.

Make the panel bigger or smaller, depending on your message.

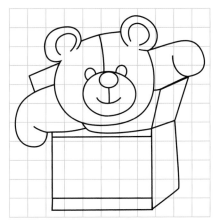

### Degree of difficulty
 Moderate

### Use for
Cake top

### Mix and match
Wishing on a star, *page 213*
Balloons, *page 220*

### Motif uses
Low relief

Flat

### Fondant colours
Green
Light brown
Dark brown
White
Red

### Tools
Plastic sleeve
Rolling pin
Palette knife
Ball tool
Veiner

### See also
Making a template, *page 38*

# *Girl in the snow*

**Degree of difficulty**

Moderate

**Use for**

Cake top

**Mix and match**

Christmas tree,
*page 121*

**Motif uses**

Low relief

**Fondant colours**

Red

Purple

Blue

Light brown

Yellow-brown

White

**Tools**

Plastic sleeve
Piping nozzle
Veiner

*See also*
Making a template,
*page 38*

This fun motif is ideal for a winter celebration cake for a young girl — or adapt it for a boy's cake.

## Order of work

1 Adjust the design to the size required. Make a template and place in a plastic sleeve.

2 Cover the body area with three squashed balls of red fondant. Roll two tubes of purple fondant, and smooth these onto the template to form the legs. Make shoes from two cones of blue fondant with tiny purple tubes added for the soles. Roll two thin purple tubes for arms.

3 Roll a small ball of light brown fondant and press it onto the face. Add a tiny tube of light brown fondant for the neck. Use the broad end of a piping nozzle to mark a mouth. Place a tiny light brown nose above the mouth, and indent two eyes with the veiner. Add a purple ball pressed down onto the top of the head to create the hat, then add a thin tube of purple for the brim. Texture the hat with the veiner.

4 Roll some very thin, pointed carrot shapes of yellow-brown fondant and tuck them under the hat on both sides for 'windswept' hair. Complete the motif by adding two flattened cones of light brown fondant, indented at the wrist and thumb with the veiner to make hands. Pile some tiny balls of white fondant into the girl's arms, and position one in her hand as if she's just about to throw it.

5 Transfer the motif to the cake when dry.

Make extra snowballs to add to the cake.

# Gone fishing

A little drop of rain doesn't deter a fishing enthusiast — as this cute motif goes to show!

**Degree of difficulty**

Moderate

**Use for**

Cake top

**Mix and match**

Fishy friends, *page 88*
Rope and shells, *page 205*

**Motif uses**

Low relief

Flat

**Fondant colours**

Yellow

Dark blue

Brown

Green

## Order of work

1 Adjust the design to the size required. Make a template and place in a plastic sleeve.

2 Roll a ball of yellow fondant, smooth it down over the shape of the jacket, and trim the bottom. Add a tube of yellow fondant for the arm.

3 Use a small ball of yellow fondant to shape the crown of the hat, leaving some depth in the centre. Roll a tube of yellow fondant for the brim. Cut the ends at an angle, and tap into shape. Add a flattened blue tube around the crown of the hat.

4 Roll two equal-sized tubes of blue fondant for the boots. Bend each boot at the ankle and mark the top of the foot with a veiner. Flatten the base with the side of the palette knife and press into the fondant to define the heel. Trim the tops of the boots so that they sit at an angle to the jacket.

5 Roll a small ball of brown fondant for the hand. Use the veiner to separate the thumb and fingers. Colour a length of angel-hair spaghetti with black food colouring to make the fishing rod. Add an uncoloured length for the fishing line. Shape a tiny green fish to fit on the end of the line.

6 Transfer the motif to the cake when dry. Place the rod and line separately.

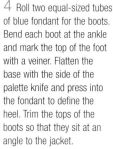

**Tools**
Plastic sleeve
Palette knife
Veiner
Angel-hair spaghetti
Black food colouring

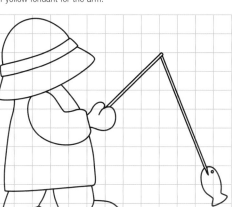

Use bright colours for the outerwear.

*See also*
Making a template, *page 38*

197

# Classic car

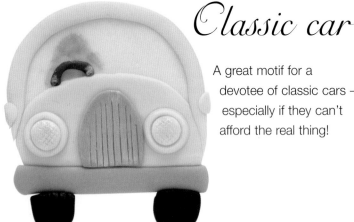

A great motif for a devotee of classic cars – especially if they can't afford the real thing!

**Degree of difficulty**

Moderate

**Use for**

Cake top

**Mix and match**

Convertible car,
*page 180*

**Motif uses**

Low relief

**Fondant colours**

White

Yellow

Grey

Black

Brown

Gold lustre

**Tools**

Plastic sleeve
Rolling pin
Palette knife
Ball tool
Sieve
Soft brush
Brown food colouring

*See also*

Making a template,
*page 38*

## Order of work

1 Adjust the design to the size required. Make a template and place in a plastic sleeve.

2 Thinly roll out enough white fondant to cover the whole template, and tap it into position with the side of the palette knife. Move the pattern in the plastic sleeve so that it is visible again.

3 Cut a semicircle of yellow fondant for the bonnet. Shape it on the template, and attach it to the white background. Roll a long tube of yellow fondant and curve it around the top of the car. Trim to fit. Add two yellow side mirrors. Roll two balls of yellow fondant and flatten them onto the bonnet for headlights. Indent them with a ball tool, and insert a white ball, textured by pressing against a sieve, in the centre of each. Use a soft brush to dust the headlights with gold lustre.

4 Between the headlights, place a flattened oval of grey fondant for the radiator. Trim the bottom flat, then indent vertical lines. Lightly brush with gold lustre.

5 Roll a tube of grey fondant for the front bumper. For the wheels, roll a small tube of black fondant, cut it in half, and place the cut edges against the bumper.

6 Brush brown food colouring onto the white background to indicate a figure inside the car. Roll a tiny tube of brown fondant and place it in front of the figure for the steering wheel.

7 Transfer the motif to the cake when dry.

Change the car colour to red or racing green.

# Little boy

This amusing caricature of a young boy is easy to mix and match.

## Order of work

1 Adjust the design to the size required. Make a template and place in a plastic sleeve.

2 Make the chest first from light orange fondant, then shape the arms and put these to one side. Use light blue fondant to make the overalls. Flatten a ball of fondant onto the template and smooth it into shape. Imagine where the body dips and curves and allow extra thickness in places. Mark a seam through the front and two lines for the trouser hems.

3 Flatten a ball of pink fondant onto the face. Smooth it into shape to form a slight dome. Indent a curved mouth with the veiner and make a hole for a tiny pink nose. Use a cocktail stick to make eye sockets. Roll out some light brown fondant, position it for hair, and indent with the veiner. Position the arms and indent the sleeves.

4 Make the cap from small balls of light blue and green fondant, pressed together and flattened. Trim the base and position over the hair. Use green fondant to make the peak of the cap. Attach so it comes right down the nose, then curve it up to one side.

5 Roll very small balls of pink and white fondant for the hands and socks, respectively, and mould them as shown. Roll a small ball of dark blue fondant and divide it into two for the shoes. Place the cut side down onto the template and ease the fondant into shape. Add the markings with the veiner as shown.

6 Transfer the motif to the cake when dry.

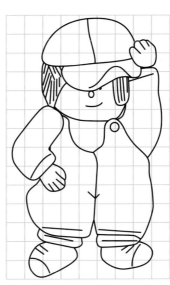

Change the colours of the outfit to suit the design of the cake.

## Degree of difficulty

 Complex

## Use for

◯ Cake top

## Mix and match
Bucket and spade, *page 179*

## Motif uses
◯ Low relief

## Fondant colours

◯ Light orange

◯ Light blue

◯ Pink

◯ Light brown

◯ Green

● Dark blue

◯ White

## Tools
Plastic sleeve
Palette knife
Veiner
Cocktail stick

*See also*
Making a template,
*page 38*

# Clown

This cheeky clown motif is ideal for a child's birthday cake.

**Degree of difficulty**

Complex

**Use for**

Cake top ⊙

**Mix and match**

Balloons, *page 220*

**Motif uses**

Low relief ◯

**Fondant colours**

Orange ●
Yellow ●
Light pink ●
Red ●
Blue ●
White ●
Green ●

**Tools**

Plastic sleeve
Palette knife
Veiner
Rolling pin
Vegetable shortening
Garlic press
Sieve
Food colouring pens

Attach some balloons to one hand.

## Order of work

1 Adjust the design to the size required. Make a template and place in a plastic sleeve.

2 Roll a sausage of orange fondant to make the right side of the body. Fold it at right angles to create the arm, and crease at the base of the leg. Trim any surplus with the palette knife. Roll a sausage of yellow fondant for the left side and position it against the orange fondant. Crease and fold as shown and trim away any surplus.

3 Roll a small ball of light pink fondant. Smooth it onto the face template, forming a slight dome. Use the veiner to make a hole for the red nose and indent the blue eyes. Mark the mouth with a curved shape.

4 Roll two small cones of blue fondant. Place them on the template as feet, and tap into shape with the side of the palette knife. Make the hands from two smaller blue cones. Flatten them and mark the thumbs with the veiner. Roll out a strip of blue fondant, and fold it into a zigzag for the frill.

5 Trim the top of the head. Soften some orange fondant with vegetable shortening and push it through a garlic press to make hair. Make a flattened cone of white fondant for the hat. Trim a flat edge to fit to the head.

6 Press scraps of green and blue fondant through a sieve to make pompons. Add these to the costume and hat, as shown. Use food colouring pens to mark features.

7 Transfer the motif to the cake when dry.

# Acrobat

This cheerful fellow
has great impact as
a cake-top feature.

## Order of work

1 Adjust the design to the size
required. Make a template and
place in a plastic sleeve.

2 Roll two tubes of yellow fondant. Smooth
them onto the legs, and indent stripes with
the veiner. Make the arms with two tubes of
orange fondant. Keep the wrists quite thick,
and texture the cuffs. Use the veiner to press
holes into the ends of the legs and arms.

3 Roll a small ball of light brown fondant for
hands. Cut it in half and form two flat rectangles.
Make a cut on one side of each to make the
thumb and turn the cut edge back. Insert a
hand into each wrist socket. Add lines for the
fingers on one hand with the veiner.

4 Roll two red tubes and bend them at right
angles to make the feet. Indent the space
between the sole and heel, and position the
feet into the trouser holes. Add a small ball
of red fondant to each shoe and texture
these with the veiner to make pompons.

5 Move the template in the plastic sleeve
so that the head shows. Roll a ball of light
brown fondant and smooth it onto the face.
Indent holes for the nose and eyes with the
veiner. Use the broad end of a piping nozzle
to indent a smiley mouth.

6 Soften some red fondant with a small
amount of vegetable shortening, and
squeeze it through a garlic press to make
strands of hair. Add these to either side of
the face. Model a flat cone hat from green
fondant and attach to the template. Add a

thin green tube for the brim and indent this
with the veiner. Attach the face to the body.

7 Finish the hat with a white ball of fondant
pressed against a sieve to texture it. Complete
the eyes with tiny blue and black balls of
fondant. Using red food colouring and a cotton
bud, paint two red cheeks.

8 Transfer the motif to the cake when dry.

Use bright, vibrant colours for this motif.

## Degree of difficulty

 Complex

## Use for

◯ Cake top

## Motif uses

▱ Low relief

## Fondant colours

● Yellow

● Orange

● Light brown

● Red

● Green

○ White

● Blue

● Black

## Tools

Plastic sleeve
Veiner
Palette knife
Piping nozzle
Vegetable shortening
Garlic press
Sieve
Red food colouring
Cotton bud

# Multi-looped bow

**Degree of difficulty**

Easy

**Use for**

Cake top ◯

Side design ▭

**Mix and match**

Bouquet, *page 102*

**Motif uses**

Low relief ◯

**Fondant colours**

Any

**Tools**

Plastic sleeve
Rolling pin
Palette knife

This versatile motif could be a central feature on a cake top, or a smaller addition to a bouquet of flowers.

## Order of work

1 Adjust the design to the size required. Make a template and place in a plastic sleeve.

2 Roll out some fondant and cut it into strips for the loops. Cut the thickest strip into five pieces, and cut the ends into points. Cut a slightly thinner, shorter strip into four equal pieces and cut their ends into points. Finally, cut a piece for the central loop.

3 Fold the loop pieces and press their ends together. Stand each loop on its side to dry. Make five of the large size and four of the smaller. The single, central loop is curled into a round shape.

4 When the fondant components are dry, soften a small amount of the remaining fondant with some water.

5 Use the softened fondant mixture to stick the bow components together. First, arrange the five base loops in a circle, with the points facing inward. Add a bulb of sticky fondant in the middle. Position the four smaller loops at an angle into it. Add another bulb of sticky fondant in the middle and place the top loop right in the centre.

6 Transfer the motif to the cake when dry.

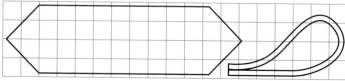

Adjust the size of the bow loop template for the outer and inner loops.

*See also*
Making a template,
*page 38*

# Flat-looped bow

This bow can be used either around the side of a cake or on the cake top.

## Order of work

1 Adjust the design to the size required.

2 The loops are made in descending sizes and placed on top of the tails. Roll out some fondant and cut several strips the width of the ribbon desired.

3 Cut lengths for the ribbon tails, cutting one end into a V. Place the flat ends together.

4 Next, create the first layer of loops – these are the largest – measuring against the template and bending to fit. Press the ends of the loops together and stand them on their sides to dry. Then make two smaller loops that will fit on top of the first set, and put these on their sides to dry also. Finally, make the central loop that will stand upright, and set aside on its side to dry.

5 Soften some of the same fondant with a little water, to make a mixture to stick the bow components together. When all the loops have dried, the bow can be assembled on the cake surface, either on the cake top or around the side to finish off a band of ribbon.

**Degree of difficulty**

⬦ Easy

**Use for**

◯ Cake top

▭ Side design

**Mix and match**
Bouquet, *page 102*

**Motif uses**
⬠ Low relief

**Fondant colours**
Any

**Tools**
Rolling pin
Palette knife

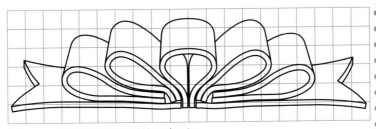

Try these bow loops placed sideways at the base of a cake.

203

*See also*
Making a template, *page 38*

# *Gift box*

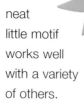

**Degree of difficulty**

Easy

**Use for**

Cake top ◯

**Mix and match**
Seasonal sleigh,
*page 118*
Party crackers,
*page 130*

**Motif uses**

Low relief ⬭

Flat ⬭

**Fondant colours**

Blue ●

Orange ●

**Tools**
Rolling pin
Palette knife
Veiner

This neat little motif works well with a variety of others. It can be successfully made quite tiny or fairly large.

## Order of work

1 Adjust the design to the size required. Make a template of the box shape without the ribbon.

2 Roll out some blue fondant and cut out the box shape. Mark lines on the box with the palette knife to form a Y shape, to indicate the sides and top of the box.

3 Roll out some orange fondant, and cut out some strips for the ribbon. Cut and fit lengths of orange fondant to the top and sides of the box.

4 Cut single lengths of the ribbon for the tails. Cut a V shape in one end of each, and assemble on the box, hanging over the top as shown.

5 Cut two diamond shapes from the ribbon strip. Fold them, sharp point to sharp point, and place these loops on top of the tails. Use the veiner to indent a couple of creases in the bow loops. Roll a small ball of orange fondant, mould into a slightly rectangular shape, and press it onto the join to complete the bow.

6 Transfer the motif to the cake when dry.

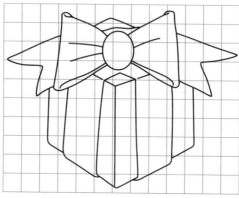

A gift box could be added to many other motifs.

*See also*
Making a template,
*page 38*

# Rope and shells

Use these little motifs to add interest or accents to a nautical design.

## Order of work

1 Adjust the design to the size required. Make a template and place in a plastic sleeve.

2 Roll out two very long, thin tubes of dark brown fondant. Lay them side by side, and twist the tubes together into a rope. If the rope breaks, twist to make sure that the join is at the back.

3 Curve the rope around, and tie a loose, overhand knot, as shown.

4 Roll a long carrot shape of light brown fondant, and curl this around on itself into a spiral shape, starting with the pointed end.

5 Press a ball tool into the side of the spiral shell to make the hole.

6 Flatten a ball of light brown fondant to fit the other shell template, and trim the hinge edge with the palette knife to form the required shape. Use the side of the palette knife to indent all the long markings, then use the tip of the knife to fill in the markings going across the shell. Use a soft brush to dust the shell with a little gold lustre.

7 Assemble the motifs on the cake when dry.

Vary the sizes of the shells, as they would be on the beach.

205

### Degree of difficulty

◇ Easy

### Use for

◯ Cake top

▭ Side design

### Mix and match

Fishy friends, *page 88*
Sailing boat, *page 190*

### Motif uses

◁ Low relief

◯ Flat

### Fondant colours

● Dark brown

● Light brown

Gold lustre

### Tools

Plastic sleeve
Palette knife
Ball tool
Soft brush

*See also*
Making a template,
*page 38*

# *Inscription banner*

**Degree of difficulty**

Easy

**Use for**

Cake top ⊙

**Mix and match**

Any motif with a message

**Motif uses**

Low relief ⬭

**Pastillage colours**

Any

**Tools**

Plastic sleeve
Rolling pin
Palette knife

Use a banner to add an inscription to your cake. As well as forming a striking design, the banner can be replaced easily if you make a mistake with the writing.

### Order of work

1 Adjust the design to the size required. To be sure the banner is big enough to hold the inscription, write out the message first and design the banner around it. Make the banner deeper if you need two lines, or longer for a word with many letters, such as 'Congratulations'. Make a template and place it in a plastic sleeve.

2 This design is best made with pastillage, which will give it added strength. Roll out the fondant to a medium thickness. Cut a strip the width of the banner, and curve it into shape over the template.

3 Cut two short strips, also the width of the banner. Cut a V shape from one end of each. Position these at either side of the large, curved strip, so that the strip is slightly above and overlaps them.

4 Let the whole banner dry before adding the message and assembling it on the cake.

Make several banners and store them until needed.

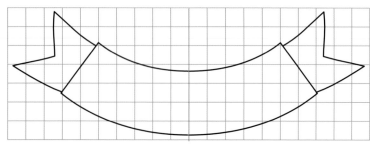

*See also*
Making a template,
*page 38*

# *Message labels*

Labels can be used to add a message to a cake. These simple shapes can be cut out quickly, using mainly straight lines.

**Degree of difficulty**

 Easy

**Use for**

Cake top

**Mix and match**
Any motif with a message

**Motif uses**

 Low relief

**Pastillage colours**
Any

**Tools**
Plastic sleeve
Rolling pin
Palette knife

## Order of work

1 Adjust the design to the size required. Write out the message first and design around it. Make a template and place in a plastic sleeve. Make a pattern from the template to cut around.

2 Use pastillage to give the label added strength. Roll out the fondant to a medium thickness and cut around the shape of the label.

3 Let the label dry before adding the message and attaching it to the cake.

Add labels with messages to flower and animal motifs.

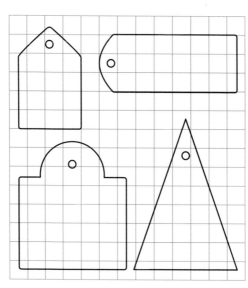

*See also*
Making a template, *page 38*

207

# Hearts

## Degree of difficulty

Easy

## Use for

Cake top

Side design

## Mix and match

Cup of love, *page 156*

## Motif uses

Low relief

## Fondant colours

Dark blue

Light blue

Red

Pink

White

## Tools

Palette knife
Veiner
Soft brush
Piping nozzle

*See also*

Making a template, *page 38*

This lovely design is suitable for the top or sides of a cake. You can make it in bright or subtle colours, as you prefer – the choice is yours.

## Order of work

1 Make a template that will fit inside the borders or along the sides of the cake. The design shown here is for a corner of a square cake, but it could be adapted to a round cake (curve the background lines around). Mark two parallel lines on the cake surface.

2 To make the hearts, roll a tube of fondant and cut it into equal portions. Roll each piece into a ball, then a cone. Press an indent into the broad end of each cone with the veiner. Place the cones on the work surface and use the blade of a palette knife to squash them flat.

You can use any combination of colours for this design.

3 Make as many heart shapes in different colours as you wish. Arrange them along the marked lines, mixing the colours and making them face in all different directions. Use a soft brush and a little water to make the hearts stick.

4 From the same colours used for the hearts, cut out tiny round shapes using the end of a round piping nozzle. Use these to fill in any gaps within the pattern area.

# ℌearts and flowers

This romantic design would suit a Valentine's Day cake, or an engagement or wedding cake.

## Order of work

1 Adjust the design to the size required. Make a template and place in a plastic sleeve.

2 This design can be created without any special tools. But if you have small heart and flower cutters, these will make the job easier and quicker. Try cutting out the flower and heart at least once before going into production, and adjust the sizes right at the start of the process if you need to. Measure around the cake and decide how many pieces you need to make.

3 Roll a long, thin tube of blue fondant and cut five small, equal pieces for each flower. Roll each piece into a ball, then a cone, and flatten with the flat surface of the palette knife to make a petal shape. Arrange the petals on the template around a tiny bulb of white fondant.

4 To make the hearts, roll out a tube of blue fondant and cut equal parts. Roll each into a ball, then a cone, and make an indent in the top of the broad part of the cone with the veiner. Flatten the heart with the blade of the

palette knife. Place onto the template and use the edge of the palette knife to tap the heart into shape, if necessary. Use a large drinking straw to indent the curved shapes into the top of each heart.

5 Assemble the motifs on the freshly coated cake. Use the veiner to make some swirls on the surface of the cake, and position one flower above one heart, then a heart above a flower. Press a serrated piping nozzle into the centre of each flower to complete the design.

### Degree of difficulty

◇ Easy

### Use for

▭ Side design

### Mix and match

Bouquet, *page 102*

### Motif uses

◯ Low relief

◯ Flat

### Fondant colours

● Blue

○ White

### Tools

Plastic sleeve
Palette knife
Veiner
Drinking straw
Serrated piping nozzle

This is a double-band motif, but a single band would also look good.

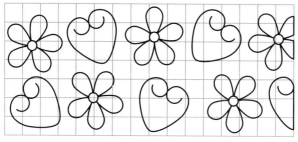

*See also*
Making a template, *page 38*

# Tassels

**Degree of difficulty**
Easy

**Use for**
Side design

**Mix and match**
Draped braid,
*page 222*

**Motif uses**
Low relief

**Pastillage colours**
Any

**Tools**
Rolling pin
Cornflour
Palette knife

Where two parts of a
draped braid or similar
side decoration meet,
cover the join with a
striking tassel motif.

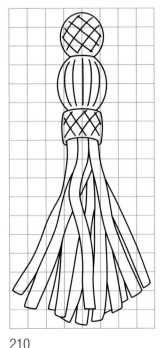

## Order of work

1 Make a template to suit the size of tassel
required – this will help you make all the tassels the
same size.

2 Use pastillage for this motif to give it added
strength. Roll out a long strip of fondant as wide
as the length of a finished tassel, and make cuts
very close together across it, leaving about
0.5 cm (¼ inch) of uncut fondant along one long
edge. Cut the strip into 5–7.5 cm (2–3 inch) lengths,
to make individual tassels.

3 Dust each tassel with cornflour. Roll up the
fondant tightly along the uncut edge, which forms the
top of the tassel. Squeeze the top together and shake
the tassel to separate the strands. Lay it down again
and cut a tiny strip of fondant to wrap around the
top. Mark this with a diamond pattern before
wrapping it around the tassel. Add two textured
balls of fondant above this, as shown.

4 Trim the base of the tassel into a slight V shape.

5 Transfer the motif(s) to the cake when dry.

Shake the tassel to separate the strands.

*See also*
Making a template,
*page 38*

# Scrolls and shells

Royal icing or buttercream icing can be used for these edging motifs, which are repeated on the edge or at the base of a cake.

## Order of work

1 Prepare the royal icing or buttercream icing to the correct consistency – so it will hold its shape.

2 Place the icing in a piping bag fitted with a serrated nozzle; do not fill it too full.

3 To practise, make a template and place into a plastic sleeve. Take time to learn the technique of piping out the icing to the required shape, and releasing the pressure when the shape is achieved.

4 Shells can be worked more easily than scrolls. To make a shell, press out a bulb of icing and pull the bag off to the side while releasing the pressure. Repeat with the beginning of the next shell, just catching the tail of the previous one. Try to make them even and the same size. When you are happy with the result, try it out on the cake.

5 To make a scroll, pressure needs to be maintained on the piping bag while the piping nozzle is moved in a circular direction; more pressure presses more icing out of the bag and the resulting swirl is bigger. Work with three or five circular movements, stop, and then start another scroll of the same size.

6 Work shells or scrolls all around the cake; they can be big and bold or neat and dainty, depending on the size of the piping nozzle.

**Degree of difficulty**

⬦ Easy

**Use for**

☐ Cake edging

**Mix and match**

All motifs

**Motif uses**

⬭ Low relief

**Icing colours**

Any

**Tools**

Piping bag with serrated nozzle
Plastic sleeve

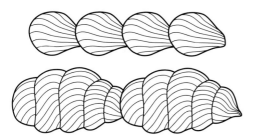

Each segment should be a similar size to the ones beside it.

211

*See also*
How to pipe, *page 42*

# Star on flag

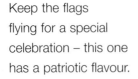

**Degree of difficulty**

Easy

Keep the flags flying for a special celebration – this one has a patriotic flavour.

**Use for**

Cake top

**Mix and match**

Fourth of July,
*page 144*
Thanksgiving turkey,
*page 145*

**Motif uses**

Low relief

**Fondant colours**

Red

White

Blue

**Tools**

Rolling pin
Palette knife
Spaghetti

## Order of work

1 Make a template to suit the size of flag required.

2 Roll out a length of fondant in red, and one in white. Cut parallel lines to make strips and then assemble these strips alternately on the pattern, curving them to fit.

3 Trim away a corner at the top left edge and replace it with a square of blue fondant. Add a white fondant star (or several if they will fit).

4 Cut a length of spaghetti for the flagpole. Add a bulb of white fondant to the top.

5 Transfer the motif to the cake when dry.

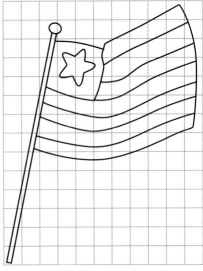

Curve the flag to make it appear to blow in the wind.

*See also*
Making a template,
*page 38*

212

# 𝒲ishing on a star

Stars of all sizes and colours can be added to a cake in different ways; if no cutter is available, here is an easy way to make them from a template.

## Order of work

1 Adjust the design to the size required. Make a template.

2 Roll out some fondant, not too thin. Place the template on top of the fondant and roll over the top with a rolling pin. Carefully lift up the template, and you will see that it has embossed the star shape onto the fondant.

3 Use a scalpel or the side of a small, pointed palette knife to trim away any surplus pieces; just fit the point of the knife to the base of the V between the points, cut downward, and lift away. Be careful not to drag the knife and pull the fondant out of shape. Work all the way around each star before removing the surplus fondant.

4 Slide the blade of the palette knife under the stars to lift them off the work surface.

5 Transfer the motifs to the cake.

Make several sizes of templates and use them again and again.

### Degree of difficulty

◇ Easy

### Use for

◯ Cake top

▭ Side design

### Mix and match

Top hat and shamrock, *page 136*

### Motif uses

⬭ Low relief

### Fondant colours

Any

### Tools

Rolling pin
Scalpel or small, pointed palette knife

*See also*
Making a template, *page 38*

213

# *Strips and flowers*

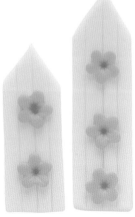

**Degree of difficulty**

Easy

**Use for**

Side design

**Mix and match**

Floral basket,
*page 146*
Inscription banner,
*page 206*

**Motif uses**

Low relief

**Pastillage colours**

White

Yellow

**Tools**

Rolling pin
Palette knife
Small blossom cutter
Foam pad
Large, round tool
Pointed, serrated tool

This repeat border decoration can be made to fit both straight and curved cake sides.

### Order of work

1 Prepare a template for one section.

2 The design is made from an odd number of strips, cut to a point at the top. Roll out some white pastillage, not too thin. Cut strips to fit the template and cut the pointed tops. Lay the strips on the template with the points in position, and make one cut across the bottom of the strips to level them.

3 Use the palette knife to indent the strips with vertical lines.

4 Cut out tiny blossoms from rolled-out yellow pastillage (or any other colour). Set them on a foam pad, and press the large round tool into the centre to soften the edges and cup the flower. Press the pointed, serrated tool into the centre of the blossom – use this to pick up the blossom and press it into position on the design.

5 Make enough sections to fit the cake. Transfer the motifs to the cake when dry.

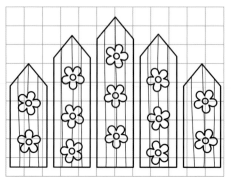

The width and height of the strips can be adjusted to fit your cake.

*See also*

Making a template,
*page 38*
Working with fondant,
*page 44*

# Formal bow

This elegant bow can be used
on its own or to gather a
bouquet of flowers.

## Order of work

1 Adjust the design to the size required. Make a template and place in a plastic sleeve.

2 This motif is made from segments of a circle, so several can be made at the same time. Roll out some yellow fondant and cut out two circles, one slightly smaller than the other. Cut the circles into segments – the smaller one into quarters and the larger one into six.

3 Assemble two quarter segments opposite one another, and indent with suitable patterns. Over each segment, place one 'sixth' piece, and again mark with a suitable pattern.

4 Roll a ball of the same fondant and attach in the centre for the knot.

5 Transfer the motif to the cake when dry.

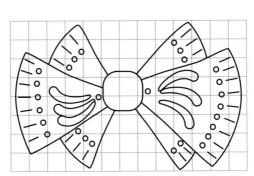

The bow can be made any colour to match the design of the cake.

**Degree of difficulty**

△ Easy

**Use for**

○ Cake top

▭ Side design

**Mix and match**
Bouquet, *page 102*

**Motif uses**

◯ Low relief

**Fondant colours**

 Yellow

**Tools**
Plastic sleeve
Rolling pin
Round cutters
Palette knife
Indenting tools

*See also*
Making a template,
*page 38*

215

# *Rounded scroll*

This repeated, rounded scroll motif is suitable for edging a round cake.

**Degree of difficulty**

Easy

**Use for**

Cake edging

**Mix and match**

Any motif

**Motif uses**

Low relief

Linework

**Icing colours**

White

Blue

**Tools**

Piping bag and very fine serrated piping nozzles

## Order of work

1 This motif involves overpiping. Choose piping nozzles that have very fine serrations rather than large indents, as this allows the overpiped scrolls to sit more comfortably on top of the larger scrolls beneath. Overpiping has been shown here in a contrasting colour to illustrate the shape, though it could equally well be done in the same, or a co-ordinating colour for a more delicate effect.

2 Prepare some fresh royal or buttercream icing to a full peak consistency. Load two piping bags fitted with the appropriate size nozzles.

3 The piped motif is rather like a comma – use plenty of pressure to push out the bulb at the beginning, then slowly release the pressure while pressing out the tail. Work all around the cake with the first bag of icing to make the base piped scrolls.

4 Use the bag of icing with the smaller nozzle to pipe over the original scrolls in the same manner.

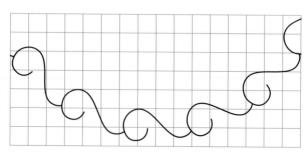

Change the colours of the scroll to co-ordinate with the rest of the cake.

*See also*
How to pipe, *page 42*

216

# *Rosebud circle*

This neat little decoration has a variety of uses, from surrounding a letter initial to acting as a border for the top of the cake itself.

## Order of work

1 Prepare a template and place in a plastic sleeve. For a large design, it is best to work in sections.

2 Roll a very long, thin tube of green fondant and place on the template.

3 Roll another tube of green fondant and cut about 30 equal pieces from it. Roll each piece into a ball, and then a cone. Use a veiner tool to press down the centre of each cone. Set them aside.

4 Roll out a tube of yellow fondant. Cut it into 12 equal pieces. Roll each piece into a flattened tube and squeeze one long edge between finger and thumb. Roll the tube up tightly and press in the base, and trim off any waste at the bottom. All the rosebuds should be the same height when finished.

5 Imagine a clock face, and set the rosebuds onto the tube shape at each hour marker. Place a leaf facing outward on either side of each bud.

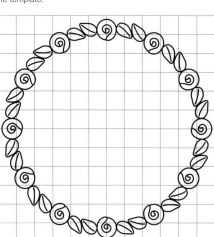

Change the colour of the rosebuds to suit the design of your cake.

### Degree of difficulty

⌂ Easy

### Use for

◯ Cake top

▢ Cake edging

### Mix and match

Floral motifs

### Motif uses

⬭ Low relief

### Fondant colours

● Green

● Yellow

### Tools

Plastic sleeve
Palette knife
Veiner

*See also*

Making a template, *page 38*

# Cutout lace

**Degree of difficulty**

Easy

**Use for**

Side design

**Mix and match**

Piped lace,
*page 225*

**Motif uses**

Low relief

**Pastillage colours**

Any

**Tools**

Plastic sleeve
Foam pad
Sharp knife

This easy-to-make lace is made from
tiny cutouts and can be adapted to fit
all kinds of designs.

## Order of work

1 Adjust the design to
the size required. Make a
template and place in a
plastic sleeve.

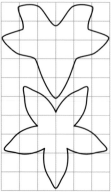

Make more pieces than you need.

2 This design is best made
with pastillage, which will
give it strength. Roll out the
fondant as thin as possible to
give it a delicate appearance.

3 The lace pieces can
consist of the whole cutout –
as with the ivy leaves – or a
trimmed cutout, as with the
calyx shape where the two
bottom segments have been
removed. Arrange the cutouts
along the length of the
patterned section to see how
many are required.
This determines the number
you need to make, but
remember to add some
extras in case of breakages.

4 Cut out the pieces until
there are enough for your
needs. These components
will dry more quickly if you
set them on a foam pad. By
the time they are all cut out,
the first cutouts should be
dry enough to assemble.
Alternatively, dry components
can be stored until needed.

5 Scribe the pattern onto
the side of the cake. Use
royal icing to add tiny dots
of icing to the components,
and place them around the
design. Tiny dots can also be
added onto the scribed line
to give space between the
cutout components.

*See also*
Making a template,
*page 38*

# Chunky lace

This chunkier method of making lace produces a useful addition to a bolder, heavier cake design.

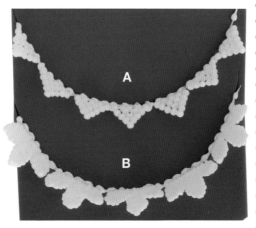

## Order of work

1 The top type of chunky lace ('A') is piped directly onto the cake, so scribe a line on the cake where the lace will go. For the bottom kind ('B'), make repeated copies of the lace pattern on a template, and place in a plastic sleeve. Prepare some fresh royal icing to soft peak stage. Mark a line where the lace will go.

2 Lace A is made up of bulbs. To make these, place a small round nozzle into an icing bag and half-fill the bag with royal icing. Pipe a line of bulbs (see page 43) on the scribed line on the cake, and work this single line all around the cake to give the first bulbs time to set. Next, between the bulbs and slightly in front of them, pipe four bulbs between five bulbs in the original line. Repeat this all around the cake. Next, pipe three bulbs between the four of the second line, once again slightly in front. Then pipe two bulbs between the three of the third line and finally one bulb between the two of the previous line. As the bulbs have been piped in front of the previous set each time, they should stand out from the cake

3 Lace B is made as 'off-pieces' and added to the cake when it is dry. Use the template to create a line of pattern pieces. Prepare some soft-peak royal icing and place it in a piping bag with a small round piping nozzle. Over each teardrop shape, pipe zigzag lines. Pipe the right and left teardrops and then the middle one, ensuring that the edges meet along the joins. Make sufficient lace pieces for the cake, plus a few spares in case any get damaged. Allow them to dry, then pick them up on the blade of a palette knife, and attach to the cake along the scribed lines with freshly piped royal icing. Adjust the angle with a soft brush.

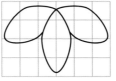

Lace B

Add the lace in curves or a straight line around the cake sides.

## Degree of difficulty

△ Easy

## Use for

▭ Side design

## Mix and match

Cutout lace, *page 218*

## Motif uses

◁▷ Low relief

## Icing colours

Any

## Tools

Sharp knife
Plastic sleeve
Piping bag and nozzle
Palette knife
Soft brush

*See also*
Making a template, *page 38*
How to pipe, *page 42*

219

# *Balloons*

**Degree of difficulty**

Easy

**Use for**

Cake top ◯

**Mix and match**
Over the moon,
*page 194*
Clown, *page 200*

**Motif uses**

Low relief ◯

**Fondant colours**

Red ●

Blue ●

Gold lustre

**Tools**
Plastic sleeve
Angel-hair spaghetti
Kettle
Shallow,
ovenproof dish
Kitchen towel
Soft brush

*See also*
Making a template,
*page 38*

Balloons add a touch of fun
to many kinds of celebratory
cakes – and they combine well
with a variety of other motifs.

## Order of work

1 Adjust the design to
the size required. Make
a template and place
in a plastic sleeve.

2 Prepare some strings
from angel-hair spaghetti.
Boil some water, pour it into
a shallow, ovenproof dish
and add some lengths of
angel-hair spaghetti. After a
few minutes, they will soften.
Remove them from the water
and place in curvy patterns
on kitchen towel to dry.

3 Take a fairly large ball
of fondant and roll it into an
oval shape. Press it down
onto the template, leaving
some depth in the centre and
smoothing out the edges. At
the base of each balloon,
place a tiny rolled ball and a
little semicircular piece of
fondant for the balloon's tie.
Use a soft brush to dust the
balloon with gold lustre.

4 Arrange the motif on the
cake with a curly piece of
spaghetti for string.

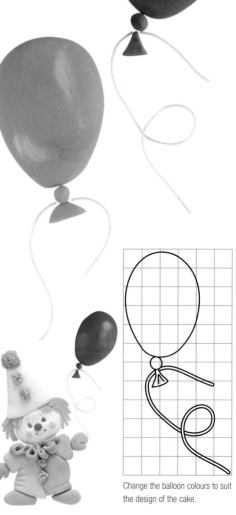

Change the balloon colours to suit
the design of the cake.

# *Pleated drape*

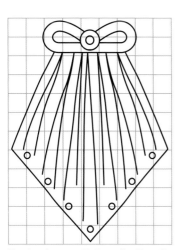

This motif adds texture
and interest to the
sides of many kinds of
celebratory cakes.

## Order of work

1 Adjust the design to the size required.
Make a template and place in a plastic sleeve.

2 This motif is designed to drape down the
side of a cake. Make it on the template, then
immediately move it to the cake. This means
the cake needs to be prepared first.

3 Roll out some fondant to a medium
thickness and cut out a rectangle the height
and width of the finished drape. Dust both
sides of the fondant with cornflour. Lay the
skewers alternately under and over the
fondant, close together, to produce a
corrugated effect.

4 Remove the skewers and squash the top
of the drape tightly together. Trim the top in a
straight line and the base into a V shape.

5 Roll a long, thin tube of the same colour
fondant, place it across the top of the drape
and curve it upward and into the middle so
that it meets. Roll a small ball of fondant and
place it over the join. Indent the centre with a
small piping nozzle.

6 Make several drapes to sit at intervals
around the sides of the cake. Transfer them
to the cake before they dry.

Have the cake prepared before making this motif.

### Degree of difficulty

 Moderate

### Use for

Side design

### Mix and match
Draped braid,
*page 222*

### Motif uses

Low relief

### Fondant colours
Any

### Tools
Plastic sleeve
Rolling pin
Palette knife
Cornflour
Round skewers
Small piping nozzle

*See also*
Making a template,
*page 38*

221

# Draped braid

Draped braids make an attractive decoration for the side of a cake, joined with a neat plume trim.

**Degree of difficulty**

Moderate

**Use for**

Side design

**Mix and match**

Tassels, *page 210*

**Motif uses**

Low relief

**Pastillage colours**

Any

**Tools**

Plastic sleeve
Rolling pin
Clingfilm
Palette knife
Large drinking straw

## Order of work

1 Adjust the design to the size required. Make a template and place in a plastic sleeve.

2 This design is best made with pastillage for added strength. Roll out a length of fondant, and cut into three equal strips. Cover any unused fondant with clingfilm.

3 Lay the three strips side by side and braid them to the desired length. Place the braid on the template and gently curve into shape. Trim off any surplus from either end. This braid can be placed straight on the cake, or left to dry, in which case it can stand out over the side of the cake to make an extension.

4 The plume is made in three pieces. Roll one long, carrot-shaped piece of fondant and two slightly shorter ones. Turn the broad end of the longer piece onto itself, and press down. With the two shorter carrot shapes, press the broad end of one over onto itself and slightly to the right, and the other slightly to the left. Squash all three carrot-shaped pieces together. Use a large drinking straw to define the curved marks.

5 Add the plumes to the braid motifs to hide the joins.

Make the drapes long or short to fit the cake size.

*See also*
Making a template,
*page 38*

# Basketweave

This method for making a basketweave texture provides a base for other decorations.

## Order of work

1 Adjust the design to the size required. Make a template and place in a plastic sleeve.

2 This design is best made with pastillage, which will give it strength. Make the weaving larger than the finished piece – it can then be trimmed to size with a cutter.

3 Roll out the fondant. Cut strips of equal width from the fondant with the palette knife and leave them lying against one another. These are the 'A' strips (the warp).

4 Roll out and cut a set of similar strips. These are the 'B' strips (the weft).

5 Lay a ruler across the 'A' strips near one end, and turn back every other strip against the ruler. Lay a 'B' strip across the 'A' strips that haven't been turned back. Bring all the 'A' strips back to their starting position and now bend back the ones that were left in place the first time. Lay another 'B' strip across these and then bring the strips back to their original position. Continue this process until you have made a woven area large enough for your needs.

6 Use a cutter to cut an area out of the weaving to the required shape. Leave the cutter in place while you remove any excess basketweave. Vary the effect by cutting either at right angles to the pattern or on a diagonal.

7 Once they are dry, the basketweave designs can be moved easily.

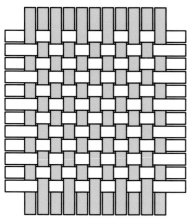

The weaving needs to be done quite quickly, before the pastillage dries and hardens. Cover any spare strips with clingfilm.

### Degree of difficulty

 Moderate

### Use for

◯ Cake top

▭ Side design

### Mix and match
Rose, *page 111*
Pretty pansy, *page 116*

### Motif uses

◯ Low relief

### Pastillage colours
Any

### Tools
Plastic sleeve
Rolling pin
Palette knife
Ruler
Cutter

*See also*
Making a template, *page 38*

# Flat lace embroidery

Add a delicate piece of lace embroidery to enhance a special cake. These motifs can be repeated around a flat-sided cake.

**Degree of difficulty**

Moderate

**Use for**

Side design

**Mix and match**

Piped lace,
*page 225*

**Motif uses**

Low relief

Linework

**Icing colours**

Any

**Tools**

Net fabric
Piping bag and small
piping nozzle
Plastic sleeve
Vegetable shortening
Foam pad
Pins
Damp brush
Veiner

*See also*
Making a template,
*page 38*
How to pipe, *page 42*

## Order of work

1 Cut out a shape from net fabric that will contain the embroidery pattern. Ensure there is room to position it on the cake. This motif is for a cake with flat sides. (See Curved lace embroidery, page 229 for a curved motif.)

2 Prepare some fresh royal icing for this motif. It should have a soft peak consistency. Put the icing in a piping bag fitted with a small piping nozzle.

3 Place the pattern in a plastic sleeve. Lightly grease the surface with vegetable shortening. Stretch out the net on this surface – the shortening should hold it in place. If not, place the whole sleeve on a foam pad and pin through the pattern into the foam to position the net.

4 Pipe over the design; for denser areas and larger pieces, pipe a zigzag over the design. Have a damp brush ready. If there are any areas that go wrong, remove them with the brush and re-pipe; if there are any peaks, tap them down with the edge of the brush.

5 While the piping is still fresh, draw a line through the icing to add extra texture – for example, a vein in a leaf. Pipe a tiny border around the edge of the net.

6 Allow the design to dry before removing it and placing it on the cake. To make more of the same pattern, gently ease the pattern from its position in the plastic sleeve and reuse in another sleeve. Attach the motif to the cake with a little royal icing.

Use coloured net fabric with contrasting icing to great effect.

# Piped lace

Decorative piped lace, such as
this looped version, adds a delicate
quality to a cake.

## Order of work

1 Prepare a page of lace
templates to the size required
and place them in a plastic
sleeve. This design is one of
the easiest patterns to make
– it can be completed
simply by piping three
continuous loops.

2 Use fresh royal icing in a
piping bag fitted with a small
piping nozzle.

3 Starting from the centre,
pipe the left-hand loop,
immediately followed by the
middle and right-hand loops
– all in one action. Add a tiny
bulb to each loop.

4 Pipe a considerable
number of lace pieces,
allowing plenty of spares
for breakages. Set them
aside to dry.

5 Scribe a line onto the
cake where the lace pieces
are to be placed with a sharp
knife. Attach each lace piece
at an angle to the cake, with
a tiny bulb of royal icing.
Adjust the angle of the lace,
if needed, by lightly moving
the lace with a soft
paintbrush. Continue adding
the lace pieces until the
entire scribed line is full.

6 At the end of a line, it
may be necessary to space
out the lace pieces a little to
ensure that there is no gap;
judge this by eye when there
are three or four pieces left
to position.

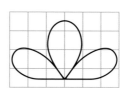

All three loops are piped in
one action.

 **Degree of difficulty**

Moderate

**Use for**

 Side design

**Mix and match**

Cutout lace,
*page 218*

**Motif uses**

Low relief

Linework

**Icing colours**

Any

**Tools**

Plastic sleeve
Piping bag and small
piping nozzle
Sharp knife
Soft paintbrush

*See also*
Making a template,
*page 38*
How to pipe, *page 42*

# Repeated stencil

**Degree of difficulty**

Moderate

**Use for**

Cake top ◯

Side design ▭

**Mix and match**

Girl in the snow,
*page 196*

**Motif uses**

Low relief ⬭

**Icing colours**

Any

**Tools**

Stencil
Palette knife

Repeated stencils are a great way to add a pattern over a large area. You will need to use a shop-bought stencil for this motif, or cut out your own stencil design with a scalpel.

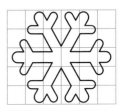

Patterns can be stencilled on the top and sides of a cake.

## Order of work

1 Stencils are applied directly onto the cake, so have the cake coated before preparing to stencil. It is important to have a flat surface for the stencil to sit on. If you decide to stencil onto buttercream icing, the surface must be semi-frozen.

2 Mix a batch of royal icing or buttercream icing, to match the cake's coating. The mixture must be stiff enough to hold a peak when a palette knife is drawn through it.

3 Position the stencil on the surface of the cake. Spread a small amount of icing along the blade of the palette knife, and smooth it across the stencil. Make a second pass if some of the stencil has not been covered.

4 Remove the stencil with a quick upward movement to keep the edges clean. Wash and pat the stencil dry before a second use.

5 Allow the stencilled area to dry.

*See also*
Royal icing, *page 20*
Buttercream icing,
*page 21*

226

# Individual stencil

Individual stencils look particularly good when they are placed on labels – keep them in readiness for the right occasion. This motif was made with a brass stencil from a craft shop.

**Degree of difficulty**

Moderate

**Use for**

Cake top

**Mix and match**

Baby's bib, *page 147*

Message labels, *page 207*

**Motif uses**

Low relief

**Icing colours**

Any

**Tools**

Stencil
Palette knife

## Order of work

1 Stencils are applied directly onto the cake, so have the cake coated before preparing to stencil. It is important to have a flat surface for the stencil to sit on. If you decide to stencil onto buttercream icing, the surface must be semi-frozen.

2 Mix a fresh batch of royal icing or buttercream icing, to match the cake's coating. The mixture must be stiff enough to hold a peak when a palette knife is drawn through it.

3 Position the stencil on the surface of the cake. Spread a small amount of icing along the blade of the palette knife, and smooth it across the stencil. Make a second pass if some of the stencil has not been covered.

4 Remove the stencil with a quick upward movement to keep the edges clean. Wash and pat the stencil dry before a second use.

5 Allow the stencilled area to dry. Extra details can be added by direct piping.

Stencils can be combined with other motifs.

*See also*
Royal icing, *page 20*
Buttercream icing, *page 21*

# *Rosette*

**Degree of difficulty**

Moderate

**Use for**

Cake top

**Mix and match**
Horse's head,
*page 77*

**Motif uses**

Low relief

**Fondant colours**

Yellow

Red

Green

**Tools**
Plastic sleeve
Rolling pin
Palette knife
Round cutter
Cornflour
Ball tool or small,
pointed dowel

*See also*
Making a template,
*page 38*

228

This rosette is a versatile motif, and it also shows how to make frills. These make splendid side decorations when used on their own or layered.

## Order of work

1 Adjust the design to the size required. Make a template and place in a plastic sleeve.

2 Roll out some yellow fondant and cut out a round shape for the rosette frill using the template as a guide. Use a plain round cutter to cut away the centre.

3 Liberally dust the work surface with cornflour. Move the yellow fondant frill to the edge of the work surface. Use a ball tool or a smooth, pointed dowel to roll the outside edge of the frill backwards and forwards, to thin and curl it. Repeat this action and keep rotating the fondant and stretching and curling the edge until the whole circle is frilled.

4 Roll out the red fondant and cut out a circle with the cutter. Position it inside the frill. Now make and place a green star for the centrepiece. (A star has been used here, but a number would be equally appropriate.)

5 Cut two rectangles from the rolled-out green fondant, then cut a V shape at one end of each for ribbon tails. Place these under the base of the rosette.

6 Transfer the motif to the cake when dry.

Change the colours of the rosette to suit the cake.

# Curved lace embroidery

This lace motif is curved to fit on the side of a round cake. It can be adapted and repeated as many times as required for the design of the cake.

## Order of work

1 Adjust the design to the size required. Make a template and place in a plastic sleeve. Tape the plastic sleeve onto a curved surface, such as a cake pan. If necessary cut the plastic sleeve so that it fits.

2 Cut out an oval of net fabric to fit the design. Smooth a thin layer of vegetable shortening onto the sleeve and lay the net in position – the shortening should hold it in place.

3 Place some fresh white royal icing into a bag fitted with a small piping nozzle and pipe the design, working from the centre outwards. For the larger areas, fill in with a zigzag pattern.

4 Tap the tops of any dots that have a point on top with a dampened soft brush to create smooth spheres.

*For the correct curve, form the motif on the side of the cake tin.*

5 Add a border around the edge of the net and set the motif aside to dry before removing from the curved surface. Make as many as needed to fit around the cake. Remove the motif before cutting the cake.

## Degree of difficulty

 Moderate

## Use for

 Side design

## Mix and match

Piped lace, *page 225*

## Motif uses

 Low relief

 Linework

## Icing colours

 White

## Tools

Plastic sleeve
Net fabric
Vegetable shortening
Piping bag and small piping nozzle
Soft brush

*See also*
Making a template,
*page 38*

# *Pair of hearts*

Make these cupcakes as a romantic addition to a traditional wedding cake.

**Degree of difficulty**

Easy ⬭

**Use for**

Cupcakes ⬭

**Mix and match**
Horseshoes,
*page 231*

**Motif uses**

3-D ⬭

**Icing colours**

Bright pink
pastillage

Light yellow
fondant or
buttercream
icing

Pink lustre

**Tools**
Rolling pin
Palette knife
Soft brush
Vegetable shortening
Coloured cake cases
Piping bag (optional)

## Order of work

1 Roll out the pink pastillage very thinly and cut out two hearts for each cake. Cut a tiny rectangular strip of pastillage, 2.5 x 0.5 cm (1 x ¼ inch), for each pair of hearts. Set all the pieces aside to dry for 24 hours.

2 Use a soft brush to cover each heart with a thin coat of vegetable shortening. Use the brush to dust each heart with pink lustre.

3 Bake as many cakes as you need in coloured cake cases. Cover each cupcake with a disc of fondant or pipe with a swirl of buttercream icing.

4 Use fondant adhesive (see page 22) to attach a strip of fondant to the top of each cupcake. Attach a heart to the front and back of it. Press the whole decoration down onto the centre of the cupcake top.

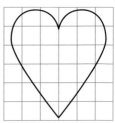

A small strip of fondant added between the hearts helps to support them.

*See also*
Pastillage, *page 23*

230

# ƀorseshoes

Make a clustre of these cupcakes to wish a happy couple good luck for the future.

## Order of work

1 Roll out the white pastillage very thinly and cut out two circles for each cake using the larger round cutter. Use the smaller round cutter to remove the centre of each circle. Make a single cut in each ring with the palette knife and trim the ends at an angle, to make horseshoe shapes. Mark each horseshoe with a plain piping nozzle to make the nail holes. Cut a tiny rectangular strip of pastillage, 2.5 x 0.5 cm (1 x ¼ inch), for each cake. Set all the pieces aside to dry for 24 hours.

2 Use a soft brush to cover each horseshoe with a thin coat of vegetable shortening. Use the brush to dust each horseshoe with mother-of-pearl lustre.

3 Bake as many cupcakes as you need in coloured cake cases. Cover each cupcake with a disc of fondant or pipe with a swirl of buttercream icing.

4 Use fondant adhesive (see page 22) to attach a strip of fondant to the top of each cupcake. Attach a horseshoe to the front and back of it. Press the whole decoration down onto the centre of the cupcake top.

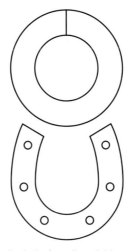

Use the tip of a small, round piping nozzle to mark the nail holes.

### Degree of difficulty

◌ Easy

### Use for

○ Cupcakes

### Mix and match

Pair of hearts, *page 230*

### Motif uses

◯ 3-D

### Icing colours

◯ White pastillage

◯ White fondant or buttercream icing

● Mother-of-pearl lustre

### Tools

Rolling pin
Two small, round cutters of different sizes
Palette knife
Small, round piping nozzle
Soft brush
Vegetable shortening
Coloured cake cases
Piping bag (optional)

*See also*
Pastillage, *page 23*

# 3-D bootees

**Degree of difficulty**

Easy

Celebrate a new arrival with some little pink or blue bootees, according to whether the baby is a girl or a boy.

**Use for**

Cupcakes

**Mix and match**
Pair of hearts,
*page 230*

**Motif uses**

3-D

**Icing colours**

Pink or blue fondant

Pink or blue
buttercream icing

White royal icing

**Tools**
Palette knife
Bulbous cone tool
Veiner
Coloured cake cases
Piping nozzle
(optional)

## Order of work

1 The bootees are each made from two teardrops of fondant. For each cake, roll two balls of paste the size of marbles, cut each in half, and roll again into teardrops.

2 Place one teardrop sideways on the work surface. Press the other onto a bulbous cone tool, and texture the outer surface all around with the veiner. Press the tool onto the pointed end of the first teardrop to make the leg of the bootee. Repeat with the other two pieces of fondant to make the other bootee. Make a pair of bootees for each cupcake.

3 Bake as many cupcakes as you need in coloured cake cases. Cover each cupcake with a disc of fondant or pipe with a swirl of buttercream icing.

4 Position two bootees on the centre of each cupcake.

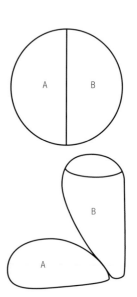

Add a rib texture to the bootees and pipe a contrasting bow in royal icing.

*See also*
Fondant, *page 22*

# Certificate

Celebrate a graduation or other educational achievement with a party featuring these congratulatory cupcakes.

## Order of work

1 Roll out very thin rectangles of pastillage, about 4 x 6 cm (1½ x 2½ inches), one for each cupcake. Keep the spare ones covered with clingfilm, and roll up one at a time starting from a short edge.

2 Wrap a tiny string of paste around the centre of the certificate and overlap the ends. Use a soft brush to dust the ends of the certificate and the tie with gold lustre.

3 Bake as many cupcakes as you need in coloured cake cases. Cover each cupcake with a disc of fondant or pipe with a swirl of buttercream icing.

4 Mount a certificate across the centre of each cupcake.

**Degree of difficulty**

Easy

**Use for**

Cupcakes

**Mix and match**

Mortarboard and diploma, *page 152*

**Motif uses**

3-D

**Icing colours**

⬤ White pastillage

⬤ Blue fondant or buttercream icing

⬤ Gold lustre

**Tools**

Rolling pin
Palette knife
Clingfilm
Soft brush
Coloured cake cases
Piping nozzle (optional)

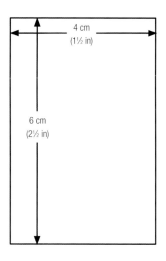

4 cm
(1½ in)

6 cm
(2½ in)

Embellish the edges of the certificate with gold lustre.

233

*See also*
Fondant, *page 22*

# Wedding bells

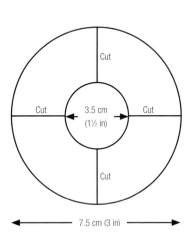

**Degree of difficulty**

Easy

**Use for**

Cupcakes

**Mix and match**
Horseshoes,
*page 231*

**Motif uses**

3-D

**Icing colours**

White pastillage

Light yellow
fondant or
buttercream
icing

Gold lustre

**Tools**
Rolling pin
Palette knife
Ball tool
Soft brush
Coloured cake cases
Piping nozzle
(optional)

Whether for a bridal
shower or the wedding
itself, these bells will
surely ring with joy.

## Order of work

1 Roll out the white pastillage finely
and cut out a 7.5 cm (3 inch) circle,
then cut out a 3.5 cm (1½ inch) circle
from the centre of this, so that the
pastillage resembles a pineapple ring.
Divide the ring into four segments.

2 Moisten one straight side of a segment
and wrap it around a ball tool, overlapping the
two straight edges to form the bell shape.
Pinch the top of the bell together and remove
any spare pastillage.

3 Pinch the base of the bell all around to
make it finer and spread it outward a little,
then set aside to dry. Make three bells for
each cupcake. Make some fine loops, tails
and bell clappers from spare pastillage, and
set these aside to dry. When they are dry,
use a soft brush to dust them all over with
gold lustre.

4 Bake as many cupcakes as you need in
coloured cake cases. Cover each cupcake
with a disc of fondant or pipe with a swirl
of buttercream icing.

5 Arrange three bells in a circle on each
cupcake top with some pastillage loops
and tails placed in between.

Cut

Cut    3.5 cm
(1½ in)    Cut

Cut

◀─────── 7.5 cm (3 in) ───────▶

Always place the bell clapper at the bottom edge
of the finished bell.

*See also*
Pastillage, *page 23*

# *Golden keys*

Moving to a new home is always a major event, so decorate cupcakes with a pair of golden keys to mark the occasion.

## Order of work

1 Roll out the white pastillage finely and cut out the shape of the keys with a sharp knife. Make two keys for each cupcake. Use the side of a palette knife to indent the grooves into the keys. Set them aside to dry.

2 Roll a fine tube of pastillage and curl it into a circle. Thread two keys onto the ring, and press the ends together to form a join. Set aside again to dry. Use a soft brush to coat the keys with gold lustre.

3 Bake as many cupcakes as you need in coloured cake cases. Cover each cupcake with a disc of fondant or pipe with a swirl of buttercream icing.

4 Arrange the keys on the ring in the centre of each cupcake.

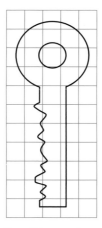

You could trace around real keys to make your own templates.

## Degree of difficulty

◇ Easy

## Use for

◯ Cupcakes

## Mix and match
Pair of hearts, *page 230*

## Motif uses

◯ 3-D

## Icing colours

⬤ White pastillage

⬤ Yellow fondant or buttercream icing

Gold lustre

## Tools
Rolling pin
Palette knife
Soft brush
Coloured cake cases
Piping nozzle
(optional)

*See also*
Pastillage, *page 23*

# *Linked lines*

This alphabet makes a bold statement. The spaces enclosed by the double lines could be filled in with flooding icing or icing gel for extra effect.

Use the diagrams on pages 238–239 to prepare a template for your message, marking the outlines with a bold, dark pen. Prepare some finely rolled pastillage tiles, each large enough for a single letter, and allow them to dry. Place a tile over each letter of the template. The letter outline should show through (a lightbox may help with this). Use a no. 2 piping nozzle to pipe over the lines with royal icing. Allow the icing to dry thoroughly before attaching each tile to the cake with a little of the remaining royal icing. The tiles could lay flat on the cake or stand upright for extra effect. They can be arranged in a straight or curved line to suit the style of the cake.

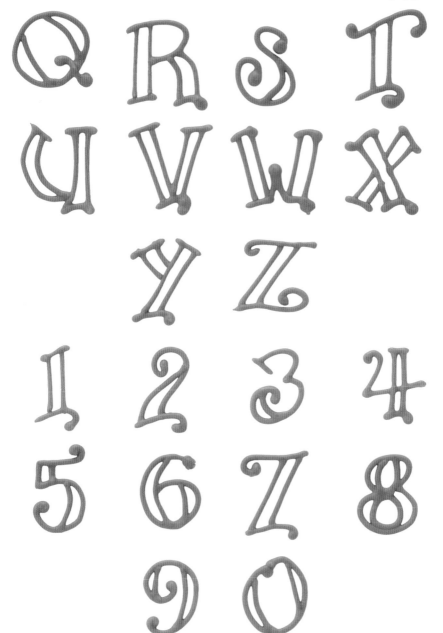

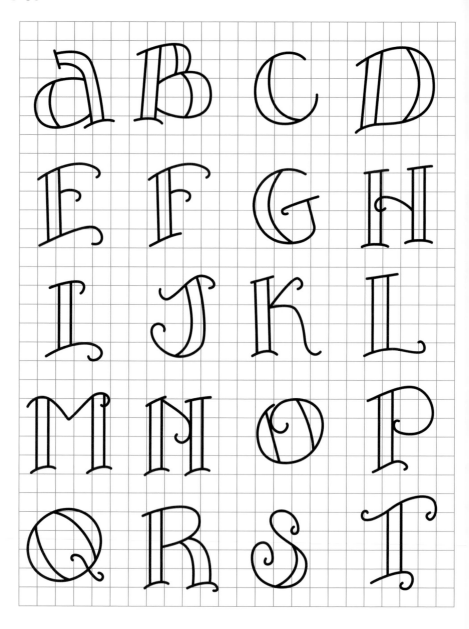

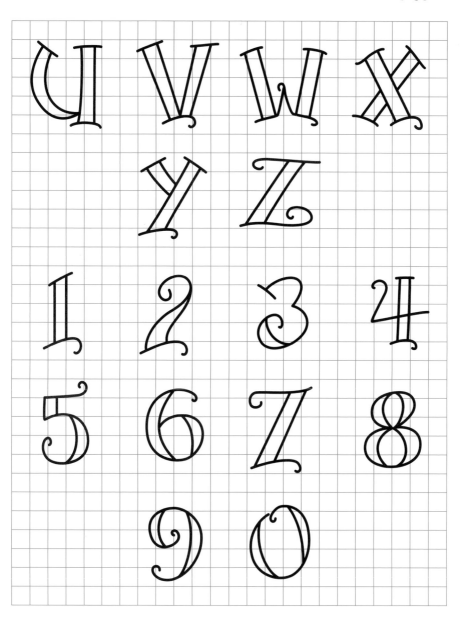

# Flower fun

These decorated letters are perfect for initials or numbers. If you are showing a whole word, try adding the flowers to a few selected letters.

Prepare some finely rolled pastillage tiles, each large enough for a single letter, as on page 236. Prepare some rolled roses and leaves (as for Rosebud circle, page 217). Pipe the letter outlines onto the tiles with a plain no. 4 nozzle, and position the roses on the letter while the icing is still fresh. Allow the icing to dry thoroughly before attaching each tile to the cake with a little of the remaining royal icing. These letters are very effective as a cake side decoration. This design is also suitable for piped buttercream icing.

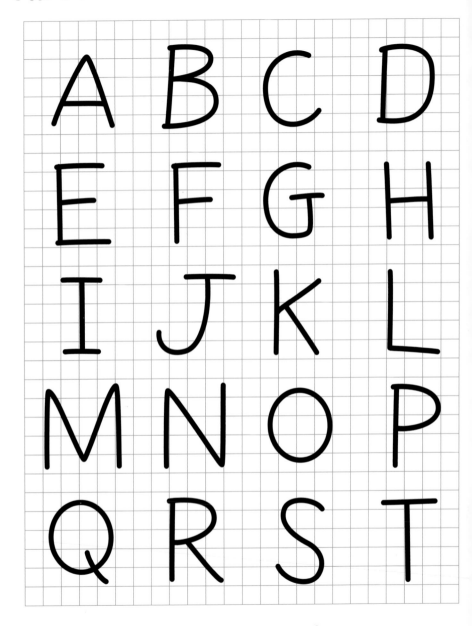

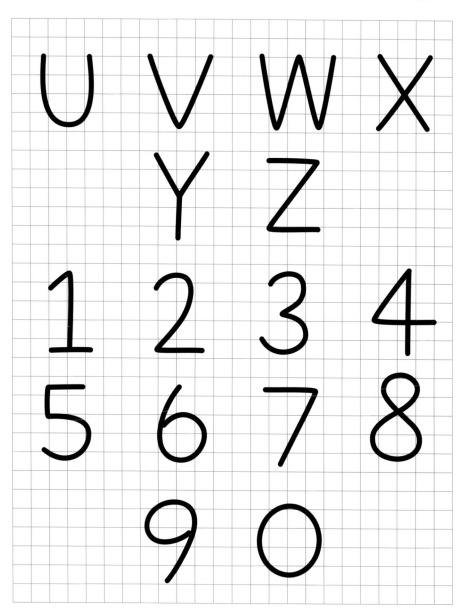

# Lots of dots

These letters and numbers embellished with dots may be piped onto individual pastillage tiles, or directly onto the cake top if you prefer.

Prepare some finely rolled pastillage tiles, each large enough for a single letter, as on page 236. Pipe the letter outlines onto the tiles (or directly onto the cake top) with a no. 2 piping nozzle. Add dots at the beginning and end of each line or curve as shown.

Use a damp brush to tap down any take-off points on the dots. Allow the icing to dry thoroughly before attaching each tile to the cake with a little of the remaining royal icing. This style also lends itself to piping with buttercream icing.

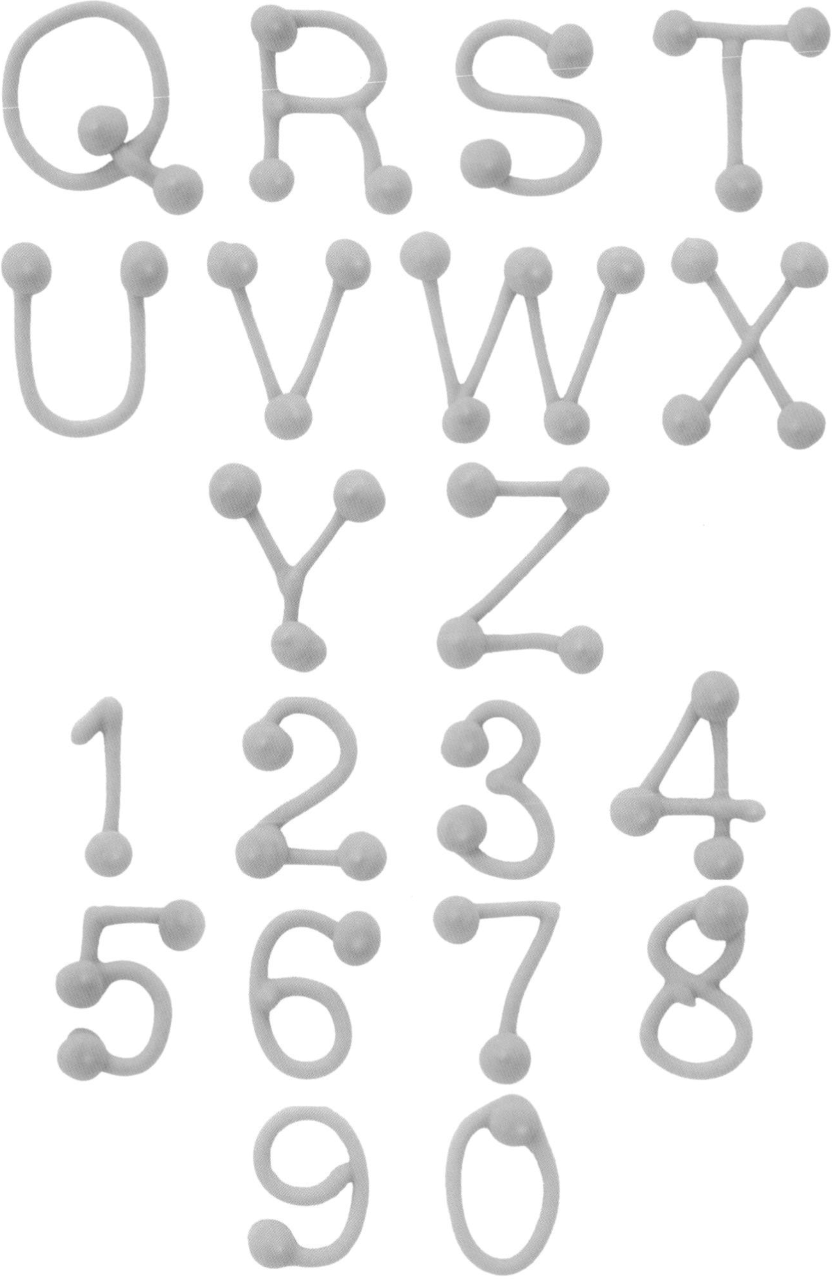

Q R S T
U V W X
Y Z
1 2 3 4
5 6 7 8
9 0

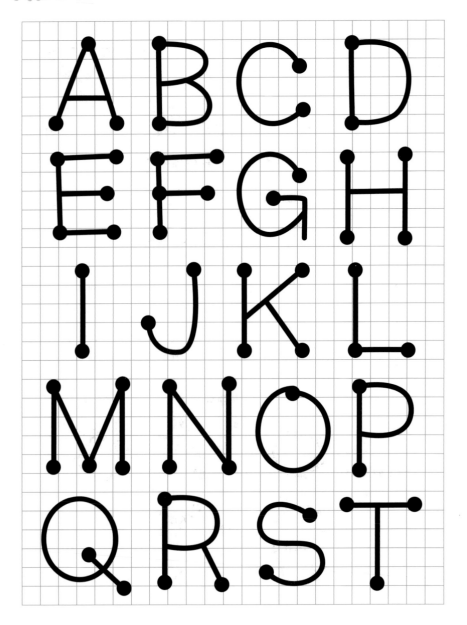

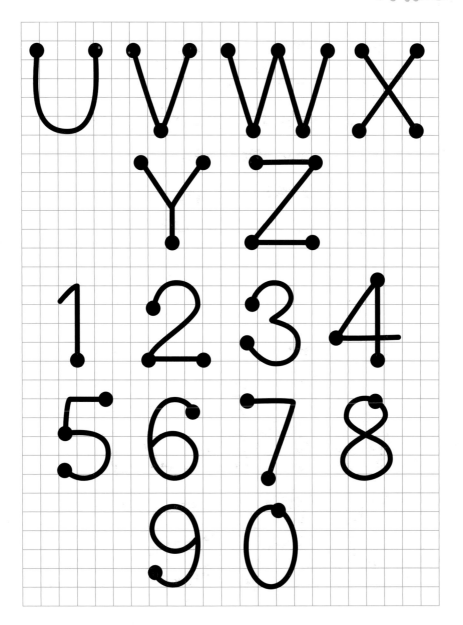

# Conversions

You may find you need to convert units of measurement into their metric or imperial equivalents.
On these pages the conversions for some common quantities are given.

## Weight

| Imperial | Metric |
|----------|--------|
| 1 oz | 28 g |
| 1 lb | 454 g |

| Metric | Imperial |
|--------|----------|
| 100 g | 3½ oz |
| 1 kg | 2¼ lb |

| Cups | Imperial | Metric |
|------|----------|--------|
| 1 cup butter | 8 oz | 230 g |
| 1 cup brown sugar | 7 oz | 200 g |
| 1 cup white sugar | 6¾ oz | 190 g |
| 1 cup chopped pecans | 4¼ oz | 120 g |
| 1 cup flour | 3½ oz | 100 g |
| 1 cup ground almonds | 3 oz | 85 g |

## Length

| Imperial | Metric |
|----------|--------|
| 1 inch | 25.4 mm |

| Metric | Imperial |
|--------|----------|
| 100 mm | 4 inches |

## Volume

| Imperial | Metric |
|----------|--------|
| 1 fl. oz | 30 ml |
| 1 pint | 568 ml |

| Cups | Imperial | Metric |
|------|----------|--------|
| ⅛ cup | 1 fl. oz | 30 ml |
| 1 cup | 8 fl. oz | 240 ml |

| Metric | Imperial |
|--------|----------|
| 100 ml | 3½ fl. oz |
| 1 litre | 2 pints |

| Spoons | Imperial | Metric |
|--------|----------|--------|
| 1 teaspoon | ⅙ fl. oz | 5 ml |
| 1 dessertspoon | ⅓ fl. oz | 10 ml |
| 1 tablespoon | ½ fl. oz | 15 ml |

## Oven temperatures

|  | Fahrenheit | Celsius |
|--|-----------|---------|
| Cool | 200° | 90° |
| Very slow | 250° | 120° |
| Slow | 300–325° | 150–160° |
| Moderately slow | 325–350° | 160–180° |
| Moderate | 350–375° | 180–190° |
| Moderately hot | 375–400° | 190–200° |
| Hot | 400–450° | 200–230° |

# *Glossary*

**Apricot glaze**
Apricot glaze is brushed onto the cake surface
to act as a 'glue' for the decorative icing layer.
An alternative is piping gel.

**Ball tool**
A ball tool is a rounded tool used to curve and shape
the petals of a flower or in other modelling applications.

**Blossom cutters**
Blossom cutters are used to make small flowers with
several petals. Some types incorporate a spring-loaded
plunger to eject the flower cleanly once it is cut.

**Buttercream icing**
Buttercream icing is made from a mixture of butter
and icing sugar beaten together, sometimes with
meringue powder added to make it smoother.
Buttercream icing may be flavoured and coloured.
It may be spread over a cake or used for piped borders.

**Calyx**
The calyx is made up of the sepals of a flower
(where the petals join the stem).

**Clingfilm**
Clingfilm is used to wrap fondant and
cakes to keep them from drying out.

**Cornelli work**
Cornelli work is a decorative piping technique
where lines are piped in curved shapes close
to each other to fill in a space.

**Cornflour**
Cornflour is used for dusting the work
surface when rolling out fondant and pastillage.

**Cranked palette knife**
A cranked palette knife has a handle angled in
such a way as to keep your fingers from hitting
the cake surface.

**Crimping**
Crimping is a decorative design made by special
patterned metal tweezers (crimpers) designed to
squeeze the fondant between them.

**Edible glue (sugar glue)**
Edible glue is used as an adhesive between
modelled sugar components.

**Embossing**
Embossing is the term given to creating a texture
on fondant with different tools.

**Firm peak**
Firm peak describes prepared royal icing when
it has been beaten to a firmness where the icing
will stay standing up in a peak.

**Fondant icing**
Fondant icing is a soft, pliable paste suitable for
covering cakes or modelling. It may be coloured and
flavoured. It is often shop-bought and ready-to-roll;
alternatively you can make your own.

**Gum tragacanth**
Gum tragacanth is a hardener used in the
preparation of pastillage.

**Icing sugar**
Icing sugar is a very finely ground sugar that is used for
cake decorating. Sometimes it is labelled "10XXX."

### Liquid glucose (corn syrup)

Liquid glucose is sometimes used as an ingredient in fondant icing to keep it pliable.

### Lustre

Lustre is used to add colour or a shimmering effect to fondant. It can be brushed on.

### Meringue powder (albumen powder )

Meringue powder is powdered egg white and is used for making royal icing and sometimes as an addition to buttercream icing (to make it smoother). Dissolve in water following the packet instructions before use.

### Pastillage

Pastillage is a firm white paste (which can have colour added to it) used to make models, plaques and cards. It sets hard.

### Royal icing

Royal icing is a beaten mixture of egg white and icing sugar suitable for coating cakes and piping. It sets firm and crisp.

### Smoothers

Smoothers are flat plastic tools used to smooth over a fondant surface to even out any undulations. Work with two smoothers to achieve the best finish.

### Soft peak

Soft peak is a description of prepared royal icing that has softened a little – so that when a peak is pulled up from the surface, the top curves over slightly.

### Stamens

Stamens are the central parts of flowers that fit into the throat – imitation plastic stamens can be bought for cake decorating.

### Turntable

A turntable holds a cake during decoration. It revolves so that the top and sides of a cake can be worked on.

### Veiner (Dresden tool)

Veiners originated as pottery tools but have become essential to the cake decorator. They create lines and creases in the surface of fondant.

# Index

## A

alphabets 61, 236–47
  Flower fun 240–43
  Linked lines 236–39
  Lots of dots 244–47
animals 52–53, 62–89
  Birdhouse 87
  Cock-a-doodle-doo 86
  Cool kitten 73
  Creel and fish 64
  Dapper dog 80
  Dragonflies 67
  Fishy friends 88
  Fluttering butterfly 63
  Friendly elephant 75
  Frisky frog 81
  Happy tortoise 70
  Horse's head 77
  Ice-bucket bunny 72
  Jumping dolphin 66
  Leo the lion 78
  Little dog 65
  Lovebirds 84
  Lovely duck 68
  Pair of geese 82
  Party penguin 76
  Playful panda 74
  Pretty parrot 83
  Prickly hedgehog 89
  Puppy love 85
  Sparkling butterfly 62
  Thinking of ewe! 69
  Wacky whale 71
  Wise owl 79
apricot masking 34

## B

ball tool 28
blade/shell tool 28
bone tool 28
bowls 24
brushes 26
bulbous cone tool 28
buttercream icing 21, 42
  covering a cake with 36–7

## C

cake cases 25
cake mix 11
carrot cake 11, 14–15
celebrations 146–73
  Baby bootees 148
  Baby in a cradle 151
  Baby's bib 147
  Book 165
  Candle power 173
  Champagne bottle 149
  Champagne glasses 150
  Cup of love 156
  Do-it-yourself 161
  Flower basket 146
  Golf bag 154
  Golf ball and club 167
  Holding the key 172
  Little girl 168
  Lucky horseshoes 170
  Mailbox 155
  Mortarboard and diploma 152
  Ocean liner 169
  Pink rabbit 171
  Pram 157
  Rattle 158
  Rubber boots 163
  Sending a message 153
  Shirt and tie 159
  Signpost 160
  Torah scroll 164
  Watering can 166
  Wedding bells 162
chilling cakes 49
chocolate cake 18–19
cocktail sticks 27, 33
colouring, types of 29, 32
colours
  adding colour to fondant 33
  colour wheel 30
  complementary 30
  manipulating 31
  non-colours 31
  primary 30
  secondary 30
  tertiary 30
  variables 31
cooling the cake 10
cotton buds 27
covering cakes 34–37

with buttercream 36–37
with fondant 34–35
crimpers 29
crimping 35
crumb coat 36, 37
cupcake stand 29
cupcakes 61, 230–35
  3-D bootees 232
  Certificate 233
  Golden keys 235
  Horseshoes 231
  Pair of hearts 230
  Wedding bells 234
cutters 26
cutting wheels 28
cutting wire 25

D

design ideas
  adding embellishments 48
  mix and match 49
  motif positions 48

E

electric mixer 24
embossing tools 29, 36, 46
equipment *see*
  tools and equipment

F

flowers, fruits and leaves
  54–5, 90–117
  Arum lily 106
  Bamboo canes 90
  Blossom basket 104

Blossom frame 91
Bouquet 102
Bunch of grapes 113
Colourful cosmos 92
Daisy spray 114
Dogwood branch 112
Exotic orchid 115
Fan with roses 117
Fancy fuchsias 107
Holly sprig 96
Ivy ring 94
Lilypads 95
Oak leaves and acorns 109
Pine cones 109
Poppy 105
Pretty pansy 116
Pretty parasol 103
Rose 111
Rose leaves 97
Rudbeckia 98
Snazzy sunflowers 99
Spring daffodils 93
Springtime tulips 100
Wild rose 110
With love 101
foam pads 27
fondant 22
  adding colour to 33
  adding detail to a complex
    motif 46–47
  basic modelling shapes 44
  covering a cake with 36–7
  order of work for a simple
    motif 45
food colouring pens 32
freezing cakes 11

fruit cakes
  cooking time before
    decoration 11
  storage 11
full peak consistency 20

G

garlic press 27
gel colours 32
greaseproof paper 10, 11, 17, 28
gum tragacanth 22, 23

I

icing
  buttercream 21
  royal 20
  tubes of 32
icing sugar 25, 34

L

lettering 32, 43
levelling the cake 11
lining the pan 10
liquid colours 32
lustres 26, 32, 41

M

making cakes 10–11
  cooling the cake 11
  levelling the cake 11
  lining the tin 10
  storing 11
marbled effect 33
marzipan 26, 34
measuring spoons 25

modeling tools 28
moulds 25
motif selector 52–61
  alphabets 61
  animals 52–53
  celebrations 56–58
  cupcakes 61
  flowers, fruits and leaves
  54–55
  novelty ideas 58–59
  seasonal 55–6
  surfaces and textures 59–60

**N**

novelty ideas 58–59, 174–201
  Acoustic guitar 182
  Acrobat 201
  American heart 174
  Anchor 175
  Ballet slippers 176
  Baseball mitt 177
  Beer mug 178
  Bucket and spade 179
  Classic car 198
  Clown 200
  Convertible car 180
  Dashing stetson 192
  Drum 193
  Flying high 183
  Footsteps in the sand 181
  Girl in the snow 196
  Gone fishing 197
  Helicopter 189
  Little boy 199
  Mobile phone 191
  Over the moon 194
  Racing car 186

Sailing boat 190
Teddy bear in a box 195
Tennis racquet 188
Top hat and gloves 184
Toy steam train 185
Umbrella 187

**P**

palette knives 27, 35, 36, 37, 41,
  45, 46
paste colours 32
pastillage 23, 32, 43
pastry brush 26, 34
piping
  bulb 43
  cornelli 43
  making a piping bag 42
  pressure 43
  scroll 43
  twisted rope 43
  zigzag 43
piping bags 28, 37
piping nozzles 28, 45
piping tools 28
pizza cutter 27
plastic wrap 11, 17, 20
portion size 10
pound cake 12–13
powder colours 32

**Q**

quilting tool 28

**R**

rich fruit cake 16–17
rolling pins 26, 34, 35
royal icing 20, 42, 43

**S**

scallop/comb tool 28
scissors 27
scriber needle 28
seasonal 55–56, 118–45
  Christmas angel 141
  Christmas bells 122
  Christmas candle 140
  Christmas rose 142
  Christmas stocking 127
  Christmas tree 121
  Easter bunny 143
  Easter chick 133
  Easter egg 132
  Fourth of July 144
  Halloween ghosts 138
  Jolly snowman 129
  Menorah 134
  Mistletoe 123
  Party crackers 125
  Peace dove 124
  Plum pudding 126
  Prayer book 131
  Pumpkin family 139
  Pumpkin witch 137
  Red-nosed reindeer 120
  Robin redbreast 130
  Santa Claus 128
  Seasonal sleigh 118
  Star of David 135
  Sugar cane 119
  Thanksgiving turkey 145
  Top hat and shamrock 136
serrated/taper cone tool 28
side scrapers 28
sieves 25
smoothers 28, 35

# Using the Design Directory

Open the flap for a quick-reference guide to the symbols used in the Design Directory (pages 50–247), to use alongside the instructions for making each motif.

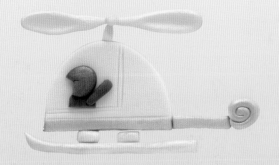

# Using the Design Directory

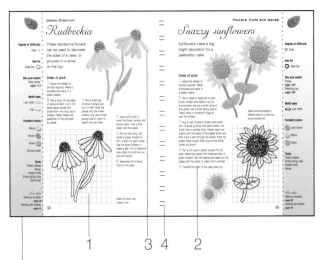

## 1 Template
Template for copying and scaling the motif up or down (full instructions given on page 38).

## 2 Order of work
Detailed instructions for assembling the motif.

## 3 Full-colour photograph
The finished motif is shown.

## 4 Spiral binding
The binding prevents the book from snapping shut!

---

## Key to symbols used in the Design Directory

There are more than 200 motifs organized into categories and arranged by degree of difficulty.

### Degree of difficulty
Skill level required on a scale of 1–3:

- Easy
- Moderate
- Complex

### Use for
Ideas for designing with decorative elements:

- Cake edging (for borders)
- Side designs (for deep cakes)
- Cake tops (for all shapes of cake: circular, square or rectangular)
- Cupcake (individual cake designs)
- Whole cake (integral motifs that act as coverings)

### Mix & match
Ideas for mixing the featured motifs with others in the directory.

### Motif uses
The motifs divide into four categories, providing very different finished effects, from flat to three-dimensional. Different types of icing (see pages 20–23) are suitable for each.

- Flat (rolled-out fondant or pastillage)
- Low relief (moulded fondant or pastillage)
- 3-D (moulded fondant)
- Linework (piped buttercream or royal icing)

### Tools
Lists the tools you will need.

sponge cakes
  cooking time before
  decoration 11
  storage 11
spoons 25
stamens 26
storage
  drawers 29
  motifs 41
  storing the cake 11
straws 27
sugar shaker 28
sugarcraft knife 28
surfaces and textures 59–60,
  202–29
  Balloons 220
  Basketweave 223
  Chunky lace 219
  Curved lace embroidery 229
  Cutout lace 218
  Draped braid 222
  Flat lace embroidery 224
  Flat-looped bow 203
  Formal bow 215
  Gift box 204
  Hearts 208
  Hearts and flowers 209
  Individual stencil 227
  Inscription banner 206
  Message labels 207
  Multi-looped bow 202
  Piped lace 225
  Pleated drape 221

Repeated stencil 225
Rope and shells 205
Rosebud circle 217
Rosette 228
Rounded scroll 216
Scrolls and shells 211
Star on flag 212
Strips and flowers 214
Tassels 210
Wishing on a star 213

T

templates
  paired motifs 39
  using a grid 38
  using a lightbox 39
  using a photocopier 39
  using a scanner 39
  using a template 40–41, 45, 46
testing cakes 13
tools and equipment 24–29
  cake making 24–25
  cutting and modelling 26–28
  finishing touches 29
turntable 29, 37
  tilting 29

V

vegetable shortening 10, 23, 26,
  40
veiner 28, 45, 46

W

whisk 25

# *Contacts*

**Annual Cake Show at NEC**
International Craft and Hobby
Fairs Ltd
Dominic House
Seaton Road
Highcliffe
Dorset BH23 5HW

**International Cake Exploration
Societé (ICES) Annual Show**
ICES
4883 Camellia Lane
Bossier City, LA
71111-5424 USA
www.ices.org

**American Cake
Decorating Magazine**
4215 White Bear Parkway
Suite 100
St Paul, MN USA
55110-7635 USA
Tel: 651-293-1544
www.americancakedecorating.com

**Cake Craft &
Decoration Magazine**
Anglo American Media Ltd
Editorial Office, PO Box 3693
Nuneaton, Warwickshire
CV10 8YQ
Tel: 02476 738846
www.cake-craft.com

**British Sugarcraft Guild**
Wellington House
Messeter Place
Eltham
London SE9 5DP
Tel: 0208 859 6943
www.bsguk.org

# *Suppliers*

**Torbay Cake Craft**
5 Seaway Road
Preston
Paignton
Devon TQ3 2NX
Telephone 01803 550178
www.crafty-creations.co.uk

**Cake Craft Shoppe**
3530 Highway 6
Sugarland
Texas 77478
USA
Telephone 281-491-3920
www.cakecraftshoppe.com